Windows 98 Optimizing And Tro
Get In, Fix It,

MW00581998

Top 10 Optimizing Tips For Windows 98

Shorten startup time, run faster, boost hardware efficiency, and just make life with Windows 98 easier and more reliable!

10. ***Set the typical role of your computer.***
    If you have at least 32MB of RAM, select Network Server as the typical role (as described in Chapter 3).

9. ***Set both modem FIFO buffers to high.***
    Use the highest settings for both your receive and transmit buffers. See Chapter 8 for all the details.

8. ***Schedule a regular defragment task for all of your hard drives.***
    Follow the instructions in Chapter 9 to set up an automated disk-scanning and defragmenting schedule.

7. ***Use Explorer Bars.***
    Chapter 2 explains how to configure Explorer Bars to add convenience to the Active Desktop.

6. ***Enable print spooling.***
    Use a print spooler—and make it as large as possible—to allow background printing in Windows 98. Chapter 7 shows you how to enable print spooling.

5. ***Locate your virtual memory swapfile on your fastest hard drive.***
    Chapter 12 explains how to optimize your virtual memory swapfile under Windows 98.

4. ***Reduce the number of System Tray icons.***
    Windows 98 will run faster and shut down quicker if you reduce the number of System Tray icons (each of which typically represents a program running in the background) to a minimum. See Chapter 2 for more information on the System Tray.

3. ***Use floating toolbars.***
    You can customize the Windows 98 Active Desktop with floating toolbars that allow immediate access to the programs and files you use most often—you'll learn more about floating toolbars in Chapter 2.

2. ***Use a blank home page in IE4.***
    Why wait for a slow home page to load every time you run Internet Explorer 4? Instead, configure your browser to use a blank home page instead. Chapter 10 explains the process step-by-step.

1. ***Convert your drives to FAT32.***
    FAT32 is faster and more reliable than FAT16. See Chapter 3 for all the details.

Get faster Internet ... th movies, enjoy a smoother game-playing experience, create a custom Active Desktop, and more!

10. ***Support for multilink modem connections.***
    Using two modems and two telephone lines to create a single connection, Windows 98 can effectively double the speed of your Internet dial-up connection.

9. ***Support for DVD drives.***
    You can watch commercial DVD movies on your computer DVD drive with the DVD player included in Windows 98. New drivers are included for most of the popular DVD computer drives currently in use.

8. **Support for processors with MMX.**
    Windows 98 supports the MultiMedia eXtensions command set for faster display of multimedia and digital video, which also helps games run faster.

7. **Outlook Express.**
    This new email program from Microsoft offers faster performance and more features than did Microsoft Exchange included with Windows 95.

6. ***Support for multiple monitors.***
    Windows 98 allows you to view a larger "virtual desktop" by installing multiple video cards and monitors.

5. ***Support for USB devices.***
    Windows 98 supports the Universal Serial Bus, allowing you to attach external devices like video cameras, joysticks, and scanners without requiring a reboot.

4. ***Faster system startup and shutdown.***
    Windows 98 has been optimized for the fastest possible startup sequence and system shutdown.

3. ***FAT32.***
    Windows 98 will automatically convert FAT16 hard drives for faster performance, optimal cluster size, and better reliability.

2. ***Single-click navigation.***
    Windows 98 provides an easily customized system interface based on Web browser controls.

1. ***Active Desktop.***
    Windows 98 enables you to integrate content from the Internet and office intranets onto your desktop.

Top 10 Windows 98 Web Sites

Cool sites for finding Windows 98 tips, shareware, reviews, links, and more. If it's Win98-related, you'll find it here!

10. **www.download.com**
    A fine Windows 98 download site featuring one of the largest collections of shareware anywhere on the Internet.

9. **www.coriolis.com**
   Headquarters for the latest books on Windows 98 from the Coriolis Group.

8. **www.winmag.com**
   The home of *Windows Magazine Online*, a source of news and reviews for Windows 98 owners.

7. **www.shareware.com**
   Another hot download site for Windows 98 shareware.

6. **www.yahoo.com**
   Searching for information on a Windows 98 feature? Yahoo! can search the Internet for you in seconds.

5. **www.winuser.com**
   Windows 98 tips, download files, links to other Windows 98-related sites, and Windows 98 news in a single site.

4. **www.windows98.org**
   A well-designed site with Windows 98 tips, online resources such as reviews, links and newsgroups, and screen shots of Windows 98 and new applications. This site even looks like the Windows 98 desktop.

3. **www.winfiles.com**
   Need even more Windows 98 shareware and download files? This is another great download site.

2. **www.nonags.com**
   The home of nag-free shareware and freeware for the Windows platform, and one of my favorite sites on the Web!

1. **www.windows.com**
   The Microsoft official Windows site; the place for new information, updates, patches, and add-ons for Windows 98.

Top 11 Windows 98 Wizards

(Sorry, I couldn't list just ten!)

11. *Compose New Fax Wizard.*
    Creates a new fax to be sent to another location. (Available only if you've upgraded to Windows 98 from Windows 95 and had installed fax support under Windows 95.) Start|Programs|Accessories|System Tools|Fax|Compose New Fax.

10. *Install New Modem Wizard.*
    Automates the installation of a new modem. Control Panel|Modems|Add.

9. *Add Printer Wizard.*
   Installs a new printer to your system. My Computer|Printers|Add Printer.

8. *Make New Connection Wizard.*
   Creates a new dial-up network connection, which you can later customize for your Internet Service Provider. My Computer|Dial-Up Networking|Make New Connection.

7. *Scheduled Task Wizard.*
   Automates the scheduling of a system task. My Computer|Scheduled Tasks|Add Scheduled Task.

6. *Maintenance Wizard.*
   Helps you set up a regular system-maintenance schedule. Start|Programs|Accessories|System Tools|Maintenance Wizard. (Also runs from Windows Tune-Up.)

5. *MIDI Instrument Installation Wizard.*
   Enables you to specify a new general MIDI instrument or import a new instrument definition. Control Panel|Multimedia|MIDI tab, and click on Add New Instrument.

4. *Add New Hardware Wizard.*
   Automates the installation of a new hardware device. Control Panel|Add New Hardware.

3. *Drive Converter Wizard.*
   Helps you convert FAT16 hard drives to FAT32, which probably will save you both loading time for programs and hard-drive space for drives over 1 gigabyte. Start|Programs|Accessories|System Tools|Drive Converter (FAT32).

2. *Direct Cable Connection Wizard.*
   Configures two PCs running Windows 98 for fast data transfer through a direct cable connection. Start|Programs|Accessories|System Tools|Communications|Direct Cable Connection.

1. *ISDN Configuration Wizard.*
   Helps in the configuration of ISDN hardware and connections. Start|Programs|Accessories|System Tools|Communications|ISDN Configuration Wizard.

Get In, Fix It, And Get Out

When the network goes down, when a schedule-buster bug can't be found, when a whole department of new workstations must be configured, *time* is the enemy. We created the *Little Black Books* to give you a weapon in this war against time. The goal is to gather essential technical facts and techniques into single, focused volumes, and make those facts easy to find when you most need them.

Every *Little Black Book* is highly structured and focused on its topic, so you won't be furiously flipping past pages and pages of irrelevant material. Every fact and solution we publish is designed to be located quickly, with minimal searching.

Each chapter consists of two major parts: "In Brief," a short technical overview of the topic at hand (with white margins), followed by the "Immediate Solutions" section (with black margins), showing you step-by-step how to accomplish various tasks associated with the topic.

To help you go right to the solution you need, each chapter begins with a "jump table," a quick, scannable index to all the immediate solutions provided in the chapter. At appropriate places throughout the chapter, you'll find additional jump tables guiding you to solutions related to the one you're reading.

We've put a lot of thought into making this format work. Please email us at **blackbookinfo@coriolis.com** to let us know what you think.

If you're reading this, you're probably on the firing line and need to return to the battle. Good luck—with this book in your hand, time is now on your side!

Jeff Duntemann
Editorial Director
The Coriolis Group

Keith Weiskamp
President and Publisher
The Coriolis Group

Also Look For These Other Little Black Book Titles:

Windows 98 Registry Little Black Book

Black Book Series Titles:

Windows 98 Black Book

Oracle8 & Windows NT Black Book

Dynamic HTML Black Book

Michael Abrash's Graphics Programming Black Book, Special Edition

Microsoft SQL Server Black Book

Oracle8 Black Book

Oracle8 PL/SQL Black Book

Web Design & Development Black Book

Windows NT 4 Administrator's Black Book

WIN 98

Optimizing & Troubleshooting

Little Black Book

Mark L. Chambers

Windows 98 Optimizing & Troubleshooting Little Black Book

Copyright © The Coriolis Group, 1998

Publisher
Keith
Weiskamp

Limits Of Liability And Disclaimer Of Warranty

Acquisitions Editor
Stephanie Wall

Marketing Specialist
Jody Kent

Trademarks

Project Editor
Don Eamon

The Coriolis Group, Inc.
An International Thomson Publishing Company
14455 N. Hayden Road, Suite 220
Scottsdale, Arizona 85260

602/483-0192
FAX 602/483-0193
http://www.coriolis.com

Production Coordinator
Wendy Littley

Library of Congress Cataloging-in-Publication Data
Chambers, Mark
    Windows 98 Optimizing and troubleshooting little black book / by
Mark L. Chambers
        p. cm.
    Includes index.
    ISBN 1-57610-295-5
    1. Microsoft Windows (Computer file)   2. Operating systems
(Computers). I. Title.
QA76.76.063C42   1998
050.4'469–dc21   98-8324
                                                          CIP

Layout Design
April Nielsen

Printed in the United States of America
10 9 8 7 6 5 4 3 2 1

Cover Design
Anthony Stock

an International Thomson Publishing company

Albany, NY • Belmont, CA • Bonn • Boston • Cincinnati • Detroit • Johannesburg
London • Madrid Melbourne • Mexico City • New York • Paris • Singapore • Tokyo
Toronto • Washington

*I'd like to respectfully dedicate this book to
another author in my family: My grandfather,
William "Bill" Liggett, Sr., whose book*
My Seventy-Five Years Along the Mexican Border
has provided me with many hours of enjoyment.

Thanks, Dada!

About The Author

Mark L. Chambers has been an author, computer consultant, BBS sysop, and game programmer for more than a decade. He spends entirely too much time on the Internet. His favorite pastimes include LSU football, collecting gargoyles, playing his pinball machines, fixing and upgrading computers, rendering 3D flights of fancy, and listening to just about every type of music imaginable. In the physical world, he lives in Columbia, Missouri—in cyberspace, you can reach him at **markc@computerland.net**, or visit his Web page at **www.geocities.com/SiliconValley/Bay/4373/index.html**.

Mark is also the author of the Coriolis book *Official Netscape Guide To Web Animation*, as well as *Building A PC For Dummies*, *Recordable CD Bible*, and *Running A Perfect BBS*.

Acknowledgments

This book has been a first for me in a number of areas: For example, it's the first book I've written in the Coriolis *Little Black Book* series. This series is truly a gem when it comes to design and ease-of-use, and it's a pleasure to see my words arranged in a format that allows the reader to locate and follow a particular project in seconds.

This book is my first true "quick reference guide" meant especially for desktop use. I've learned countless lessons during the writing and editing of the manuscript: What readers really want in a quick reference, what information should be presented and in what order, and how to create projects that both teach a concept *and* accomplish a task. Writing a quick-reference book like this one is no easy undertaking—in fact, in some ways it's much more of a challenge than a typical computer book.

But most important, this book was my first chance to work with a group of great people at Coriolis. Let me introduce each of them:

- My Acquisitions Editor, Stephanie Wall, who not only visualized and developed the idea for this book, but also gave me the chance to write it. I hope she'll consider me for the next Little Black Book in the series... as soon as she's thought of it, anyway!

- Toni Zuccarini, who was the initial Project Editor for my book... although she didn't stay long, she got us moving on the right track.

- Bonnie Trenga, Copy Editor.... Bonnie somehow charted the correct course through every chapter, no matter how convoluted my writing became! She has an eagle eye—much of the additional detail in this book is due to her recommendations.

- Craig Swanson, a fine Technical Editor whose knowledge of Windows 98 proved invaluable. I slept better at night knowing that if I missed a concept or tip in the text, Craig was there to make sure that we were covered—and I very much appreciated his positive feedback, too. (Thanks, Craig!)

- Production Coordinator Wendy Littley, whose hard work helped us make a series of deadlines that would have left other publishers in a state of shock... her name should appear on each and every page.

- Jody Kent, this book's Marketing Specialist, who wrote the text for the book's cover and—with April Neilsen—helped design the tear-out card. Summing up the content and high points of an entire book in 100 words or less is no simple job, but she makes it look easy.

- Tony Stock, the graphic artist whose cover design caught your eye in the bookstore... I think you'll agree that he did a fantastic job, especially since he had to start with basic black and a 6×9-inch format.

- Proofreaders Laura Poole, Sage Dillon, and Bob LaRoche, who caught mistakes that... well, weren't supposed to exist by that point! They read every word of this volume and survived to tell about it—and the accuracy of these printed pages is testimony to their work.

Finally, we come to the guy who handled my book as his first project at Coriolis: I owe a debt of sincere gratitude (and at least one expensive dinner) to Don Eamon, Project Editor. Don and I were on the right wavelength from the first, and he guided the evolution of this Little Black Book with a sure and steady hand... even when we had problems with beta software and when major formatting changes hit late in the game. Any author will tell you that the best Project Editors have two identifying characteristics—they're always ready to help, yet they give you enough space to work without interruption. (It's rather like the relationship between M and James Bond, except he's not with the British Secret Service and I don't carry a gun.)

My sincere thanks to this group for their hard work and dedication, and I hope that we can team up again in the future for another Little Black Book... the "sport cars" of quick-reference guides.

Mark L. Chambers

markc@computerland.net

Table Of Contents

Introduction

Do you miss MS-DOS? I mean, do you *really* miss MS-DOS—staying up late at night staring at that unyielding, unforgiving command prompt, with no eye-popping graphics, no online help to guide you and a different set of function keys for every program? Personally, I would have to concede that the MS-DOS world I once knew has been almost entirely swept away, and I really don't miss it very much!

By this time, the Windows operating system has pacified even the most jaded computer old-timers—those who used to make fun of Windows 3.0—must grudgingly admit that the new Windows 98 platform makes it easier than ever for everyone to connect to the Internet, browse and run programs, and tackle applications that were reserved solely for computer nerds only a few years ago. Wizards have been added to help automate just about every difficult task within Windows 98, and the system defaults and configuration settings were carefully selected to match today's computer hardware and the typical Windows 98 user.

The Reason For This Book

However, Windows 98 isn't quite a perfect fit yet—in fact, I've yet to meet the "typical" Windows user or to see a "typical" Windows PC that functions perfectly from the moment you install Windows 98. For example:

- The vast majority of PCs running Windows 98 will run with the default Windows 98 system configuration, but these computers probably won't run at the fastest possible speed.

- More strange pieces of PC hardware seem to exist on this planet than there are stars in the sky, and many of them weren't designed specifically for Windows.

- Many PCs that run Windows 98 aren't blessed with 128MB worth of system RAM or 6GB of free hard-drive territory.

That's the idea behind this *Little Black Book*: It's been specifically designed to help you fine-tune your Windows 98 system settings for the best possible performance, no matter what you've defined as your idea of the "typical"

Windows PC. Computer technowizards like to call this process *optimizing*. Whatever you call it, making the right adjustments to Windows 98 for your particular hardware and software will save you both time and trouble every time you sit in front of the monitor.

But this isn't all—in fact, optimizing is only half of this book. The other half is dedicated to the ancient art of *troubleshooting*: How to diagnose what's wrong with your computer or Windows 98 and how to fix it yourself (if possible). Some problems, such as your modem connecting at a slower speed than it should, are minor. Other problems, such as a complete lockup each time your PC starts loading Windows 98, are downright disastrous. No matter what the severity of the problem, however, this book will help you ask the right questions and find the best solution that returns your PC to working order.

I should also mention that this *Little Black Book* was expressly designed and written as a "get in, get it fixed, and get out" *quick-reference guide* for your cubicle or PC desk. Rather than teach you mundane Windows 98 applications and tasks that you probably already know, this book uses step-by-step projects that help you change a setting, optimize your PC, or fix a problem and get back to work quickly. If you want to turn on mouse trails to make it easier to locate your cursor on a laptop computer, you don't want to read a comprehensive history of mouse development! (We'll leave this kind of writing to the ponderous books that other publishers generate.) Everything about this book is arranged with speed and convenience in mind, making it the first book you'll grab when you need to answer a Windows 98 question.

How To Use This Book

I know, I know, "You turn the pages and read the words." There's more to it, however, than that, and understanding how this book is designed will help you use it more efficiently.

Each chapter in this book is a self-contained reference to a single *subsystem* within Windows 98—for example, *file and CD-ROM access* or *graphics and video*. This arrangement makes it easy for you to jump directly to the chapter that covers the material you need.

Here's a quick list of features contained in this book that will help you:

- At the beginning of each chapter, you will see a "jump table," a list of immediate solutions that point to sections that address the most common questions posed by Windows 98 users. Always check this table first to see if it points you to the solution you need.

- Next, you will find the In Brief section, which includes—appropriately enough—a brief overview of the chapter's subsystem coverage.

- Following the In Brief section, you get into the meat of the chapter—Immediate Solutions. Here, you will find the answers that you can use to optimize your Windows 98 computer.

- Every chapter in the *Windows 98 Optimizing And Troubleshooting Little Black Book* ends with a troubleshooting guide that will help you diagnose and fix common problems that can affect the subsystem that chapter covers.

- Looking for a specific topic? Cross-references throughout the book point you to other chapters that include additional information.

- Finally, each chapter contains tips on using Windows 98, as well as tips that cover different types of hardware and software. If you read and heed the occasional warning that appears in the section you are currently investigating, it just might save you time, money, and some of your sanity!

Throughout this book, specific choices were made to make this book easy to read. All email and Internet addresses, for example, are shown in boldface, as in **www.microsoft.com** and **www.coriolis.com/**. Additionally, new terms are introduced in *italics*.

Organization

This book is organized into the following chapters:

- *Chapter 1: Optimizing Startup And Shutdown*—The Immediate solutions in this chapter help you speed up the system startup and shutdown sequences, as well as how to create hardware and user profiles.

- *Chapter 2: The Active Desktop*—You'll find a complete discussion of the Windows 98 Active Desktop in this chapter, including projects on configuring desktop elements and subscribing to Active Desktop Channels.

- *Chapter 3: Disk And CD-ROM Access*—This chapter discusses the optimization of your hard drive, CD-ROM, and DVD. You'll learn how to achieve the fastest data transfer rates, and how to diagnose and correct disk errors.

- *Chapter 4: Graphics And Video*—This chapter discusses how to set the proper color depth, display resolution, and appearance for your PC, as well as how to optimize the display of digital video.

- *Chapter 5: Sound And Music*—Windows 98 provides a rich multimedia environment, and Chapter 5 includes projects to add sound to your desktop, optimize the playback of CD-ROM audio and configure the MIDI features of your sound card.

- *Chapter 6: Your Keyboard And Mouse*—This chapter provides all the details on how to properly configure your keyboard and mouse (or other pointing device) under Windows 98.

- *Chapter 7: Printing*—If you're having problems printing under Windows 98, look no further than Chapter 7—you will find a complete discussion of how to install, configure and troubleshoot any printer.

- *Chapter 8: Communications, Faxing, And The Internet*—This chapter helps you with all facets of modem use within Windows 98: Connect to the Internet, send and receive faxes or troubleshoot a misbehaving modem.

- *Chapter 9: Automating Windows 98*—Here, you are introduced to the Task Scheduler and shown how to automate many tasks you would otherwise have to perform manually under Windows 98.

- *Chapter 10: Optimizing Internet Explorer 4*—IE4 is an important, integral part of Windows 98. This chapter provides details on optimizing Internet Explorer for speed, convenience, and security.

- *Chapter 11: Using Windows 98 Disk Compression*—If you have decided to compress a hard drive or removable media drive with DriveSpace 3, refer to this chapter for the information that you will need.

- *Chapter 12: Optimizing Windows 98 Virtual Memory*—Looking for the best performance from your PC? To achieve the fastest operation, virtual memory must be properly configured under Windows 98—and this chapter contains everything you need to know about how to properly configure your virtual memory.

- *Chapter 13: Hardware Configuration In Windows 98*—This chapter will help you install and configure new hardware, as well as diagnose and fix hardware conflicts that may arise under Windows 98.

- *Chapter 14: Using The Windows 98 Tune-Up Wizard*—Finally, Chapter 14 will show you how to create your own custom maintenance schedule that will automatically repair and optimize your hard drive.

A Final Word

I hope you will find this quick reference guide valuable whenever you need help with Windows 98. As always, I welcome your comments and suggestions for corrections, improvements, and additions to the text; please send them via Internet email to me, at **markc@computerland.net**.

Optimizing Startup And Shutdown

In Brief

Optimizing Startup And Shutdown

By default, your computer will automatically load Windows 98 when you turn it on; because most PC owners have switched over to 32-bit Windows applications, this choice is probably right for most of us. As it loads, Windows 98 runs a number of different programs and reads the contents of several important initialization files. The entire loading process that takes place—from the moment you turn on your PC until you begin using Windows 98—is known as the *startup sequence*. To safely turn off your PC, you should also allow Windows 98 to complete its *shutdown sequence*.

You can customize the startup sequence in a number of ways. For example, you can boot directly into DOS 7 instead of into Windows, or you can create a boot menu that allows you to select between DOS 7 and Windows 98 each time you start your PC. You can run Windows 98 in Safe mode, which makes fixing lockup problems easier. You can replace the standard Windows 98 startup screen, or you can turn off the startup screen completely.

At the end of the startup sequence, you can elect to automatically launch specific applications (or, if you boot directly to DOS 7, you can run DOS programs from the familiar AUTOEXEC.BAT file).

In this chapter, you learn how to take control of the Windows 98 startup and shutdown sequences. I'll show you how to save time by reducing the number of tasks your PC must complete before you can start using Windows 98, and how to reduce the amount of time it takes to shut down your PC.

Immediate Solutions

Selecting Windows 98 Boot Options

The read-only system file MSDOS.SYS provides Windows 98 with a number of initialization options that you can use to control the startup sequence, as shown in Table 1.1. By changing the options that appear in this file under the **[Options]** label, you can boot directly to DOS 7 or a startup menu.

Table 1.1   The Windows 98 startup options available in MSDOS.SYS.

Option	Default Setting	Description
AutoScan	1	When this command is set to 1, it runs ScanDisk automatically if Windows is improperly shut down. When it is set to 0, the ScanDisk utility doesn't automatically run.
BootDelay	2	This command specifies the number of seconds that Windows 98 will pause at the beginning of the startup sequence for a function key to be pressed. If you don't use the startup function keys and would like to save time during the startup sequence, set the **BootDelay** option to 0.
BootFailSafe	0	When this command is set to 0, Windows 98 boots in Normal mode. When it is set to 1, Windows 98 boots directly into Safe mode.
BootGUI	1	When this command is set to 1, the system boots automatically to the Windows 98 desktop. When it is set to 0, the system boots automatically to the DOS 7.0 command prompt.
BootKeys	1	When this command is set to 1, the function keys are enabled during startup. A setting of 0 disables the function key control.

continued

***Table 1.1   The Windows 98 startup options available in
MSDOS.SYS (continued).***

Option	Default Setting	Description
BootMenu	0	When this command is set to 0, Windows 98 doesn't automatically display the Startup menu at startup (you must press F8 to display the Startup menu). When it is set to 1, the Startup menu is always displayed at startup. If the **BootMenu** command does not currently appear in your MSDOS.SYS file, add it only if you decide to set **BootMenu** to 1.
BootMenuDefault	1, 3, or 4	This command specifies the default menu selection number on the Startup menu. The default setting of 1 is changed to 3 or 4 (Safe mode with or without network support) if Windows is not shut down correctly. You can use any menu number that currently appears in your Startup menu.
BootMenuDelay	30	This command specifies the number of seconds used in the Startup menu count-down. If you don't select a menu item by the time this delay has elapsed, Windows 98 selects the default menu item automatically.
BootMulti	1	When this command is set to 1, your system can boot to DOS version 5.x or 6.x or Windows 3.1 when you hold down the F4 or F8 key during startup. When it is set to 0, the system can only be booted in Windows 98. If the **BootMulti** command does not currently appear in your MSDOS.SYS file, your system can only be booted in Windows 98.
BootWarn	1	When this command is set to 1, Windows 98 displays a dialog box whenever it boots into Safe mode to inform you that the system is running in Safe mode. When it is set to 0, the dialog box doesn't appear.

continued

Table 1.1   *The Windows 98 startup options available in MSDOS.SYS (continued).*

Option	Default Setting	Description
BootWin	1	When this command is set to 1, the system boots automatically using Windows 98 or DOS 7 (depending on the setting of **BootGUI**). When it is set to 0, boot the system to DOS version 5.x or 6.x or Windows 3.1. A setting of 0 is only enabled if you have set up a dual-boot system with a standard FAT-16 partition.
DoubleBuffer	1	When this command is set to 1, Windows 98 uses double buffering with SCSI devices. When it is set to 0, double buffering is disabled.
DrvSpace	1	When this command is set to 1, Windows 98 loads the DriveSpace driver DRVSPACE.BIN, which will allow you to read compressed drives. When it is set to 0, the driver isn't loaded and DriveSpace cannot mount a compressed drive.
LoadTop	1	When this command is set to 1, Windows 98 loads COMMAND.COM and other low-level drivers into the top of conventional memory, allowing more free memory for programs that will run in DOS mode. When it is set to 0, these programs and drivers are not loaded into the top of conventional memory (this may be necessary to allow some older programs to run successfully).
Logo	1	When this command is set to 1, Windows 98 displays the LOGO.SYS graphic during startup. When it is set to 0, Windows 98 doesn't show the LOGO.SYS graphic. Instead, it displays the text of any status messages output by programs during startup. You can also make the startup graphic disappear during startup by pressing the Escape key after the graphic is first displayed.

continued

Table 1.1   The Windows 98 startup options available in MSDOS.SYS (continued).

Option	Default Setting	Description
Network	1	When this command is set to 1, Windows 98 will install network programs and drivers, allowing you to boot into Safe mode with Network support from the Startup menu. When it is set to 0, the Safe Mode With Network Support menu selection doesn't appear on the Startup menu.

Editing The MSDOS.SYS File

To add or remove initialization options from MSDOS.SYS, you must first change the read-only DOS attribute on the file to allow it to be edited. When the file can be edited and saved, you can make the changes with Windows Notepad. When you're finished editing, MSDOS.SYS should be restored as a read-only system file.

To edit the MSDOS.SYS file, follow these steps:

1. Double-click on the My Computer icon to display your drive icons.

2. Right-click on the C: icon and select Explore from the menu.

3. Click on the Options item under the View menu and click on the Show All Files option to enable it. Click on OK to close the dialog box.

4. Locate the MSDOS.SYS file icon in the Contents window. Right-click on the icon and select Properties from the menu.

5. Click on the Read-Only checkbox to turn off the read-only attribute and click on OK to accept the change. You can minimize the Explorer window at this point, but you'll need it again soon so don't close it.

6. Click on Start|Programs|Accessories|Notepad to run Windows Notepad.

7. Click on File on the Notepad menu and select Open. From the File Open dialog box, select All Files in the Files Of Type drop-down list box.

8. Double-click on the MSDOS.SYS file icon to open it in Notepad, as shown in Figure 1.1. You can now add, remove, or edit any of the initialization options under the **[Options]** label. Remember: Each option must appear on a line by

Figure 1.1   Notepad is an easy way to edit your MSDOS.SYS file.

itself, and do not delete the comment lines of x characters that appear in the middle of the file.

9. Click on File from the Notepad menu and select Save to save the edited file to disk.

10. Close Notepad and maximize the Explorer window.

11. Locate the MSDOS.SYS file icon in the Contents window. Right-click on the icon and select Properties from the menu.

12. Click on the Read-Only checkbox to turn on the read-only attribute, and then click on OK to accept the change. Close Explorer.

Controlling Startup With The Function Keys

By editing your MSDOS.SYS file, you can select the startup sequence defaults that suit your preferences, saving you both time and trouble. However, there will still be times when you'll need to change the startup sequence (usually, when you're diagnosing a problem with Windows 98 or trying to run a program).

If you leave the function keys enabled during the startup sequence, it's easy to change how Windows 98 boots without changing your default options. By default, Windows 98 pauses for two seconds immediately after it displays the text message "Loading Windows

98...", and you must be relatively quick to press the desired function key—but you can change the delay period by editing the **BootDelay** value in the MSDOS.SYS file.

Controlling Startup With The Windows Startup Menu

Table 1.2 describes the function keys available during the startup sequence.

Table 1.3 describes the options available on the standard Windows 98 Startup menu (invoked with the F8 key, or by setting **BootMenu=1** in your MSDOS.SYS file.

Table 1.2*   *You can change the startup sequence with these function keys.

Key	Description
F4	Loads version 5.x or 6.x of DOS instead of Windows 98. This key is only available if your MSDOS.SYS file contains the **BootMulti=1** option, which indicates that your installation of Windows 98 supports a multiboot configuration.
F5	Boots Windows 98 in Safe mode. This key is especially helpful when you're diagnosing a problem with new device or network drivers, or if you need to remove a program from the Startup group that's locking up your PC. Network support is not loaded.
F6	Boots Windows 98 in Safe mode with network support.
F8	Displays the Windows 98 Startup menu, allowing you to select a startup configuration.
Ctrl+F5	Boots to the DOS 7 command prompt without loading the DRVSPACE.BIN driver, so you will be unable to mount or use compressed drives. Any commands present in your CONFIG.SYS or AUTOEXEC.BAT files are ignored.
Shift+F5	Boots to the DOS 7 command prompt, with system support for DriveSpace. Any commands present in your CONFIG.SYS or AUTOEXEC.BAT files are ignored.
Shift+F8	Boots Windows 95 step by step, allowing you to select which programs and drivers are loaded. Windows 98 will prompt you to press Y or N after displaying each entry in your AUTOEXEC.BAT and CONFIG.SYS files; press Y to process the command or N to skip it. Step-by-step confirmation is suitable for diagnosing problems caused by programs or drivers loaded from CONFIG.SYS or AUTOEXEC.BAT.

Table 1.3   The default options offered by the Windows 98 Startup menu.

Entry	Description
Normal	Loads Windows 98. If the option **BootGUI=0** has been added to MSDOS.SYS, DOS 7 will load instead.
Logged	Loads Windows 98 and stores a record of the startup sequence in the file BOOTLOG.TXT. This file can come in handy when you are diagnosing startup problems.
Safe Mode	Loads Windows 98 in Safe mode, ignoring any drivers or programs specified in AUTOEXEC.BAT or CONFIG.SYS. Network support is not loaded. Safe mode is typically used to avoid lockups and other problems caused by conflicting hardware and software.
Safe Mode with Network	Loads Windows 98 in Safe mode, but also includes network components so that you can access your network for troubleshooting.
Step-by-Step Confirmation	Windows 98 loads normally, but it will confirm whether you want to load each program and driver in your AUTOEXEC.BAT and CONFIG.SYS files. Press Y to process the current command or N to skip it.
Command Prompt Only	Boots to the DOS 7 command prompt.
Safe Mode, Command Prompt Only	Boots to the DOS 7 command prompt, but does not process any of the commands in your AUTOEXEC.BAT and CONFIG.SYS files.

Changing Startup And Shutdown LOGO Screens

Windows 98 displays three bitmap image screens during the startup and shutdown sequences:

- *LOGO.SYS*—If a LOGO.SYS file is present on your computer, it appears during the startup sequence, unless you've set **Logo=0** in your MSDOS.SYS file or pressed Esc. The LOGO.SYS file is located in the root directory of the drive where Windows was installed, and it can be animated with a color-cycling effect.

- *LOGOW.SYS*—This screen is displayed while Windows is in the process of shutting down, and it usually warns you not to turn off the computer just yet. LOGOW.SYS is located in your Windows directory.

- *LOGOS.SYS*—This screen appears when Windows has completed the shutdown sequence, and it usually instructs you to turn off your computer. LOGOS.SYS is located in your Windows directory.

TIP: *All three of these files have the hidden attribute set, so they may not appear in a directory listing.*

It's easy to change any of these screens, and you'll find thousands of different LOGO screens on many Internet sites (one of my favorites is Nonags at **www.nonags.com**). You can also create your own LOGO screens for all the PCs on a corporate network or in a small business.

Your LOGO file should have the following characteristics:

- It must be saved as a Windows Bitmap format image file.

- It must have a color depth of 256 colors (commonly called *8-bit color*).

- The file size must be 127K. Most LOGO files are 320×400 pixels at 256 colors, which results in a file size of 127K.

Microsoft Paint is not the best tool to use for image editing, so I would recommend the excellent shareware program Paint Shop Pro from Jasc Software, Inc. (**www.jasc.com**), as shown in Figure 1.2. Most image-editing programs will allow you to resize an image to 320×400 pixels, or save a JPEG or GIF image as a Windows bitmap. You also may need to reduce the color depth of your image from 24- to 8-bit color.

Installing LOGO.SYS

After you've created your LOGO.SYS file, follow these steps to install it:

1. Double-click on the My Computer icon to display your drive icons.

2. Right-click on the drive icon where you installed Windows and select Explore from the menu.

3. Click on the View|Options and click on the Show All Files option to enable it. Click on OK to close the dialog box.

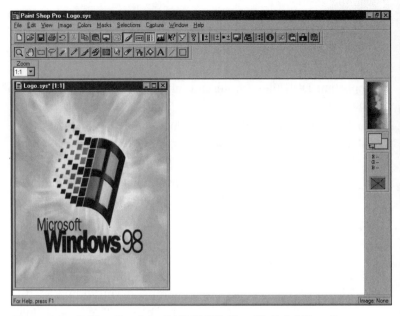

Figure 1.2   Editing the default LOGO.SYS file with Paint Shop Pro.

4. Check to see if you have a LOGO.SYS file icon in the Contents window. Right-click on the icon and select Rename from the menu.

5. Enter a new name and press Enter. This creates a backup of the original LOGO file.

6. Copy your new LOGO.SYS file into the root directory.

Installing LOGOW.SYS And LOGOS.SYS

To install your custom LOGOW.SYS and LOGOS.SYS files, follow these steps:

1. Double-click on the My Computer icon to display your drive icons.

2. Right-click on the drive icon where Windows 98 resides and select Explore from the menu.

3. Double-click on the Windows folder.

4. Right-click on the LOGOW.SYS file icon and select Rename from the menu.

5. Enter a new name and press Enter.

6. Repeat Steps 4 and 5 using the LOGOS.SYS file icon.

7. Copy your new LOGOW.SYS and LOGOS.SYS files into the Windows directory. Close Explorer.

Optimizing DOS Startup Files

Although 32-bit Windows 98 and DOS are generally considered to be two separate operating systems, Windows 98 still checks two important DOS files for certain initialization and configuration commands:

- *AUTOEXEC.BAT*—Runs any required conventional DOS 16-bit real-mode programs at the beginning of the startup sequence and sets up your DOS environment.

- *CONFIG.SYS*—Loads certain conventional DOS real-mode 16-bit device drivers at the beginning of the startup sequence.

Windows 98 doesn't need either of these files to run, and it no longer needs most of the commands once found in these files under DOS or Windows 3.x. In an optimal Windows 98 installation, AUTOEXEC.BAT should include only a handful of commands, and CONFIG.SYS may be completely empty. If you've upgraded to Windows 98 from an older version, however, or you've installed older MS-DOS programs, these files can become "clogged" with unnecessary commands that reduce the efficiency of your Windows 98 system.

TIP: *Before you change anything—Always save backup copies of your DOS startup files onto a floppy for safekeeping before you begin optimizing! Although most modern computer hardware is recognized within Windows 98, older hardware may require those drivers or support programs and refuse to run without them. With a backup copy of AUTOEXEC.BAT and CONFIG.SYS, you can always restore your startup files should problems occur.*

An optimal AUTOEXEC.BAT file under Windows 98 may include:

- **SET** environment variable statements that pass information to DOS programs (like a sound card's hardware settings)

- A **SET PATH** statement that specifies directories

- A virus-scanning program

An optimal CONFIG.SYS file under Windows 98 should be empty. However, the drivers built into Windows 98 may not support some hardware—for example, SCSI devices such as hard drives, scanners, or CD recorders; some network cards; and older tape drives. These devices will still require 16-bit device drivers in CONFIG.SYS to run at all in Windows 98.

TIP: *Why doesn't my CD-ROM install this program?—Unfortunately, loading a 16-bit device driver for a CD-ROM or hard drive during the startup sequence might result in that drive being accessed in MS-DOS compatibility mode, which is much slower than standard 32-bit file access within Windows 98. MS-DOS compatibility mode can also lead to problems with Windows 98 recognizing long filenames or running a CD-ROM automatically. For this reason, it's a good idea to routinely check the Web for upgraded drivers to any of your hardware, especially if that hardware currently requires 16-bit drivers in CONFIG.SYS.*

Checking Your DOS Startup Files

To check your DOS startup files for unnecessary clutter, follow these steps:

1. Click on the Start button and select Shut Down.

2. Click on Restart the Computer and click on Yes. Windows 98 will shut down and reboot your PC.

3. When the "Loading Windows 98..." prompt appears, press Shift+F8 to begin loading the statements in your CONFIG.SYS and AUTOEXEC.BAT file step by step.

4. Press Y to load the system Registry.

5. Windows 98 will ask for confirmation before loading your CONFIG.SYS file; press Y to begin processing the file. If any device drivers are mentioned, press N to skip them.

6. When Windows 98 prompts you, press Y to continue processing your startup command file (otherwise known as AUTOEXEC.BAT). If any programs are mentioned besides disk or anti-virus utilities, press N to skip them.

7. After Windows 98 has completed the startup sequence, check each hard drive and device on your system. If your system is working normally, you can safely optimize your DOS startup files by disabling all unnecessary statements.

Optimizing Your AUTOEXEC.BAT File

To remove unneeded statements from your AUTOEXEC.BAT file, follow these steps:

1. Double-click on the My Computer icon to display your drive icons.

2. Right-click on the drive icon where Windows 98 resides and select Explore from the menu.

3. Locate your AUTOEXEC.BAT file icon in the Contents window. Right-click on the icon and select Edit from the menu to edit the file within Windows Notepad.

4. Check each statement in the file. **SET** statements and programs that run and quit, such as virus scanners and disk-recovery utilities, are fine. Your AUTOEXEC.BAT file, however, should not load programs such as mouse drivers, the DOS program SHARE.EXE, or any program that remains running within Windows 98. If your CONFIG.SYS file is loading a 16-bit CD-ROM driver, your AUTOEXEC.BAT file may run the program MSCDEX.EXE—if this is the case, this statement should remain for now.

5. Insert the abbreviation **REM** (short for remark) and a space at the beginning of any statement for which testing has proven unnecessary; this effectively disables the statement, and Windows 98 will not process that line. For example, the line

```
C:\MOUSE\MOUSE.EXE
```

will become:

```
REM C:\MOUSE\MOUSE.EXE
```

6. After you make all the changes, save the file and close Notepad.

Optimizing Your CONFIG.SYS File

To optimize your CONFIG.SYS file, follow the same procedures outlined in the previous section, but substitute CONFIG.SYS for AUTOEXEC.BAT.

Restoring Statements To Your Startup Files

If your system locks up or hardware devices no longer work after you've made changes to your DOS startup files, you should trouble-shoot both files by restoring the statements that you disabled one by one until you find the statement that needs to load. To restore a statement in either of your DOS startup files, simply follow Steps 1 through 3 in the previous section "Optimizing Your AUTOEXEC.BAT File" and remove the **REM** and accompanying space from the front of the statement that needs to be processed.

Configuring Hardware During Startup

Are you constantly juggling hardware on your system? It can be a real hassle to reconfigure your system each time you change hardware—for example, connecting an older laptop computer to a docking station, or adding different combinations of external peripherals like a Zip drive, a flatbed scanner, and a printer to a desktop PC.

With Windows 98, you can solve this problem by creating multiple hardware configuration *profiles* to handle each combination of hardware that can be attached to your PC. If you're using a laptop with a docking station, you can select one profile to use while docked and another profile to use when you're on the road.

TIP: *It's not necessary to create a hardware profile for "plug and play" hardware because Windows 98 can automatically detect when these peripherals are added or removed.*

You can select which profile you'd like to use during the startup sequence; Windows 98 displays a menu with the profiles you've defined and pauses until you've selected one.

Creating A Hardware Profile

To create a new hardware profile, follow these steps:

1. Click on Start|Settings|Control Panel.

2. Double-click on the System icon to display the System Properties dialog box.

3. Click on the Hardware Profiles tab to display the Hardware Profiles pane, as shown in Figure 1.3.

4. In the profile list, click on the configuration that most closely matches your new profile to highlight it and click on Copy.

5. Enter a unique name for the new profile and click on OK.

6. Click on OK to exit the System Properties dialog box.

Adding Or Removing Hardware Within A Profile

To add or remove hardware within a hardware profile you've created, follow these steps:

1. Click on Start|Settings|Control Panel.

2. Double-click on the System icon to display the System Properties dialog box.

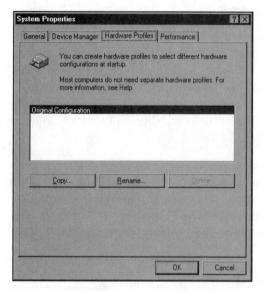

Figure 1.3   The Hardware Profiles pane is accessed from the System Properties dialog box.

3. Click on the Device Manager tab to display the Device Manager pane, as shown in Figure 1.4.

4. Click on the plus sign that appears beside the desired hardware class, and then double-click on the specific device to display its Properties dialog box, as shown in Figure 1.5.

5. Click on the desired profile name in the Device Usage list to add the device to the profile; a check mark will appear next to the profile name. To remove a device from a profile, click on the check mark beside the entry to clear the box.

6. Click on OK to confirm your changes and click on OK again to exit the System Properties dialog box.

7. Depending on the device, Windows 98 may require you to reboot before your changes are applied.

Removing Or Renaming A Hardware Profile

To remove or rename an existing hardware profile, follow these steps:

1. Click on Start|Settings|Control Panel.

2. Double-click on the System icon to display the System Properties dialog box.

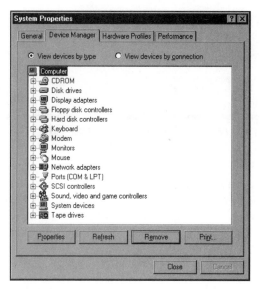

Figure 1.4   *You can add hardware to a profile from the Device Manager pane.*

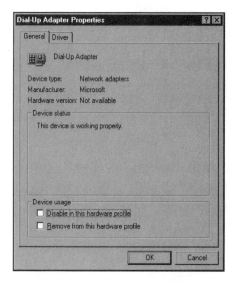

Figure 1.5   *Add hardware to a profile from the Device Usage list.*

3. Click on the Hardware Profiles tab to display the Hardware Profiles pane.

4. In the profile list, click on the configuration that you want to delete or rename.

5. To remove the profile, click on Delete.

6. To rename the profile, click on Rename. Enter a unique name for the new profile and click on OK.

7. Click on OK to exit the System Properties dialog box.

Configuring Multiple Logons With User Profiles

User profiles enable more than one person to customize their Windows 98 environment on the same computer—a good idea for office workstations, laptops that get passed around from salesperson to salesperson in an office, or computers that are used for shift work.

During the logon sequence, entering a username and password with a matching user profile will automatically load the Windows 98 desktop preferences associated with that user profile. User profiles are also supported within Internet Explorer 4 (IE4). Windows 98 keeps track of all changes a user makes and records the preferences automatically.

Enabling The User Profile System

By default, user profiles are disabled within Windows 98. To enable user profiles, follow these steps:

1. Click on Start|Settings|Control Panel.

2. Double-click on the Passwords icon.

3. Windows 98 displays the Password dialog box; click on the User Profiles tab.

4. Click on Users Can Customize Their Preferences And Desktop Settings.

5. Click on the Profile Settings options that you want to include in each user profile.

6. Double-click on the Passwords icon.

7. Click on OK; Windows 98 will reboot your PC.

Disabling The User Profile System

To completely disable all user-profile processing, follow these steps:

1. Click on Start|Settings|Control Panel.

2. Double-click on the Passwords icon.

3. Windows 98 displays the Password dialog box; click on the User Profiles tab.

4. Click on All Users Of This Computer Use The Same Preferences And Desktop Settings.

5. Click on OK; Windows 98 will reboot your PC.

Creating Your User Profile With The User Wizard

If no user profiles are currently set up, you can run the User Profile Wizard both to lead you through the process and to enable the user-profile system automatically. To run the User Profile Wizard, follow these steps:

1. Click on Start|Settings|Control Panel.

2. Double-click on the User icon.

3. Windows 98 launches the User Profile Wizard, as shown in Figure 1.6. Click on Next to continue.

4. Enter a username and password for your personal profile.

5. Click on Finish to exit the Wizard and reboot your PC.

TIP: *Adding and editing user profiles.—The easiest method of adding a new user profile is to log on to the computer with a new username; Windows 98 will automatically create a new user profile with that name. You can also add a new user from the Users icon in the Control Panel, or create a copy of an existing user profile under a new name. After you have created the first user profile under Windows 98, that profile acts as the administrator for all profiles created afterwards. Any user who wants to make changes to another user's profile will need to know the administrator's password that was used to create the first profile.*

Figure 1.6   The first user profile is created by the User Profile Wizard.

Adding Profiles From The User Settings Dialog Box

To add a new user, follow these steps:

1. Click on Start|Settings|Control Panel.

2. Double-click on the User icon.

3. Windows 98 displays the User Settings dialog box, as shown in Figure 1.7.

4. Click on New User—or, if you would like to copy an existing profile under a new name, highlight the profile name in the list and click on Make A Copy. Enter a username and password for the new personal profile.

5. Click on OK to add the profile and click on Close to exit the User Settings dialog box.

Editing Profiles From The User Settings Dialog Box

To edit an existing user's profile, follow these steps:

1. Click on Start|Settings|Control Panel.

2. Double-click on the User icon. Windows 98 prompts you for the administrator password.

3. After the correct password is entered, Windows 98 displays the User Settings dialog box.

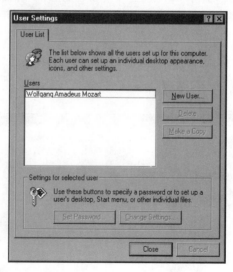

Figure 1.7   You can add, edit, and remove profiles from the User Settings dialog box.

4. Highlight the profile name you would like to edit. To change the logon password for the selected profile, click on the Set Password button and enter the new password. To change the desktop settings for that profile, click on Change Desktop.

5. Click on Close to exit the User Settings dialog box.

Removing User Profiles

To remove a user profile from the Users icon within the Control Panel, you will need the administrator's password, and you must *not* be currently logged on as that user. Follow these steps:

1. Click on Start button|Settings|Control Panel.

2. Double-click on the User icon.

3. After the correct password has been entered, Windows 98 displays the User Settings dialog box.

4. Highlight the profile name you would like to remove and click on Delete.

5. Click on Close to exit the User Settings dialog box.

TIP: *Deleting profiles using RegEdit.—You can remove one or all of the user profiles on your computer through the System Registry. The Registry subkey*

```
HKEY_LOCAL_MACHINE
\Software\Microsoft\Windows\CurrentVersion\Profilelst
```

contains the names of all users with user profiles.

Deleting Individual Profiles

To delete an individual profile, follow these steps:

1. Click on Start|Run. Enter "REGEDIT.EXE" and click on OK.

2. From the RegEdit main window, click on Edit and select Find.

3. Enable only the Keys search option and enter the text "Profilelst".

4. Highlight the username keys you want to remove in the right side of the RegEdit window and press Delete.

5. Exit the RegEdit program.

6. Double-click on the My Computer icon to display your drive icons.

7. Right-click on the drive icon where you installed Windows and select Explore from the menu.

8. Click on View|Options and click on the Show All Files option to enable it. Click on OK to close the dialog box.

9. Switch to your Windows folder and double-click on the Profiles subfolder to open it. Windows 98 displays the different folders for each user profile.

10. Highlight the folders with the same names as the username keys you deleted in RegEdit and press Delete to delete them. Close Explorer.

Deleting All Profiles

To delete all profiles, follow these steps:

1. Click on Start|Run. Enter REGEDIT.EXE and click on OK.

2. From the RegEdit main window, click on Edit and select Find.

3. Enable only the Keys search option and enter the text "Profilelst".

4. Highlight the **Profilelst** subkey in the left side of the RegEdit window and press Delete.

5. Exit the RegEdit program.

6. Double-click on the My Computer icon to display your drive icons.

7. Right-click on the drive icon where you installed Windows and select Explore from the menu.

8. Click on View|Options and click on the Show All Files option to enable it. Click on OK to close the dialog box.

9. Switch to your Windows folder and double-click on the Profiles subfolder to open it. Windows 98 displays the different folders for each user profile.

10. Highlight all of the folders within the Profile folder and press Delete to delete them. Close Explorer.

Optimizing The Shutdown Process

Does it seem to take forever for your PC to shut down? One of the features of Windows 98 is a faster shutdown process than with Windows 95—however, there are a number of tricks you can use to optimize the shutdown process. It never hurts to shave a few additional seconds off your wait time.

To reduce the amount of time it takes to shut down in Windows 98, you must complete the following tasks:

- *Reduce Taskbar items and background tasks*—Before the shutdown process can complete, Windows 98 must first close each of the Taskbar programs and background tasks. Some of these programs can take several seconds to quit and unload, which is extra time you spend waiting. (Also, loading too many programs on your Taskbar eats up valuable memory and system resources; I recommend you load no more than three or four Taskbar items on your PC.)

- *Close all open applications first*—Before you click on Shut Down, take a second or two to close any unnecessary applications that are still running—for example, Outlook or Microsoft Word 97. It typically takes longer during the shutdown process to close applications than it does to close them manually.

- *Log off manually*—If you have an active dial-up Internet connection or your modem is connected to a BBS, it will save time if you disconnect before you shut down.

- *Reduce the size of your Registry*—Because the Registry is accessed often during both the startup and shutdown sequences, you'll notice a big difference if you run a utility to optimize the Registry file. Several third-party programs are available that can remove unneeded data from the Registry and compress it to the smallest possible size—for example, Norton Utilities from Symantec and Nuts and Bolts from McAfee.

Troubleshooting

Troubleshooting Startup Errors

Startup errors can be caused by a wide range of problems, including device driver conflicts, system file and Registry corruption, network configuration errors, and ill-behaved applications. Unfortunately, under certain conditions, Windows 98 can grind to a halt during startup without displaying a single error message. This section discusses a number of tools that will help you to troubleshoot errors that occur during startup.

TIP: *Take note of error messages.—It's always a good idea to write down any error messages that Windows 98 displays during the startup sequence. Although these messages are often cryptic, they usually include at least a short text description and a mention of the specific file that's causing the problem. Any error message will usually be helpful if you need to call for technical support.*

Troubleshooting With Safe Mode

Troubleshooting With Safe Mode

Let's face it: It's hard to troubleshoot your system if your PC consistently locks up during the startup sequence! If you suddenly find that your system can't complete startup and never displays the desktop, you still have a card to play: You can boot Windows 98 in Safe mode, which corresponds to a "vanilla" system with nothing extra.

In Safe mode, your PC uses a standard VGA video driver; any extraneous device drivers or programs in your Startup folder are not loaded (which often bypasses the source of the problem). Often, Safe mode is the only method of making a change to your system if it's experiencing a severe lockup; from within Safe mode, you can disable misbehaving hardware, edit system-initialization files, and troubleshoot problems.

To activate Safe mode from the Windows 98 Startup menu, press F8 when the Windows 98 loading prompt appears to display the menu. If you're connected to a network, select Safe Mode With Network, and Windows 98 will attempt to load the necessary drivers and components so that you can access your network resources. If you're not connected to a network, select Safe Mode.

Troubleshooting With Step-By-Step Confirmation

If your startup problem is due to a driver automatically added by a program to either your AUTOEXEC.BAT or CONFIG.SYS files, running the startup sequence step by step often can pinpoint the problem. You can use this technique to disable each statement in both files. If disabling a driver or program results in a successful boot without the error, you've isolated the problem, and you can follow the steps in the section "Optimizing Your AUTOEXEC.BAT File" in this chapter to disable that statement.

Follow the steps outlined in the section "Checking Your DOS Startup Files" in this chapter to disable one entry at a time in your DOS startup files. It's recommended that you begin with CONFIG.SYS, since a serious lockup is more likely to be caused by a driver conflict.

Creating And Viewing BOOTLOG.TXT

If you press F8 to display the Windows 98 Startup menu at the beginning of the startup sequence, you can select the Logged option to create the file BOOTLOG.TXT. BOOTLOG.TXT is a hidden file in the root directory of the drive where Windows 98 was installed; although the file may appear very technical and cryptic, it can provide valuable information if you're experiencing problems during the startup sequence.

To view BOOTLOG.TXT within Windows 98, follow these steps:

1. Start Windows 98 in Logged mode by pressing F8 during startup and selecting the Logged menu item.

2. After the startup sequence has completed, double-click on the My Computer icon to display your drive icons.

3. Right-click on the C: icon and select Explore from the menu.

4. Click on View|Options and click on the Show All Files option to enable it. Click on OK to close the dialog box.

5. Locate the BOOTLOG.TXT file icon in the Contents window and double-click on the icon to open the file in Notepad, as shown in Figure 1.8.

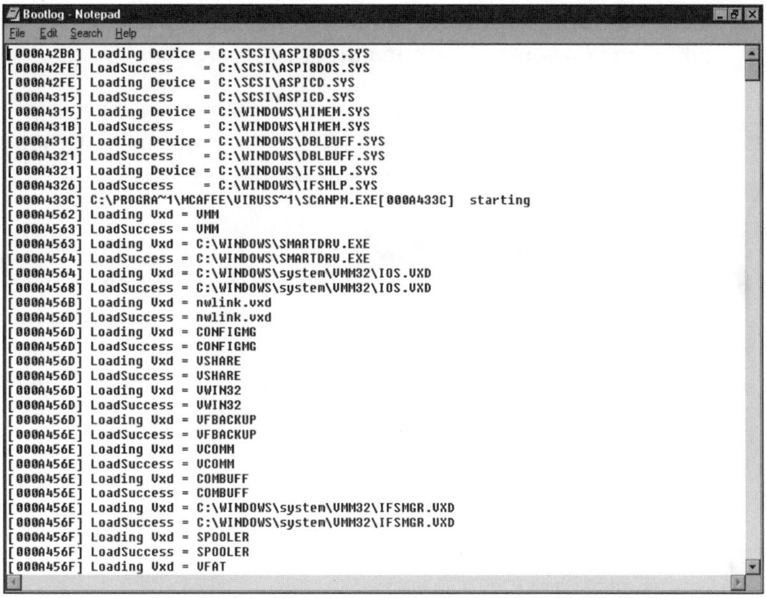

Figure 1.8   Viewing the record of a startup sequence in Notepad.

Note that each entry marks the loading of a device driver or system file, while the next entry in the file indicates whether or not that component was loaded successfully. This makes it easy to locate programs or drivers that may be causing problems; Windows 98 marks loading failures and generally provides a short error description, similar to the following line:

```
[000AFC33] Dynamic load failed serwave.vxd : [000AFC33] File
not found
```

Although BOOTLOG.TXT may not include enough information in every case, it's useful for pinpointing problem areas. Microsoft technical support will often refer to it as a debugging tool.

Troubleshooting With The Windows 98 Command Line

Windows 98 will recognize the following command line parameters if you run the program from the DOS prompt:

- *win /d:f*—Disables 32-bit file access.
- *win /d:v*—Disables some of the advanced hard drive I/O routines within Windows 98.

- *win /d:x*—May help avoid problems with upper memory allocation on some older computers.

If you're encountering startup problems and any of these command line switches allows Windows 98 to boot normally without error, I recommend calling Microsoft technical support.

Disabling Startup Programs

If a startup sequence lockup occurs after Windows 98 has started to display the desktop, then one of the programs in your Startup folder may be causing the problem. To disable all Startup programs for a single session of troubleshooting, simply hold down the Shift key when you see the Windows 98 startup graphic, and hold it down throughout the startup sequence until the Taskbar appears. Windows 98 will ignore all Startup programs. If this action solves your startup problem, one of the programs in your Startup folder is causing the error.

Checking Your System Registry With SCANREG

The Windows 98 Registry file can become corrupted and cause severe problems or system lockups during start up. The MS-DOS program SCANREG.EXE, which is provided with Windows 98, can check your Registry file for problems even if you can't boot Windows 98. Simply type SCANREG at the DOS prompt and press Enter; the program will prompt you if there are problems with the Registry that it can detect and fix.

The Active Desktop

In Brief

The Active Desktop

The Active Desktop is one of the key features that separates Windows 98 from Windows 95; it's the first step in combining elements of the traditional Windows desktop, the Internet (or, more specifically, the World Wide Web), and the information and entertainment content of television. Both individual Web surfers on the Internet and employees on a corporate intranet can display active channels on their Windows 98 Active Desktop—but rather than broadcasting over the air, these content providers are *webcasting* over the network.

Active Desktop technology has also changed the traditional elements of the desktop that we have used since the days of Windows 3.0. For example, you can now do the following:

- Display folders in the same format as a Web page within a browser.
- "Paste" HTML applets and graphics directly on your desktop.
- Add application-specific toolbars to the Taskbar or allow them to "float" on top of the desktop.
- Customize the appearance of menus.

However, this new look and feel may not appeal to everyone who switches from Windows 95 to Windows 98. If you feel that the familiar Windows 95 desktop is better and HTML technology should remain within your browser window, don't despair—you can select a number of options that disable most of the Active Desktop's functions and return you to more comfortable waters.

The projects in this chapter show you how to either take full advantage of the Active Desktop or disable as much of it as possible. You'll learn how to customize the various elements of the Active Desktop, and also how to configure Active Channels that receive information from content providers on the Web and your company intranet.

Immediate Solutions

Disabling The Active Desktop

Although the default Active Desktop that ships with Windows 98 will appeal to many people, some users may not want the extra functionality; for example, users with little experience on the World Wide Web may find the older Windows 95 interface to be faster and easier to use.

If you want to restore your Windows 98 system to the "look and feel" of Windows 95, follow the projects in this section.

Removing Active Wallpaper

Windows 98 can incorporate HTML elements into its background wallpaper, but the animation used on Active Desktop wallpaper can often significantly slow the performance of older PCs (especially machines with less video memory, and 486 or early Pentium processors). The first step in disabling the Active Desktop is to reload a plain bitmap as your background. To do so, follow these steps:

1. Click on Start|Settings.

2. Click on Control Panel to open the Control Panel window and double-click on the Display icon to open the Display Properties dialog box, as shown in Figure 2.1.

3. Click on the Background tab.

4. Highlight a plain bitmap or choose (None) from the Wallpaper list.

5. Click on OK to apply your changes.

Changing Folder Options

Unlike in Windows 95, the default Windows 98 Active Desktop uses a single click to open folders—if you've spent the last few years double-clicking to open a folder in Windows Explorer or on your Windows 95 desktop, this can be quite disconcerting! To return to the Windows 95 method of opening folders, follow these steps:

1. Click on Start|Settings.

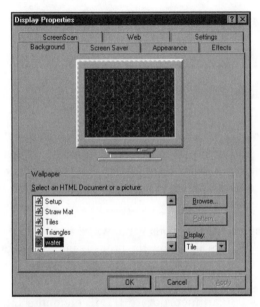

Figure 2.1   The Display Properties dialog box.

2. Click on Folder Options to open the Folder Options dialog box, as shown in Figure 2.2.

3. Click on the Classic Style option.

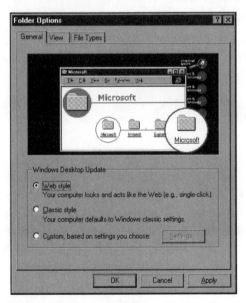

Figure 2.2   The Folder Options dialog box.

4. Click on OK to apply your changes.

TIP: *Disabling Web Items—By default, Windows 98 includes a number of HTML items (usually referred to as controls) on the Active Desktop, including the Internet Explorer Channel bar. You can disable each of these controls individually, or you can choose to disable the entire Web page functionality of the Active Desktop.*

Disabling A Single Web Control Within The Active Desktop

To disable one or more Web controls on your Active Desktop without disabling Web functionality completely, follow these steps:

1. Click on Start|Settings.

2. Click on Control Panel to open the Control Panel window, and double-click on the Display icon to open the Display Properties dialog box.

3. Click on the Web tab.

4. In the Web Control list, click on each entry you want to disable; this will remove the checkmark beside each entry.

5. Click on OK to apply your changes.

Disabling All Web Controls Within The Active Desktop

To disable Web functionality completely within the Active Desktop, follow these steps:

1. Click on Start|Settings.

2. Click on Control Panel to open the Control Panel window and double-click on the Display icon to open the Display Properties dialog box.

3. Click on the Web tab.

4. Click on the View My Active Desktop As A Web Page field to disable it. Note that the Web Control list is also disabled automatically.

5. Click on OK to apply your changes.

Removing Custom Toolbars

If you have created a custom toolbar on the Windows Taskbar, you can follow these steps to remove it:

1. Move the mouse cursor over the custom toolbar and right-click on it.

2. Click on Close from the menu to remove the toolbar.

Removing The Quick Launch Toolbar

The default Windows 98 Quick Launch toolbar adds four buttons next to the Start button that will perform four functions with a single click: Launch Outlook Express, Show Desktop, View Channels, and Launch Internet Explorer Browser. To remove these Quick Launch buttons from the Taskbar, take the following steps:

1. Move your mouse cursor over the toolbar and right-click on it.

2. Click on Toolbars from the menu.

3. Click on Quick Launch to remove the checkmark, which disables the Quick Launch toolbar.

Arranging Desktop Elements

Each Active Desktop element can be individually arranged—and many elements can appear in more than one location. This section discusses how to activate each element (and place elements, where necessary).

Adding Web Items

You can add HTML controls to your Active Desktop background, including Java and ActiveX applets written for use as Active Desktop items. To do so, follow these steps:

1. Click on Start|Settings.

2. Click on Control Panel to open the Control Panel window, and then double-click on the Display icon to open the Display Properties dialog box.

3. Click on the Web tab.

4. In the Web Control list, click on New.

5. Windows 98 displays the New Active Desktop Item dialog box, as shown in Figure 2.3. To load an item from a different location, click on No; Windows 98 will allow you to browse for the location of the new item. To connect to the Active Desktop Gallery on the Web, click on Yes.

Figure 2.3   The New Active Desktop Item dialog box gives you the chance to connect to the Microsoft Active Desktop Gallery.

Windows 98 opens Internet Explorer and displays an index of items. If you decide to add one or more of these items, they will be automatically downloaded.

Adding HTML Wallpaper

To use an HTML page located on your local PC or network, follow these steps:

1. Click on Start|Settings.

2. Click on Control Panel to open the Control Panel window and double-click on the Display icon to open the Display Properties dialog box.

3. Click on the Background tab.

4. Highlight the desired HTML page from the Wallpaper list.

5. Click on OK to apply your changes.

Adding Explorer Bars

The Active Desktop allows you to include *Explorer bars*, which can display one of five drop-down lists from the My Computer window or the Windows Explorer; the display appears within a separate pane on the left side of the window. Explorer bars allow the integration of traditional browser functionality within your Windows 98 file system (for example, you now can search the Internet or connect to a favorite site without launching Internet Explorer or Netscape Navigator).

The five lists are:

• *Favorites*—A list of the favorite Web addresses, folders, and programs you've accumulated within Internet Explorer.

- *Search*—A shortcut to one of several Web search engines, where you can enter keywords to search for information on the Web. Figure 2.4 shows the My Computer Search bar.

- *History*—A list of links you've recently visited within Internet Explorer.

- *Channels*—A list of the active c hannels you've joined as a subscriber.

- *All Folders*—A list of all local and network folders (this bar is available only within Windows Explorer).

To activate Explorer bars within the My Computer window or Windows Explorer, follow these steps:

1. Click on View|Explorer Bar.

2. Click on the type of Explorer bar that you want to display. To disable Explorer bars, click on None.

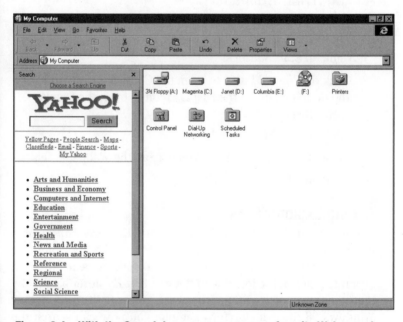

Figure 2.4   *With the Search bar, you can use your favorite Web search engine within the My Computer window.*

Adding Custom Toolbars And Taskbar Controls

The Active Desktop adds functionality to the traditional Windows Taskbar, but it also allows you to create brand-new custom toolbars that "float" above the desktop. These new toolbars let you run any program or load almost any data directly from the desktop with a single click, and it's easy to create a custom toolbar with the contents of any folder on your system.

Adding Quick Launch Icons

To add applications, Web URL addresses, files, or file folders to the Quick Launch area of the Taskbar, follow these steps:

1. Double-click on My Computer to open the My Computer window. (Alternately, you can right-click on My Computer and select Explore from the menu to open Windows Explorer.)

2. Click on the desired icon within the window and drag it to the Quick Launch toolbar.

Windows 98 displays a small version of the same icon within the Quick Launch toolbar.

Adding Icons To The Windows Taskbar

To add applications, Web URL addresses, files, or file folders to the Taskbar, follow these steps:

1. Double-click on My Computer to open the My Computer window. (Alternately, you can right-click on My Computer and select Explore from the menu to open Windows Explorer.)

2. Click on the desired icon within the window and drag it to the Taskbar.

Windows 98 displays a small version of the same icon within the Taskbar as a new custom toolbar. If the icon is of a drive or folder, the contents also will be displayed on the toolbar.

Creating A New Toolbar From A Folder

You can create a brand-new toolbar with the contents of a folder, including applications, Web URL addresses, files, and other file folders. To do so, follow these steps after you've set up the contents of the folder:

1. Right-click on the Taskbar and select Toolbars from the menu.

2. Click on New Toolbar.

3. Windows 98 displays the New Toolbar dialog box, as shown in Figure 2.5.

4. Navigate to the desired folder, highlight it, and click on OK.

Windows 98 displays the contents of the folder within the Taskbar as a new custom toolbar.

Adding A Floating Toolbar

To transfer an existing custom toolbar to the Active Desktop as a floating toolbar, follow these steps:

1. Click on and drag the desired toolbar from the Taskbar and place it anywhere on the Active Desktop background.

2. Resize the toolbar as desired.

Figure 2.5   Creating a new custom toolbar with the contents of a folder from the New Toolbar dialog box.

Customizing The Windows 98 Menu System

It's now easier than ever to customize three of the familiar menus within Windows 98: the Start menu, the Programs menu, and the Favorites menu. All three can be changed to provide a custom Active Desktop menu system.

Adding An Item To The Start Menu

To add an item to the Start menu, follow these steps:

1. Double-click on My Computer to open the My Computer window. (Alternately, you can right-click on My Computer and select Explore from the menu to open Windows Explorer.)

2. Navigate to the location of the item icon on your system.

3. Click on the desired icon within the window and drag it to the Start button.

Windows 98 automatically adds the item to the top of the Start menu.

Removing An Item From The Start Menu

To remove an item from the Start menu, follow these steps:

1. Click on the Start button to display the Start menu.

2. Right-click on the desired icon within the Start menu and select Delete from the menu.

Arranging An Item On The Start Menu

To change the position of an item on the Start menu, follow these steps:

1. Click on the Start button to display the Start menu.

2. Right-click on the desired icon and drag the item to the new location within the menu.

Adding An Item To The Programs Menu

To add an item to the Programs menu, follow these steps:

1. Click on Start|Settings.

2. Click on Taskbar & Start Menu to display the Taskbar Properties dialog box.

3. Click on the Start Menu Programs tab to display the pane shown in Figure 2.6, then click on Add.

4. Click on Browse and navigate through your system to the location of the program you wish to add.

5. Highlight the desired program and click on Open|Next.

6. Select the Programs folder where the icon should appear, or click on New Folder to create a new Programs folder. Click on Next to continue.

7. Type the name for the item in the Programs menu and click on Finish.

8. Click on OK to close the Taskbar Properties dialog box.

The new item is created within the target folder you selected.

Removing An Item From The Programs Menu

To remove an item from the Programs menu, follow these steps:

1. Click on Start|Settings.

2. Click on Taskbar & Start Menu to display the Taskbar Properties dialog box, and then click on the Start Menu Programs tab.

3. Click on Remove to display the Remove Shortcuts/Folders dialog box. Click on the small plus sign next to the folder that contains the item you want to remove.

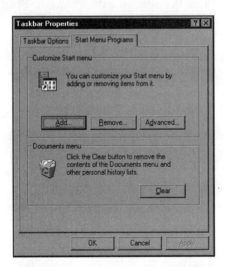

Figure 2.6   You can add or remove items from the Start or Programs menus from this dialog box.

4. Windows 98 displays the contents of the folder. Highlight the icon you want to remove and click on Remove.

5. Click on Close to exit the Remove Shortcuts/Folders dialog box, and then click on OK to exit the Taskbar Properties dialog box.

Arranging An Item On The Programs Menu

To change the position of an item on the Programs menu, follow these steps:

1. Click on the Start button to display the Start menu, and then click on Programs.

2. Right-click on the desired icon and drag the item to the new location within the menu.

Arranging An Item On The Favorites Menu

To change the position of an entry in your Favorites menu, follow these steps:

1. Click on the Start button to display the Start menu, and then click on Favorites.

2. Right-click on the desired icon and drag the item to the new location within the menu.

Configuring Active Channel Subscriptions

Windows 98 has standardized the "server push" technology often used by larger Web sites to provide updated news, weather, or information automatically to your PC over the Internet. In the past, this push information has been displayed within a screen saver or a small display window on the desktop. With the arrival of Active Channels, however, the data is supported seamlessly within the operating system, allowing Web authors to customize the entire appearance of the channel on their desktop (and even the delivery times for updated channel information).

You can configure any Active Desktop items or channels you've subscribed to from the Display Properties dialog box; for example, items that display news content should be scheduled for regular updates, whereas sites with content that's not as timely can be updated once a week.

Subscribing To A Site

To subscribe to an Active Desktop channel site, follow these steps:

1. Run Internet Explorer and load the Web page for the site. The site should feature an Add to Channels button; click on it to begin the subscription process.

2. Windows 98 displays the Subscribe Channel dialog box, which offers you two options. To receive notification through email of updates to this channel, click on the Only Tell Me When Updates Occur field. To receive notification through email and automatically download future updates, click on The Notify Me Of Updates And Download The Channel For Offline Viewing field.

3. Click on OK to save your changes.

Unsubscribing From A Site

To unsubscribe from an Active Desktop item or channel, follow these steps:

1. Click on Start|Settings.

2. Click on Control Panel to open the Control Panel window, and then double-click on the Display icon to open the Display Properties dialog box.

3. Click on the Web tab.

4. In the Web Control list, select the desired entry and click on Properties.

5. Click on the Subscription tab.

6. Click on Unsubscribe, and then click on OK to save your changes.

Scheduling Subscription Updates

To schedule the updates for an Active Desktop item or channel, follow these steps:

1. Click on Start|Settings.

2. Click on Control Panel to open the Control Panel window, and then double-click on the Display icon to open the Display Properties dialog box.

3. Click on the Web tab.

4. In the Web Control list, select the desired entry and click on Properties.

5. Click on the Schedule tab.

6. Windows 98 displays the Schedule pane, as shown in Figure 2.7. This pane offers several options, as follows:

- To schedule an item automatically, click on Scheduled and select the frequency (daily, monthly, or weekly).

- To create a custom schedule, click on New and select from the options in the Custom Schedule dialog box.

- To edit an existing schedule, click on it to select it and then click on Edit. (If you use a dial-up connection to the Internet, click on Dial As Needed If You Are Connected Through A Modem field so that, if necessary, Windows 98 can establish an Internet connection.)

- To update the item manually, click on Manually. The update takes place whenever you select the Update All Subscriptions item from the Favorites menu. You also can update immediately by clicking on the Update Now button.

7. If you'd rather not be interrupted by the update process while you work with your computer, click on the Don't Update This Subscription When I'm Using My Computer checkbox. (Note, however, that enabling this field may interfere with automatic updating.)

8. Click on OK to accept the changes, and then click on OK to exit the Display Properties dialog box.

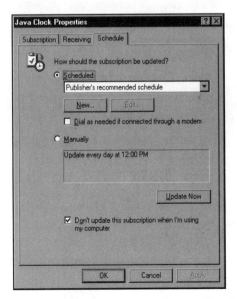

Figure 2.7   You can schedule updates for Active Desktop items automatically or manually.

Using Desktop Themes

Another powerful method of customizing your Active Desktop
under Windows 98 is the *desktop theme*, which was originally introduced with the Windows 95 Plus Pack. A complete desktop
theme can contain everything from a background image and animated cursors to custom sound effects for events and a custom
color scheme. Desktop themes come in handy if the following situations exist:

• An entire office wants to standardize the appearance of
  company PCs or workstations

• You want to feature a favorite topic or hobby on your desktop

• Multiple people are using a PC, and at least one person needs
  larger fonts and higher contrast colors for better readability

Loading A Desktop Theme

To load an existing desktop theme, follow these steps:

1. Click on Start|Settings.

2. Click on Control Panel to open the Control Panel window,
   and then double-click on the Desktop Themes icon to open
   the Desktop Themes dialog box, as shown in Figure 2.8.

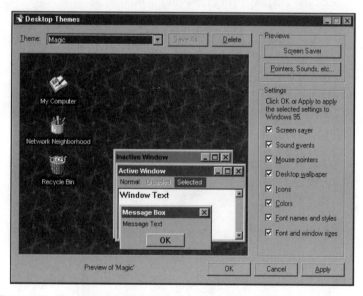

*Figure 2.8   From the Desktop Themes dialog box, you can load and apply
different themes.*

3. To load all the elements of a desktop theme, check all the boxes under Settings and select a theme name from the Theme drop-down list. To load only certain elements of the theme, check only the elements you want to load.

4. Windows 98 displays an example of the desktop's new appearance in the preview window. If you approve of the scheme, click on OK to accept the change.

5. Windows 98 automatically loads all the theme elements you selected.

Removing Tray Icons

The Taskbar *system tray* has been a favorite Windows timesaver since its debut in Windows 95, and many applications automatically add icons to your system tray when you install them. These icons represent programs that are running "in the background," performing tasks behind the scenes such as scanning for viruses or monitoring your Internet connection.

However, each one of these icons in the system tray takes a certain amount of CPU time and memory to run—too many tray programs can appreciably slow your system and reduce the amount of free memory available to Windows 98. To help optimize the performance of your PC, you may decide to eliminate some of these programs permanently, or you can simply disable one or more of these programs until you restart your PC.

TIP: *Do I really need this system tray program?—Removing a clock or a calendar program from your system tray won't harm anything, but beware! Remember, some programs in your system tray may be required to use some hardware devices or applications, so always be careful when removing a program—generally, you should try disabling the program first. If you're not certain what a particular system tray icon does, move your mouse cursor over the icon (sometimes a left- or right-click may be required), and see if it displays any information or a menu.*

Disabling System Tray Programs

To temporarily disable system tray programs until you restart Windows 98, follow these steps:

1. Move your mouse cursor directly over the icon you wish to disable. (Depending on the program, you may need to click, right-click, or double-click in order to display the icon's menu.)

2. Select Close, Exit, or Disable from the icon's menu.

Removing System Tray Programs From The StartUp Folder

Some system tray programs are loaded from the StartUp folder. To permanently remove one of these program icons from your Windows 98 system tray, follow these steps:

1. Click on Start|Settings.

2. Click on Taskbar & Start Menu to display the Taskbar Properties dialog box, and then click on the Start Menu Programs tab.

3. Click on Remove to display the Remove Shortcuts/Folders dialog box. Click on the small plus sign next to the StartUp folder.

4. Windows 98 displays all programs stored in the StartUp folder, as shown in Figure 2.9. Highlight the icon you want to remove and press the Delete key. Click on OK to exit the Taskbar Properties dialog box.

Figure 2.9   Preparing to remove a program from the StartUp folder.

Removing System Tray Programs From WIN.INI

If a program is being automatically loaded during the startup sequence and it doesn't appear in the StartUp folder, the chances are good that the program was added to your WIN.INI file. To permanently remove one of these program icons from your Windows 98 system tray, follow these steps:

1. Click on Start|Programs|Accessories|Notepad.

2. Within Notepad, click on File|Open to display the File Open dialog box. Navigate to your Windows directory.

3. In the File Name field, type "win.ini" and click on Open.

4. Search through WIN.INI for the [Windows] label; under this label, delete the program names you want to remove from the **Run=** and **Load=** statements.

5. Click on File|Save to save your edited WIN.INI file under the same name.

6. Click on File|Exit to exit Notepad.

Optimizing The Desktop

With all the new elements available within the Active Desktop, the possibilities for optimizing your Window 98 desktop seem endless. This section covers four configurations; each configuration is designed around the type of work you perform on your PC and what resources are available to your computer.

Deactivating The Active Desktop

If you fall into one of the following categories, I recommend that you optimize Windows 98 by disabling most of the Active Desktop altogether:

• Users who have extensive experience with Windows 95 and have grown accustomed to it may feel more comfortable with most of the Active Desktop disabled.

• Users with less powerful computers—such as laptop PCs or older 486 computers—may not want to devote system resources and CPU power to the Active Desktop display.

• Users with no connection to the Internet or an office intranet will find little benefit in the Active Desktop.

For more information on disabling the default Active Desktop elements installed with Windows 98, see the previous section, "Disabling The Active Desktop," in this chapter.

Optimizing For Speed

This configuration is designed for the Windows 98 user who wants the fastest possible response from the Active Desktop. To optimize the desktop for speed, take the following steps:

1. Disable the HTML background (see the previous section, "Disabling The Active Desktop"). For the fastest redraw speed and the lowest memory requirements, I recommend a plain, single-color background.

2. Drag the applications, files, and folders you use the most to the Taskbar and create custom toolbars. It's faster to use toolbars when they appear on the Taskbar, because the Taskbar is always available (even if you're using a program full screen).

3. Add an All Folders Explorer bar to speed your navigation in Windows Explorer. (If you use the Internet heavily for research, you might also consider a Search Explorer bar as well, which will make browsing the Web a much simpler process.)

4. If you subscribe to any Active Channels or controls, you can avoid interruptions to your work by scheduling them for manual updates. Using the manual updates scheduling option allows you to start the update process when your PC will be idle (such as a lunch break).

Optimizing For The Manager Or Workgroup Member

Another kind of Windows 98 user must manage or participate in multiple tasks, keeping everything organized but within the reach of one or two mouse clicks. If you fit this description, follow these steps to optimize your desktop:

1. If you have a local intranet connection through your network, you'll find it easy to stay updated by adding your project's Web pages as Active Desktop items.

2. Create a custom floating toolbar for each of your projects by loading the contents of your project folder. You'll be able to access the important data required for any of your projects from your desktop, and everything remains organized. Figure 2.10 shows such a desktop configuration.

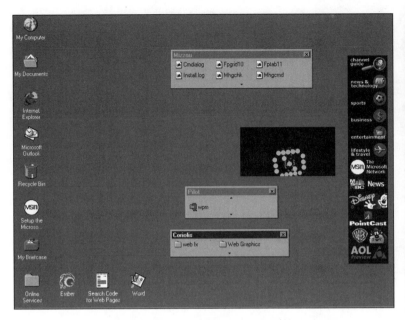

Figure 2.10   An Active Desktop optimized for a project manager.

3. Add an All Folders Explorer bar to speed your navigation in Windows Explorer; this will allow you to quickly navigate throughout the entire network while exploring.

4. If your intranet offers Active Channels with changing content, make sure that your schedule for this channel includes at least one daily automatic update (or create a custom update schedule). If you're away from your desk or on the road, Windows 98 can send an email message signaling each update. Often, this email can be sent to a pager or retrieved remotely from a portable computer.

Optimizing For The High-Speed Internet Connection

Whether you're surfing the Web for fun, for research, or as part of your job, it makes a big difference to your Active Desktop if you have a dial-up connection of 56Kbps, an ISDN link, or a direct network connection. To optimize the Windows 98 desktop for a high-speed link, follow these steps:

1. Configure your Active Channel subscriptions at a daily update interval (or less), and allow your channel subscriptions to update your PC while you're using it.

2. Add a Favorites Explorer bar to your Windows Explorer. This action will allow you to connect to any of your favorite links from the Explorer window.

3. Add a Search Explorer bar to your Windows Explorer. With the Search bar, you can access your favorite Internet search engine directly from the Explorer window.

4. Stay on top of the latest information by using an Active Channel screen saver. Many channels offer screen savers, and Windows 98 will automatically switch the display between each of your subscribed savers every 60 seconds. You can click on a link displayed by the screen saver to open a browser window for more information on that topic.

5. Make full use of Active Desktop items on your desktop background.

Troubleshooting

Troubleshooting Desktop Problems

If you're experiencing problems with the Active Desktop, you may be able to locate the source of the trouble with the following troubleshooting tips.

Problems With The Windows Background

If you can't load a background file within Windows 98 or if it looks wrong after it loads, check the following possible trouble areas:

- *The image is not in the proper format*—Windows 98 recognizes standard Windows bitmap format for image files (usually ending with the extension .BMP) and HTML files for active backgrounds. You will have to use an image editor to convert image files in other formats to Windows bitmaps.

- *The image is stretched*—If your background image looks grainy or distorted, you've probably selected Stretch as your background display setting and Windows has changed the resolution to fit your screen. To fix this, follow these steps:

  1. Click on Start|Settings.

  2. Click on Control Panel to open the Control Panel window and double-click on the Display icon to open the Display Properties dialog box.

  3. Click on the Background tab.

  4. Highlight the desired bitmap image or HTML page from the Wallpaper list, and select Center from the Display drop-down list box.

  5. Click on OK to apply your changes.

Intranet Active Channels Return Errors

If you've subscribed to an Active Channel on your office intranet and receive errors from Windows 98 or your intranet server, check these possible sources:

- *Incorrect (or nonexistent) CDF file*—The Channel Definition Format file created by the system administrator or Web author controls the data sent to every subscriber, as well as the update timetable and the display format. An error within this file can either block access to a channel or cause a display problem on your system.

- *Logon profiles are required*—If you haven't configured your workstation with the correct logon profile—typically created by the system administrator—you won't be able to receive content from an intranet Active Channel.

Active Desktop Items Return Errors

Active Desktop Items Return Errors

Active Desktop items and Active Channels that you've downloaded from the Internet can often cause the following problems on the desktop:

- *The program returns errors*—This situation can be caused by a poorly written item that doesn't trap for error conditions, especially if the program requires a live Internet or intranet connection and you're currently working offline. If the error message doesn't provide a solution or recommend a course of action, try downloading the latest update to see if the problem has been fixed. If not, contact the item's developer.

- *The program can't connect for updates*—Dial-up connections are strictly controlled within Windows 98. To ensure that the item can automatically initiate a dial-up connection, follow these steps:

    1. Click on Start|Settings.

    2. Click on Control Panel to open the Control Panel window, and then double-click on the Display icon to open the Display Properties dialog box.

    3. Click on the Web tab.

    4. In the Web Control list, select the desired entry and click on Properties.

    5. Click on the Schedule tab.

    6. Windows 98 displays the Schedule pane. Make sure that you've enabled The Dial As Needed If Connected Through A Modem option so that Windows 98 can establish an Internet connection if necessary.

    7. Click on OK to accept your changes, and then click on OK to exit the Display Properties dialog box.

Applications Won't Automatically Load

Sometimes, you try to double-click on a data file or document used by an application you've installed under Windows 98, but you cannot open it. This may occur for several reasons:

- *The program has moved*—If you move the location of a file or program to another folder on your hard drive, all shortcuts that you created on the desktop or within a toolbar will no longer point to the right place. Windows 98 will automatically attempt to find the original program by scanning your drive, but if that doesn't succeed, follow these steps:

  1. Right-click on the icon and select Properties from the menu.

  2. Click on the Shortcut tab, and then click on the Find Target button.

  3. Navigate to the new location and double-click on the original file or program.

  4. Click on OK to close the Properties dialog box.

- *The file type is not recognized*—This indicates that Windows 98 doesn't recognize the file's extension as "belonging" to an application. Windows 98 displays the dialog box shown in Figure 2.11. To change the file type, follow these steps:

  1. Scroll down the list of recognized applications within Windows 98, and then select the program that always should be used to open a file with this extension. If the file is a standard ASCII text file, you can use Notepad.

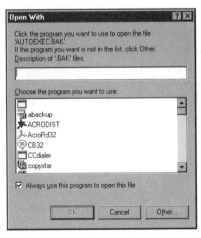

Figure 2.11   You can create file associations from this dialog box.

2. Click on the Always Use This Program To Open This File checkboxto enable it.

3. Click on OK to save the file association and open the specified application.

- *The wrong program appears*—Sometimes, the installation process of a new application will nullify the association created by an earlier program. For example, installing a new graphics editor might change the association so that it opens a JPEG image rather than your favorite image slideshow program. To restore or change an association, follow these steps:

  1. Double-click on My Computer to open the My Computer window. (Alternately, you can right-click on My Computer and select Explore from the menu to open Windows Explorer.)

  2. Click on View|Folder Options from the menu.

  3. Click on the File Types tab and scroll down the list of recognized file extensions until you locate the extension you want to edit.

  4. Click on Edit to display the Edit File Type dialog box, and then highlight Open within the Actions list.

  5. Click on Edit to display the Editing Action dialog box, and then click on Browse to navigate through your system. After you select the application file (with an .EXE or .COM extension), click on Ok To Load The Path In The Application Used To Perform Action option.

  6. Click on OK to exit the Editing Action dialog box, and then click on OK to exit the Edit File Type dialog box. Click on OK in the Folder Options dialog box to save your changes and return to the My Computer window.

Problems
With
Windows
Explorer
Or My
Computer

Problems With Windows Explorer Or My Computer

If you can't locate or edit a file or program within Explorer or My Computer, check the following:

- *The program is marked hidden*—If a file doesn't appear and it should, the file type is probably marked with the Hidden DOS attribute. To view all programs within My Computer or Explorer—including system files and hidden files—follow these steps:

1. Click on View|Folder Options.

2. Under Advanced Settings, click on the Show All Files option to enable it.

3. Click on OK to close the Folder Options dialog box.

- *The program is marked read-only*—If you can't open a file within My Computer or Explorer to edit it, follow these steps:

1. Right-click on the icon and select Properties from the menu.

2. On the General pane, click on the Read-Only checkbox to disable it.

3. Click on OK to close the Properties dialog box.

WARNING! *About read-only files—Most files within Windows 98 that are marked with the read-only attribute should not be edited, such as the Windows swapfile or the operating system kernel files. Remove the read-only attribute only when you are certain that you can safely edit the file.*

Chapter 3

Disk And CD-ROM Access

In Brief

Disk And CD-ROM Access

Since the days of Windows 3.0, hard drives and CD-ROM drives have been multitasking "data bottlenecks" on the PC. It takes much longer for a typical hard drive to read data than your PC's RAM memory, and CD-ROM drives are worse. While your computer is busy reading information from your hard drive or CD-ROM, your application is idle (and you keep waiting).

If you're a power user, Windows 98 can also take full advantage of the high data transfer rates of SCSI hardware, with built-in support for most SCSI CD-ROM drives, high-performance hard drives, tape backup units, and other SCSI devices. PCs equipped with fast SCSI hardware can really test the full 32-bit speed of Windows 98.

TIP: *It's getting better all the time—The average access time for both hard drives and CD-ROMs has dropped over the last few years. However, you usually can see a hard drive advertised with an access time of 10 milliseconds or even less; 24× and 32× CD-ROM drives now average access times of around 100 milliseconds. When you're shopping for your next hard drive or CD-ROM drive, it's worth spending more for a drive with a significantly lower access time of 10 milliseconds or less; you'll speed up the operation of your entire system.*

Even if your PC uses older hardware, you can optimize both hardware and software in ways to provide the fastest possible file access and to avoid data bottlenecks (even with multiple applications running and accessing a hard drive simultaneously). This chapter's projects will help you fine-tune your file system under Windows 98 to maximize the performance of your file system.

Immediate Solutions

Optimizing Performance Settings

The speed of your file system can make such a difference in how Windows 98 performs overall. You can set a number of options throughout the operating system to match your system's performance.

Changing The Typical Role Of Your PC

By default, Windows 98 assumes your computer will be used in a typical desktop role, so some hard drive transfer speed is sacrificed to provide additional memory for your applications. However, if you have more than 32MB of system RAM, you may want to change the typical role of your PC to network server. This setting instructs Windows 98 to provide the fastest possible disk access and transfer rates by dedicating additional RAM for these tasks. To change the typical role of your PC, follow these steps:

1. Right-click on My Computer to display the System Properties dialog box and click on the Performance tab.

2. Under Advanced Settings, click on the File System button to open the File System Properties dialog box, as shown in Figure 3.1.

3. Click on the Hard Disk tab.

4. Change the value in the Typical Role Of This Computer drop-down list to Network Server.

5. Click on OK to apply your change and exit the File System Properties dialog box.

6. Click on OK to exit the System Properties dialog box. Windows 98 requires a reboot for your change to take effect.

Adjusting Read-Ahead Optimization

Some Windows 98 applications read data files from your hard drive in sequence (for example, a presentation graphics package may read animated slides for display on your monitor in the order that you created them). These programs benefit from Windows 98's *read-ahead* memory buffer; when a program reads data in sequence, the system automatically loads the next segment of the

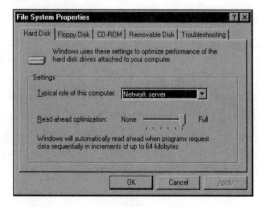

Figure 3.1   The File System Properties dialog box.

data that is required into the read-ahead buffer, where the program can retrieve it faster.

TIP: *Don't forget your CPU—The idea of a read-ahead buffer is the same general idea
behind the cache memory used by your computer's CPU, which acts as a "holding area" for
the next data segment that the CPU will likely require. The larger the cache memory, the
more likely that the CPU will be able to retrieve the required data from RAM rather than from
your hard drive (which is much slower).*

As you may have guessed, the larger the read-ahead buffer, the
more efficient and faster your file system. However, if your system has only 16MB of RAM, Windows 98 may limit the size of the
read-ahead buffer to less than the maximum of 64K. To set your
read-ahead buffer to the maximum value, follow these steps:

1. Right-click on My Computer to display the System Properties dialog box and click on the Performance tab.

2. Under Advanced Settings, click on the File System button to
   open the File System Properties dialog box.

3. Click on the Hard Disk tab.

4. Click on the Read-Ahead Optimization slider and move it as
   far to the right as possible toward Full.

5. Click on OK to apply your change and exit the File System
   Properties dialog box.

6. Click on OK to exit the System Properties dialog box.
   Windows 98 requires a reboot for your change to take effect.

Adjusting Floppy Disk Search

If your applications read data from floppy disks often, it's a good idea to allow Windows 98 to search the floppy drives for new disks whenever the system starts. Doing so will prevent disk errors while you work because your PC won't recognize a disk swap.

On the other hand, if you rarely use floppy disks, you should turn this setting off; you'll save the time it takes for Windows 98 to search your floppy drives. To adjust the floppy disk search feature, follow these steps:

1. Right-click on My Computer to display the System Properties dialog box and click on the Performance tab.

2. Under Advanced Settings, click on the File System button to open the File System Properties dialog box.

3. Click on the Floppy Disk tab.

4. Click on the Search For New Floppy Disk Drives Each Time Your Computer Starts checkbox to enable (or disable) it.

5. Click on OK to apply your change and exit the File System Properties dialog box.

6. Click on OK to exit the System Properties dialog box. Windows 98 will need a reboot for changes to take effect.

Optimizing The CD-ROM Cache

Although most CD-ROM drives have their own internal cache buffer, Windows 98 also maintains a separate read-ahead performance cache for CD-ROMs to help avoid problems with digital video and other applications that require the fastest transfer rates. If your PC has only 16MB of RAM, Windows 98 may reduce the size of the supplemental cache to less than the maximum of 1,238K. To set your CD-ROM supplemental cache to the maximum value, follow these steps:

1. Right-click on My Computer to display the System Properties dialog box and click on the Performance tab.

2. Under Advanced Settings, click on the File System button to open the File System Properties dialog box.

3. Click on the CD-ROM tab.

4. Click on the Supplemental Cache Size Optimization slider and move it as far to the right as possible toward Large.

5. Click on OK to apply your change and exit the File System Properties dialog box.

6. Click on OK to exit the System Properties dialog box. Again, Windows 98 requires a reboot to apply your change.

Adjusting The CD-ROM Access Pattern

You also can adjust Windows 98 to compensate for older CD-ROM drives slower than 4× (quad) speed; these drives can't take advantage of a larger supplemental cache, so selecting a slower drive reduces the size of the supplemental cache. To set your CD-ROM supplemental cache to the maximum value, follow these steps:

1. Right-click on My Computer to display the System Properties dialog box and click on the Performance tab.

2. Under Advanced Settings, click on the File System button to open the File System Properties dialog box.

3. Click on the CD-ROM tab.

4. Change the value in the Optimize Access Pattern drop-down list to match your drive's speed. Speeds range from single speed to quad speed and higher.

5. Click on OK to apply your change and exit the File System Properties dialog box.

6. Click on OK to exit the System Properties dialog box. Windows 98 needs a reboot before your change will take effect.

Adjusting Removable Disk Caching

Most removable media drives currently on the market support *write-behind* caching, where Windows 98 will immediately return control to you (or the application using the drive) while the data is written to the drive in the background. Owners of Zip and Jaz removable media drives should use this feature; if you're using a different brand of removable drive, check your manual to see if it supports write-behind caching.

However, some older removable media drives may have problems with write-behind caching. If your removable drive returns errors or saves data incorrectly with this feature on, you can disable it and wait until the drive writes the data completely before Windows 98 returns control of your system. To enable or disable write-behind caching, follow these steps:

1. Right-click on My Computer to display the System Properties dialog box and click on the Performance tab.

2. Under Advanced Settings, click on the File System button to open the File System Properties dialog box.

3. Click on the Removable Disk tab.

4. Click on the Enable Write-Behind Caching On All Removable Disk Drives checkbox to enable (or disable) it.

5. Click on OK to apply your change and exit the File System Properties dialog box.

6. Click on OK to exit the System Properties dialog box. Windows 98 will require a reboot to apply your change.

Enabling Direct Memory Access (DMA)

Most of the PCs in use today have Enhanced Integrated Drive Electronics (EIDE) hard drives and CD-ROM drives, which can take advantage of Direct Memory Access (DMA) to provide faster transfer rates. DMA also can reduce the load on your CPU during file reads and writes. Because most EIDE hard drives and CD-ROM drives support this standard, you should enable DMA within Windows 98 for those drives. Check the device manual or contact the device's manufacturer to check if you can enable DMA.

Unfortunately, some older IDE (not EIDE) hardware can actually "lose" data if DMA transfers are enabled. It's usually a good idea to contact the manufacturer of older IDE hard drives and CD-ROMs if you're not certain whether they can support DMA transfer. To enable or disable DMA support for a single drive, follow these steps:

1. Right-click on My Computer to display the System Properties dialog box, and then click on the Device Manager tab to display the Device Manager dialog box, as shown in Figure 3.2.

2. Click on the plus signs next to the entries for CDROM and Disk Drives to expand the branch and display your EIDE devices.

3. Highlight the desired device and click on Properties.

4. Click on the Settings tab and then click on the DMA checkbox to enable (or disable) it. Figure 3.3 shows the Settings tab for a typical EIDE hard drive.

5. Click on OK to apply your change and exit the Properties dialog box.

6. Click on OK to exit the System Properties dialog box. As you may have guessed, Windows 98 will require a reboot.

Remember to repeat this process for each IDE/EIDE hard drive and CD-ROM drive on your PC—and watch closely for file-transfer errors that may indicate your drive(s) don't support DMA.

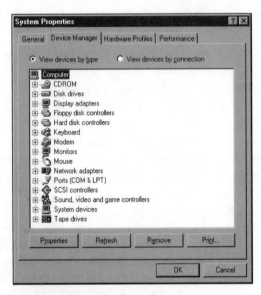

Figure 3.2   The Device Manager dialog box.

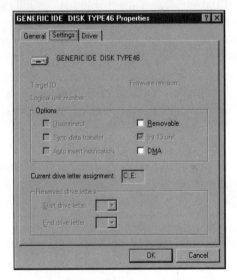

Figure 3.3   Changing the DMA settings for an EIDE hard drive.

Defragmenting Your Hard Drives

As you use your hard drive, you naturally delete files, which creates empty space. Unfortunately, however, new files that you create are practically never the same size as these empty spaces, so over time, the files on your hard drive become *fragmented*. Part of a new file is saved in one area, and part in another empty space, so the data that makes up a file is not contiguous. The information in the FAT table provides to Windows 98 the location of each of these file fragments.

When a program requests the data from a file, Windows 98 automatically reconstructs the file so the data can be read—no matter how badly it's fragmented. However, it takes more time for your PC to reassemble a file that's in 20 pieces and scattered across your hard drive than to open a file that resides in one piece on your hard drive. You can eliminate the wait by *defragmenting* your drive, and Windows 98 includes a defragmenting utility.

TIP: *Using commercial utilities—Although the defragmenting utility supplied in Windows 98 does the job, other utility program suites such as Norton Utilities offer defragmenting programs that offer more features and operate more efficiently. Norton Utilities also includes a replacement for the standard ScanDisk program. However, it's important to make sure that these utilities are expressly designed for Windows 98—not for Windows 95!*

Manual Defragmenting

To defragment one or all of your disk drives, follow these steps:

1. Click on Start|Programs|Accessories|System Tools.

2. Click on Disk Defragmenter to run the utility, as shown in Figure 3.4.

3. Select the desired drive to defragment from the pull-down menu, or pick All Hard Drives to defragment each hard drive on your PC.

4. Click on Settings to display the Disk Defragmenter Settings dialog box. Make sure that these three fields are enabled: Rearrange Program Files So My Programs Start Faster, Check The Drive For Errors, and Every Time I Defragment My Hard Drive. Click on OK to exit the dialog box. (You need to perform this step only the first time you run Disk Defragmenter.)

Figure 3.4   The Disk Defragmenter utility.

5. Click on OK to begin the defragmentation process. If you
   want to watch an animated graphic display of the process,
   click on Show Details. To stop the defragmentation process,
   click on Stop.

Automatic Scheduled Defragmenting

To defragment one or all of your disk drives automatically with
the Task Scheduler, follow these steps:

1. Click on Start|Programs|Accessories|System Tools.

2. Click on the Scheduled Tasks entry to run the Task Scheduler utility.

3. Double-click on the Add Scheduled Task entry to run the
   Scheduled Task Wizard.

4. Select Disk Defragmenter from the application list and
   follow the Wizard's prompts to schedule the task.

FAT32 Support Within Windows 98

Windows 98 includes support for the improved File Allocation
Table 32-bit (FAT32) system, which provides the following improvements over the traditional DOS FAT16 system:

- *Larger drives*—FAT32 supports drives of up to two terabytes.

- *More efficient use of space*—Drives of one gigabyte or larger
  can use four-KB clusters, which usually means that more
  information can be stored more efficiently on the same
  amount of hard drive space.

- *Faster transfer rates*—FAT32 allows faster file transfers to and from your PC's hard drive.

- *Faster program loading*—With FAT32, Windows 98 applications start faster than they would under a traditional DOS FAT16 system.

Although Windows 98 can use an existing DOS FAT16 system if required—for example, if you opt for a multiboot configuration with MS-DOS 6.22 or Windows NT 4.0—it makes sense to convert all your hard drives to FAT32 if you'll work exclusively through Windows 98.

TIP: *Another benefit of FAT32—Unlike the older DOS FAT16 system, the FAT32 file structure is less prone to catastrophic loss of data from hard drive mechanical problems. For example, a FAT32 drive can recover from the loss of root-directory and allocation-table information that renders a FAT16 drive impossible to read.*

All of this information about FAT32 sounds nifty, but a number of restrictions exist on which hard drives can be converted to FAT32. Do *not* convert your drive if the following conditions exist:

- *The drive is compressed*—Drives that are compressed with DriveSpace 3 or another commercial compression utility require a traditional DOS FAT16; a conversion to FAT32 will render these drives unreadable.

- *You need to use the drive with another operating system, including a dual boot or multiboot configuration*—Windows NT 5.0 is slated to support FAT32, but other popular operating systems such as Unix, Linux, and OS/2 will not recognize a drive that is converted to FAT32.

- *You use the "suspend" feature on a portable computer.* The suspend feature may save information to the disk in the boot sector, which is different on a FAT32 drive.

Also, remember that conversion is "one way" only: You can convert a drive from a standard 16-bit DOS FAT to FAT32, but a FAT32 drive *cannot* be converted back to a 16-bit DOS FAT. If you need to return to a traditional 16-bit DOS FAT after conversion to FAT32, you'll have to repartition and reformat the hard drive! Windows 98 cannot be uninstalled if you convert to FAT32. To convert a drive to FAT32, follow these steps:

1. Click on Start|Programs|Accessories|System Tools.

2. Click on Drive Converter (FAT32) to run the Drive Converter Wizard. Click on Next to continue.

3. The Wizard displays the screen shown in Figure 3.5, which lists all the drives on your system and the current FAT system that each drive is using. Highlight the drive you want to convert and click on Next to continue.

4. Next, the Drive Converter Wizard scans your system for anti-virus programs and disk utilities that are incompatible with FAT32. If any are found, they are displayed, and you can click on the Details checkbox for additional information on the highlighted programs. Note the names of any programs that appear, and consider deleting those programs until future versions are compatible with FAT32. Click on Next to continue.

5. On the next screen, the Drive Converter Wizard allows you to back up the drive before converting it. If you installed Microsoft Backup, you can run the program directly from the Wizard by clicking on Create Backup. A backup is not necessary, but it's certainly not a bad idea in case something goes wrong. Click on Next to continue.

6. The Wizard displays a confirmation screen, giving you one last chance to cancel the conversion process. Click on Next to continue.

7. The Wizard closes all open applications, restarts your PC in MS-DOS mode, and completes the conversion process.

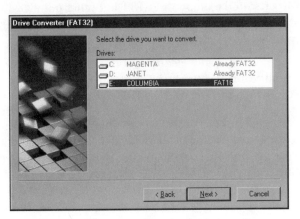

Figure 3.5   Selecting a drive to convert to FAT32.

Configuring SCSI Hardware

Traditionally, SCSI adapters and devices have been difficult to install under DOS and 16-bit Windows, but Windows 95 included built-in support for most SCSI devices. This support is improved within Windows 98, which now recognizes even more brands and models of SCSI hardware, and gives you greater control over the advanced settings available on SCSI devices.

TIP: *Shopping for a SCSI card—If you plan to add a SCSI adapter card to your PC, I recommend that you select a plug-and-play PCI adapter. You get the fastest possible file transfers through your PCI bus, and the plug-and-play feature helps ensure that your new adapter won't conflict with existing plug-and-play cards. Older 16-bit SCSI adapters will work under Windows 98, but you'll slow your fastest SCSI devices.*

Checking The Device Chain

Most SCSI configuration is now automatic within Windows 98, and the SCSI adapter card you install in your PC should either be directly recognized by Windows 98 (especially plug-and-play devices) or should come with the proper drivers and support software.

However, each piece of hardware must still meet the following requirements to successfully add a SCSI device chain to your PC under Windows 98:

- *Unique SCSI ID numbers*—Each SCSI device included on your SCSI chain (including the SCSI adapter itself) must be assigned a unique ID number. These numbers are generally set using a jumper block or a thumbwheel on the device. Some plug-and-play SCSI cards can also assign IDs automatically during the boot process.

- *Correct termination*—Each SCSI device on your chain must be correctly terminated. The two devices at each end of the SCSI chain should be terminated; all devices appearing between them must not be terminated. You usually set termination on a SCSI device through a jumper block or by fitting a resistor pack; other devices may be able to automatically set themselves for correct termination. For information on how to determine the proper termination and how to set that termination on each device, check your SCSI adapter manual and the manuals for each SCSI device on your chain.

- *ASPI software support*—Windows 98 includes 32-bit native support for Advanced SCSI Programming Interface (ASPI), so your adapter card may not require you to add 16-bit real mode SCSI drivers to your CONFIG.SYS and AUTOEXEC.BAT files. Older SCSI adapters and hardware may require you to load these drivers anyway.

SCSI hardware can coexist with an EIDE hard drive and CD-ROM, or your entire system can run with nothing but SCSI hardware.

Optimizing SCSI Settings

For the best possible performance under Windows 98, you should check the properties for each of your SCSI devices.

Enabling SCSI Disconnect. Most SCSI devices transfer data more efficiently with SCSI Disconnect enabled. To enable or disable this feature for a SCSI device, follow these steps:

1. Right-click on My Computer to display the System Properties dialog box and click on the Device Manager tab.

2. Click on the plus sign to the left of the entry for the CD-ROM and Disk Drives to expand the branch and display your SCSI devices.

3. Highlight the desired device and click on Properties.

4. Click on the Settings tab, and click on the Disconnect checkbox to enable (or disable) it.

5. Click on OK to apply your change and exit the Properties dialog box.

6. Click on OK to exit the System Properties dialog box. You need to reboot Windows 98 for your change to take effect.

Setting SCSI Sync Data Transfer. Typically, for the best performance, SCSI hard drives require the Sync Data Transfer feature to be set for hard drives and disabled for CD-ROMs. To enable or disable this feature for a SCSI device, follow these steps:

1. Right-click on My Computer to display the System Properties dialog box and click on the Device Manager tab.

2. Click on the plus sign next to the entry for the CD-ROM and Disk Drives to expand the branch and display your SCSI devices.

3. Highlight the desired device and click on Properties.

4. Click on the Settings tab. For hard drives, click on the Sync Data Transfer checkbox to enable it; for CD-ROM drives, disable the checkbox.

5. Click on OK to apply your change and exit the Properties dialog box.

6. Click on OK to exit the System Properties dialog box. Windows 98 requires a reboot for your change to take effect.

If a device no longer works correctly immediately after you make a change to the Sync Data Transfer field, reset the field to its original state immediately.

Optimizing The Recycle Bin

The Recycle Bin was a welcome addition to Windows 95, allowing you a second chance to access deleted files before they were lost. However, it is possible for the Recycle Bin to claim too much of your hard drive. Some users who are running Windows 98 would rather disable the Recycle Bin altogether. The steps in this section help you optimize your Recycle Bin.

Configuring Global Settings For The Recycle Bin

If you want to maintain the same settings for the Recycle Bin across all hard drives on your system, follow these steps:

1. Right-click on the Recycle Bin and select Properties from the menu.

2. Windows 98 displays the Recycle Bin Properties dialog box, as shown in Figure 3.6. Click on the Global tab.

3. Click on the Use One Setting For All Drives checkbox to indicate that you want to configure the settings globally.

4. If necessary, disable the Do Not Move Files To The Recycle Bin checkbox.

5. If your PC's hard drive(s) is/are over 1GB each, move the Maximum Size slider bar to 1% or 2%. If your drive(s) is/are smaller than 1GB, move the Maximum Size slider bar to 4% or 5%. (Unless you routinely recover files that are several megabytes, you can shrink the size of your Recycle Bin to free more space on your drive.)

6. If you want to save a mouse click, you can disable the Delete Confirmation dialog box that appears whenever you

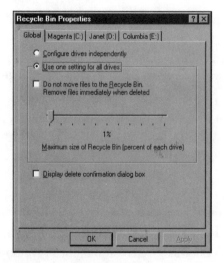

Figure 3.6   The Recycle Bin Properties dialog box.

empty the Recycle Bin by clicking on the Display Delete
Confirmation Dialog checkbox to disable it.

7. Click on OK to close the Recycle Bin Properties dialog box.

Configuring Independent Settings For The Recycle Bin

Some of your drives may contain applications that may benefit
from a larger Recycle Bin, allowing you to recover larger files. To
specify separate settings for the Recycle Bin for a single hard drive,
follow these steps:

1. Right-click on the Recycle Bin and select Properties from
   the pop-up menu.

2. Windows 98 displays the Recycle Bin Properties dialog box.
   Click on the Global tab.

3. Click on the Configure Drives Independently checkbox to
   indicate that you want to configure each drive separately.

4. Click on the tab that corresponds to the desired hard drive.

5. If necessary, disable the Do Not Move Files To The Recycle
   Bin checkbox.

6. Move the Maximum Size slider bar to indicate the maximum
   amount of hard drive space that you would like to reserve
   for the Recycle Bin on the current drive.

7. Click on OK to close the Recycle Bin Properties dialog box.

Disabling The Recycle Bin

You can also disable the Recycle Bin for all of your hard drives, or just a specific drive. If the Recycle Bin is disabled, Windows 98 will be unable to restore the file in most cases—for example; you might disable the Recycle Bin in a secure setting.

Global Disable, All Drives. To disable the Recycle Bin across all hard drives on your system, follow these steps:

1. Right-click on the Recycle Bin and select Properties from the pop-up menu.
2. Windows 98 displays the Recycle Bin Properties dialog box. Click on the Global tab.
3. Click on the Use One Setting For All Drives checkbox to indicate that you want to configure the settings globally.
4. Click on the Do Not Move Files To The Recycle Bin checkbox to enable it.
5. Click on OK to close the Recycle Bin Properties dialog box.

Specific Disable, One Drive. To disable the Recycle Bin for a specific hard drive, follow these steps:

1. Right-click on the Recycle Bin and select Properties from the pop-up menu.
2. Windows 98 displays the Recycle Bin Properties dialog box. Click on the Global tab.
3. Click on the Configure Drives Independently checkbox to indicate that you want to set each drive separately.
4. Click on the tab that corresponds to the desired hard drive.
5. Enable the Do Not Move Files To The Recycle Bin checkbox.
6. Click on OK to close the Recycle Bin Properties dialog box.

Using DVD Under Windows 98

Windows 98 provides support for the new DVD (typically identified as *Digital Video Disc* or *Digital Versatile Disc*) optical drives, which are eventually slated to replace the standard ISO-9660 CD-ROM drives. DirectShow provides mixing capabilities for this new medium, and the UDF file system used to store data on DVDs is directly supported.

Windows 98 also provides a very basic DVD viewing program, DVDPLAY, which you can use if the manufacturer of your DVD drive did not furnish a player application.

TIP: *Don't forget software—Windows 98 includes support for the Mt. Fuji specification for DVD drives, but as DVD hardware matures, new drives will probably require an external driver. When you shop for a DVD drive, make sure it contains the support software you need, including a fully featured DVD movie player for Windows 98.*

Reading DVD Data

With Windows 98, you can replace the older CD-ROM drive in your system with a DVD drive. Although the way you operate DVD quite similar to how you use the older CD-ROM technology, a single-sided, single-layer DVD can hold 4.7GB of data. Second-generation DVD drives can read an unbelievable 17GB of data from a double-sided, double-layer disc.

Loading programs and viewing files from a DVD disc is no different under Windows 98 than using a standard 680MB CD-ROM.

Viewing Commercial DVD Movies

With the right equipment, you can watch commercial movie discs within Windows 98 with Dolby Digital surround sound. Your PC must be at least a Pentium 120, with 800×600 16-bit color and 16MB of RAM. It should also be equipped with the following components:

- *MPEG-2 decoder*—The digital video on a DVD movie disc is compressed by using the MPEG-2 standard. To decompress the video stream, your PC must have an MPEG-2 decoder adapter card (or a software program that can decompress the MPEG-2 video without hardware).

- *Dolby Digital (AC-3) decoder*—Many hardware manufacturers integrate both the Dolby Digital decoder and MPEG-2 decoder onto the same adapter card. Without the Dolby Digital decoder, your computer can produce only stereo sound output.

- *A Dolby Digital stereo system*—Although your PC can create the surround sound signal with the decoders, you will still need a Dolby Digital stereo receiver and the required surround sound speakers to enjoy the true Dolby Digital effect.

TIP: *Shopping for a monitor—If you plan to watch high-resolution DVD video on your computer, I highly recommend a SuperVGA monitor with a dot pitch value of .24 or less; the lower the dot pitch, the more detail and the better the picture quality.*

Troubleshooting

Troubleshooting SCSI Errors

SCSI errors can be hard to troubleshoot, especially when you've added a new device onto an existing chain and something goes wrong. However, these troubleshooting techniques should help you identify and fix the problem.

Windows 98 Doesn't Recognize The SCSI Adapter

If you're installing a new SCSI adapter in your PC and Windows 98 doesn't recognize it, make sure that you check for these problems:

- *There are hardware conflicts*—Typically, hardware conflicts with a SCSI adapter card are due to older, non–plug-and-play adapter cards in your system that may be using the same DMA or IRQ settings. (If your system uses plug-and-play hardware exclusively, hardware conflicts are largely a thing of the past.) To check for possible conflicts, follow these steps:

  1. Right-click on My Computer to display the System Properties dialog box and click on the Device Manager tab.

  2. Click on the plus sign next to the entry for the SCSI adapter to expand the branch and display your SCSI devices.

  3. If the adapter card appears in the Device Manager list with a yellow exclamation point—as shown in Figure 3.7—or a red stop sign, you may have a conflict with another device. The other device may also have a yellow exclamation point next to it.

  4. Click on Properties to display the Adapter Card Properties dialog box and click on the General tab.

  5. Click on Update Driver to check for newer drivers for your adapter card. Windows 98 will launch the Update Device Drivers Wizard.

  6. If updating the driver doesn't work, follow the instructions in the device manual for resolving resource conflicts.

  7. Click on OK to exit the Adapter Card Properties dialog box and then click on OK to exit the System Properties

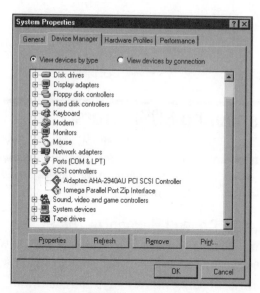

Figure 3.7   A yellow exclamation point in the Windows 98 Device Manager can signal trouble.

dialog box. If you made any changes, Windows 98 will require a reboot.

- *The card requires 16-bit drivers*—Older 16-bit ISA (*Industry Standard Architecture*) SCSI cards may require you to run their real-mode drivers within CONFIG.SYS if the card is to be recognized under Windows 98.

- *The card wasn't properly installed*—If you're using an older motherboard with 8-bit slots, check to make sure you haven't installed a 16-bit ISA card into an 8-bit slot. Additionally, the full length of the card must be firmly inserted into the matching bus slot on the motherboard.

Windows 98 Doesn't Recognize A SCSI Device

Windows 98 Doesn't Recognize A SCSI Device

If a new or existing SCSI device doesn't appear within the Device Manager (or, for SCSI hard drives or CD-ROM drives, within My Computer), check these possible problems (most of which occur during new SCSI hardware installation):

- *There are hardware conflicts*—Follow the steps outlined in the previous section to determine if your new SCSI device is trying to use hardware settings already claimed by another device. If updating the driver doesn't work, follow the instructions in the device manual for resolving resource conflicts.

- *The SCSI chain is improperly terminated*—The devices at both ends of the SCSI chain must be terminated correctly; if you're running a single SCSI device, this means your SCSI adapter card must be terminated. If a device is improperly terminated before the end of the chain, all the peripherals after that device will not be recognized. Run the SCSI diagnostic program that came with your SCSI adapter card to make sure that all devices are correctly terminated.

- *The device does not have a unique ID*—If two devices are assigned the same ID number, it's likely that both devices will refuse to work, and Windows 98 will probably recognize only one of them.

- *A device-specific driver hasn't been installed*—If Windows 98 lacks built-in support for your SCSI device, you should still install the accompanying driver.

- *The cabling is incorrect*—When connecting devices, make sure that pin 1 from the connector mates to pin 1 on the cable (which is always marked with a colored stripe or some kind of lettering). If the cable is incorrectly connected, your system will not recognize the device.

Troubleshooting With ScanDisk

Many hard drive errors are "invisible" to the naked eye—for example, lost clusters don't show up in a directory listing, and cross-linked files cause problems only for the applications that use them. However, these programs can wreak havoc on your programs and data over time, eating up hard drive territory and reducing your system's overall speed.

In this section, you learn how to run the Windows 98 ScanDisk utility both manually and automatically, as well as find out how you can use it to troubleshoot hard drive problems.

WARNING! Back it up—This phrase bears repeating: Back it up! No matter how well you maintain hard drives, they're still machines, and they'll eventually fail. Millions of PC users have never backed up a single byte of their data, and have absolutely no recourse if a hard drive crashes or a folder is accidentally deleted. The only sure protection you can take against accidentally losing your data is to back it up to tape, removable media, or a network—regularly.

If nothing else, keep the simplest level of backup handy for the document or data file you're currently working on. If the file is important, updated often, and will take a lot of effort to re-create, take a moment or two and create a copy on a 3.5-inch floppy or a Zip disk.

Running ScanDisk Manually

To scan one or all of your disk drives for errors, follow these steps:

1. Click on Start|Programs|Accessories|System Tools.

2. Click on ScanDisk to run the utility, as shown in Figure 3.8.

3. Select the desired drive to scan from the list. If you want to scan more than one drive, hold down the Ctrl key while clicking on the desired drives to select them.

4. Typically, you don't need to scan the surface of your drives for errors very often. Surface scanning takes longer, but it checks the actual magnetic surface of the drive for physical read/write errors as well as the files themselves. I recommend that you perform a thorough scan about once a month—the remainder of the time, use the Standard test option and save time. Click on Standard or Thorough to select the test type.

5. Click on Options to display the Surface Scan Options dialog box. Make sure that the System And Data Areas field is enabled. You should disable the Do Not Perform Write-Testing and Do Not Repair Bad Sectors In Hidden And

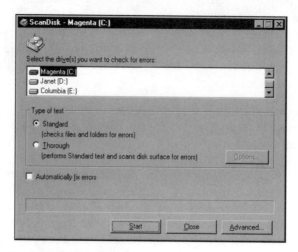

Figure 3.8   ScanDisk in action.

System Files checkboxes. Click on OK to exit the dialog box. (You need to perform this step only the first time you run ScanDisk with the Thorough test type.)

6. If you want ScanDisk to automatically fix errors on your drive without prompting you, enable the Automatically Fix Errors checkbox. (Personally, I'm a curious person, and it's harder to troubleshoot a possible problem without an error message; therefore, I leave this option disabled.)

7. It's always a good idea to stop all other activity on your PC before you start the scanning process—if another program accesses the disk while it's being scanned, ScanDisk must start all over again! To keep from having to begin again, close all other open applications before you click on Start.

8. Click on Start to begin scanning the drives you selected. ScanDisk indicates its activity with a progress bar. To stop the scanning process, click on Cancel.

9. If your drive(s) receive(s) a clean bill of health, ScanDisk simply reports that the process is complete. If an error is found, ScanDisk displays it, and you can determine whether you want to repair the disk or leave it alone for now. If you opt to repair the problem, ScanDisk allows you to make a backup so you can "undelete" the fix and restore everything.

10. After all of your disks are scanned (and fixed, if necessary), click on Close.

Scanning Disks Automatically

To scan one or all of your disk drives automatically with the Task Scheduler, follow these steps:

1. Click on the Start|Programs|Accessories|System Tools.

2. Click on Scheduled Tasks to run the Task Scheduler utility.

3. Double-click on the Add Scheduled Task entry to run the Scheduled Task Wizard.

4. Select ScanDisk from the application list and follow the Wizard's prompts to schedule the task.

Setting Advanced Options In ScanDisk

You can configure ScanDisk with a number of advanced options— ScanDisk saves these settings for future scanning sessions. To set the advanced options, follow these steps:

1. Run ScanDisk and click on the Advanced button to display the Advanced Options dialog box, as shown in Figure 3.9.

2. Under the Display Summary field, specify whether you want to see a summary of disk statistics each time you run ScanDisk, only if errors are found, or never. For trouble-shooting purposes, it's best to pick either Always or Only If Errors Found.

3. Under Log File, you can elect to overwrite the log, append the results of the current scan to the log, or disable the log entirely.

4. *Cross-linked files* are particularly troublesome file errors, because you'll almost always lose data in both of the files. Although you can ignore the problem, cross-linkage usually gets worse over time; it's best to delete the cross-linked files or make copies of the affected files and then delete the linked files.

5. Lost File Fragments can be fixed either by freeing the space the fragments occupy or by converting them to files in the root directory of the drive. If you convert them to files, you can check them with Notepad or a file editor to see if they contain anything valuable.

6. ScanDisk can perform additional checking on file names and also the date and time stamped on each file. However, because these errors usually don't cause problems under Windows 98, only the Invalid File Names field is enabled by default.

Figure 3.9   ScanDisk allows you to set a number of advanced options.

7. If you're using DriveSpace disk compression on your system, it's generally a good idea to check the uncompressed "host" drive for errors before scanning or repairing errors on the compressed data. By default, the Check Host Drive First field is enabled.

8. The final field, Report MS-DOS Mode Name Length Errors, reflects file name problems that may affect your older MS-DOS programs that are running in a DOS box or MS-DOS mode. By default, it's enabled; if you run any DOS applications, I recommended that you leave this field checked.

9. After you've set all of the desired fields, click on OK to close the dialog box and save your changes.

Troubleshooting ScanDisk Errors

You'll find that ScanDisk can help diagnose continuing problems with both your applications and your hard drive. Each error can occur during normal operation—for example, there's no reason to worry if your free space is incorrect once or twice in a month, as long as ScanDisk can fix the problem. However, a recurring ScanDisk report with the same errors over the space of a week or so indicates that it's time to troubleshoot.

TIP: *Using the ScanDisk log file—To help you troubleshoot continuing problems over a period, the designers of ScanDisk thoughtfully allow you to append the log; make sure you choose this option in the Advanced Options dialog box.*

ScanDisk Reports Lost Clusters Or Cross-Links. If ScanDisk repeatedly reports lost clusters or cross-linked files over time, make sure that you check for these problems:

- *Incorrect shutdown*—Under Windows 98, any improper shutdown will force your PC to run the DOS version of ScanDisk the next time you boot your PC. Never turn off your PC until Windows 98 properly shuts down. Any applications currently writing to disk will not be able to close data files, which can lead to problems later when the application tries to read this data.

- *Application lockup*—Typically, "misbehaving" programs that lock up your PC tend to leave behind lost clusters and cross-links. Always try to avoid running legacy DOS programs or games that consistently lock up Windows 98 either while they're running or when you exit the program.

- *Power failure*—A PC caught in a power failure almost always leads to a disk problem. If you lose your power often, I would highly recommend an uninterruptible power supply (UPS) unit, which automatically supplies a few minutes' worth of battery power during a power outage. You can use these extra few minutes to safely save your documents and data and shut down Windows 98 normally.

ScanDisk Reports Naming Problems. If ScanDisk repeatedly reports incorrect long file names or MS-DOS names, consider the following possible sources:

- *Legacy DOS programs*—If you run MS-DOS programs within a DOS box or MS-DOS mode and attempt to open or edit existing files from a Windows 98 application, you're inviting potential disaster. Windows 98 automatically handles file name conflicts whenever possible, but some MS-DOS programs read and write data using routines that Windows 98 can't control.

- *Older disk utilities*—Avoid running *any* DOS or Windows 3.x/ Windows 95 disk utilities that are not expressly written for Windows 98. Although Windows 98 can run almost all Windows 3.x and Windows 95 programs, it's a bad idea to use an older program that can change the structure of your hard drive if it hasn't been tested with Windows 98.

TIP: *FAT32 under Windows 95—It's true that later versions of Windows 95 did support FAT32, and some utility programs written for Windows 95 will recognize disks with FAT32. However, I still highly recommend that you upgrade all of your utility software to versions that have been expressly designed for Windows 98.*

ScanDisk Reports Surface Damage. If ScanDisk reports bad sectors or surface damage during a thorough scan, you may be getting an error message that indicates a drive is malfunctioning. This is one of the few error messages returned from ScanDisk that indicates that the drive's mechanism is the culprit. As a hard drive ages, the magnetic surface of the drive platters develops *bad sectors* (areas that can no longer store data), and the total capacity of your drive starts to diminish. If ScanDisk reports surface damage to your drive, the time has probably arrived to start shopping for a new drive.

Graphics And Video

In Brief

Graphics And Video

For most of us who own an Intel-based PC, the phrase "high-resolution video" and the name Microsoft Windows are synonymous. In fact, you could argue that the 16-million-color Super VGA standard in common use today was introduced on IBM systems simply to keep up with the expectations of Windows 3.0 users for better and better graphics.

The demands for higher resolution and greater detail have driven the Windows software industry to animate every button and menu (even within programs such as disk utilities and data communications software). "If it doesn't move or look good enough, we need another version!" seems to be the battle cry.

In the early days of Windows 3.0, these graphics tended to bog down the entire system. By the time Windows 3.11 arrived, however, the manufacturers of video adapter cards had already developed accelerator chipsets to speed up the display of high-resolution graphics.

What's the result of this cycle of development? Your PC can now display graphics and digital video that once required an expensive graphics workstation computer. Windows 98 supports the latest 64-bit accelerated video hardware, including 3D chipsets for the best graphics in computer games.

The projects in this chapter will help you configure a myriad of graphics settings—including resolution, color depth, and refresh rate—to achieve the optimum display for both your applications *and* your eyes. You'll also configure Windows 98 to deliver the best possible display of digital video, no matter what your PC's processor's speed. You'll learn how to select the best fonts for your desktop and applications. Finally, this chapter provides you with some troubleshooting tips for solving video problems within Windows 98.

Immediate Solutions

Configuring Video Drivers Under Windows 98

One of the most important configuration settings within Windows 98 is your video driver. If the wrong driver is selected, your PC cannot take advantage of the special features on an accelerated video adapter card or a 3D graphics video card. Additionally, you may not be able to set Windows 98 to a desired resolution or color depth; in the worst case, your PC will be unable to display graphics at all!

During installation, Windows 98 attempts to locate the exact video driver for your video adapter card in its driver database. If it can't identify the card or there's no driver for it in the database, Windows 98 may default to another card from the same manufacturer , or it may use one of the generic drivers that work with most cards.

In this section, I will discuss how you can update both your video driver and monitor selection under Windows 98; I'll also cover how you can set any advanced options offered on your video adapter card.

Updating Your Video Driver

Most manufacturers of video adapter cards are constantly updating their software drivers to keep pace with new versions of DirectX and new Windows standards. Often, an updated driver means the difference between successfully running an application and watching your PC lock up tight! If you want to check for updates for your existing video driver, follow these steps:

1. Click on Start|Control Panel.

2. Click on Display on the Control Panel menu to open the Display Properties dialog box. Click on the Settings tab, as shown in Figure 4.1. Below the sample monitor thumbnail, Windows 98 displays the name of the current video driver as "monitor type on video driver".

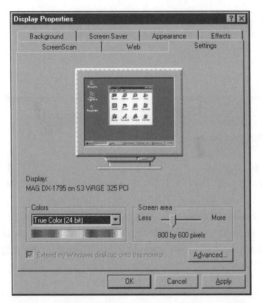

*Figure 4.1   The Display Properties dialog box, showing the
Settings information.*

3. Click on the Advanced button to display the Properties
   panel for your video driver.

4. Click on the Adapter tab and then click on the Change button.

5. Windows 98 automatically runs the Update Device Driver
   Wizard. Click on the Next button to continue.

6. Click on Search to find a better driver than the one your
   device is using and then click on the Next button.

7. The Wizard prompts you for the location(s) where it should
   search for updates. If you have an updated driver on a
   floppy disk or CD-ROM, load the update in your drive and
   make sure the corresponding checkbox is enabled. By
   default, the Wizard also searches the Microsoft Windows
   Update Web site. Finally, you can set a specific location on
   your system or a network computer by enabling the Specify
   A Location field. Click on the Next button to continue.

8. The Wizard searches the location(s) you specified. If an
   updated video driver is found, the Wizard prompts you for
   confirmation before installing it; if an update is not found,
   you can either continue to use your current video driver or
   install another driver. Windows 98 will indicate the recommended action; generally, it's a better idea to keep your

current driver rather than try another that's not specifically designed for your video adapter card. Click on the Next button to continue.

9. If you selected a new driver or decided to use the updated driver, the Wizard will load the new driver now. Click on Finish to close the Wizard.

10. Click on OK to exit your driver's Properties dialog box. Click on OK again in the Display Properties dialog box to save your changes.

Updating Your Monitor Driver

Windows 98 depends upon your monitor driver to correctly set features such as your refresh rate and power management functions. To update your existing monitor driver, follow these steps:

1. Click on Start|Control Panel.

2. Click on Display on the Control Panel menu to open the Display Properties dialog box. Below the sample monitor thumbnail, Windows 98 displays the name of the current monitor driver as "monitor type on video driver".

3. Click on the Advanced button to display the Properties panel for your video driver.

4. Click on the Monitor tab. If the Automatically Detect Plug & Play Monitors checkbox is disabled, enable it. Click on the Change button.

5. Windows 98 automatically runs the Update Device Driver Wizard. Click on the Next button to continue.

6. Click on Search for a better driver than the one your device is using now and then click on the Next button.

7. The Wizard prompts you for the location(s) where it should search for updates. Enable the checkboxes for the locations that may contain an updated driver and then click on the Next button to continue.

8. The Wizard searches the location(s) you specified. If Wizard finds an updated monitor driver, it prompts you for confirmation before installing it. If an update isn't found, you can either continue to use your current monitor driver or install another driver. Windows 98 will indicate the recommended action; it's usually recommended that you keep your current driver rather than try another that isn't specifically designed for your monitor. Click on the Next button to continue.

9. If you selected a new driver or decided to use the updated driver, the Wizard will load the new driver now. Click on Finish to close the Wizard.

10. Click on OK to exit your video driver's Properties dialog box. Click on OK again in the Display Properties dialog box to save your changes.

Selecting A New Video Driver

If Windows 98 is currently using a completely wrong video driver, it is possible to load a different driver without running the Add New Hardware Wizard (which can make mistakes when determining which video adapter card you're using). To force the selection of a different video driver, follow these steps:

1. Click on Start|Control Panel.

2. Click on Display on the Control Panel menu to open the Display Properties dialog box.

3. Click on the Advanced button to display the Properties panel for your video driver.

4. Click on the Adapter tab and then click on the Change button.

5. Windows 98 automatically runs the Update Device Driver Wizard. Click on the Next button to continue.

6. Click on the Display A List Of All The Drivers In A Specific Location field and then click on the Next button.

7. You now have three options:

   • *Use a compatible driver*—The hardware listed in the Models scrolling list box has been found to be compatible with your video driver. If the driver you want to use is listed, click on it to highlight it and click on Next.

   • *Use any driver*—Click on the Show All Hardware field to display all the video driver brands and models in the Windows 98 driver database. Scroll through the manufacturer list and click on the desired manufacturer; the Wizard updates the Models list with the corresponding models from that manufacturer. Click on the driver you want to use to highlight it and then click on the Next button to continue.

   • *Use a driver from a floppy disk or CD-ROM*—Click on the Have Disk button to display the Install From Disk dialog box. Click on the Browse button to navigate to the location of the new driver and then click on OK. The

Wizard returns to the list box to display the video drivers it found at the specified location. The Wizard updates the Models list with the drivers it found. Click on the driver you want to use to highlight it and then click on the Next button to continue.

8. The Wizard prompts you for confirmation before it installs the new driver. Confirm that you want to load the driver and then click on the Next button to continue.

9. Click on Finish to close the Wizard and close the Display Properties dialog as previously directed.

Selecting Resolution, Color Depth, And Refresh Rate

If you've used a previous version of Windows extensively for playing games, desktop publishing, or editing graphics, you're probably familiar with the terms *screen resolution*, *color depth*, and *refresh rate*; however, most owners of PCs that run Windows have never changed these three settings since they bought their computer!

If these terms are new to you, here are the quick definitions:

- *Screen resolution*—This term refers to the number of individual *pixels* (or dots) that make up an image, measured across the top of your monitor and then down the side. Therefore, a screen resolution of 800×600 displays 800 pixels horizontally and 600 vertically; the higher the screen resolution, the smaller and more detailed the image or document you're working on—and the more "area" on your desktop.

- *Color depth*—This term refers to the maximum number of colors that can appear in an image. For example, 24-bit color (usually referred to as *true color*) images can contain a *maximum* of more than 16 million colors, which yields results comparable to those you would get with a 35mm camera. (Actually, it's practically impossible to find a 24-bit image that actually has even a million different colors in it; remember, these are maximum values!) Other common color depths are 16-color, 256-color, 32,000-color, and 64,000-color. You only need to remember that the more colors there are displayed on screen, the better the color images and video will look on your PC.

- *Refresh rate*—This term refers to the number of times per second your video adapter card redraws the image on your monitor. It's necessary to keep redrawing over and over because the glowing phosphors that emit the light you see from your monitor fade very quickly. This figure is generally expressed in Hz (Hertz); for example, most computers use a standard refresh rate of about 60Hz. The higher the refresh rate, the better your display looks and the easier it is on your eyes, so it's a good idea to buy a video adapter card and monitor that can both do 72- or 80Hz.

It certainly isn't necessary to set Windows 98 optimally for either resolution or color depth to run programs or surf the Web, but the proper configuration can prevent eyestrain and add detail and realism to color images.

Selecting A Screen Resolution

If you need to change the resolution of your display—for example, to edit a high-resolution color image—follow these steps:

1. Click on Start|Control Panel.
2. Click on Display on the Control Panel menu to open the Display Properties dialog box.
3. Click on the Settings tab.
4. Click on the Settings button to display the current resolution; typical values include the standard 640×480 (measured in pixels across and down the screen), 800×600, 1024×768, and 1152×864.
5. Click on and drag the Screen Area slider bar to raise or lower your screen resolution. The maximum screen resolution on your computer depends on the amount of video

memory on your video adapter card, the current color depth, and the maximum resolution available on your monitor. Most Windows users prefer working in either 800×600 or 1024×768—both resolutions provide you with more screen area than the standard 640×480, but they also allow you to use 16- or 24-bit color.

6. Click on OK to exit the Display Properties dialog box and save your changes. You may need to reboot your computer or restart Windows 98 to switch resolutions; depending on the settings you selected, Windows 98 may also allow you to apply the changes without restarting.

Selecting A Color Depth

Many games and multimedia programs will only run in 256 colors, so you may have to change your color depth often if you're a game player. To change the number of colors displayed within Windows 98, follow these steps:

1. Click on Start|Control Panel.

2. Click on Display on the Control Panel menu to open the Display Properties dialog box.

3. Click on the Settings tab.

4. Click on the Colors drop-down list to display the color levels available on your PC; typical values include 16 colors, 256 colors, 32,000 colors (High Color), and over 16 million colors (True Color).

5. Select the desired color depth. The maximum color depth on your computer depends on the amount of video memory on your video adapter card and the maximum resolution available on your monitor. Most Windows owners prefer working in either 16- or 24-bit color.

6. Click on OK to exit the Display Properties dialog box and save your changes. Depending on the settings you chose, Windows 98 may allow you to apply the changes without restarting or rebooting your PC.

TIP: *The Great Tug-Of-War—If you're shopping for a video adapter card, make sure that your card of choice has at least 4MB of video RAM. Why? Unfortunately, if your video adapter card has less than this amount, you'll probably have to juggle the importance of a higher screen resolution vs. more colors on screen. The higher the value for either number, the more video RAM your system needs. Windows 98 automatically decreases the number of colors you can choose as your resolution increases, and the reverse also is true. In addition, you may have to make adjustments for different applications. For example, if you're editing or displaying images, you'll need 24-bit color, but you may have to drop your resolution to 800×600, or even 640×480.*

To find out how much video RAM is available on your video adapter card, follow the first four steps in the following section, "Selecting A Refresh Rate." Windows 98 displays the total amount of video RAM on your system on the Adapter pane.

Selecting A Refresh Rate

To change the refresh rate—for example, if your monitor flickers noticeably—follow these steps:

1. Click on Start|Control Panel.

2. Click on Display on the Control Panel menu to open the Display Properties dialog box.

3. Click on the Settings tab.

4. Click on the Advanced button and then click on the Adapter tab.

5. Select the refresh rate from the Refresh Rate drop-down list. Windows 98 provides an Optimal setting, which usually provides the best image, but you can choose any refresh rate available on both your monitor and video adapter card. Click on OK to save your changes.

TIP: *It is possible to damage your monitor by selecting too high of a refresh rate; if you're unsure of what rates are supported by your monitor, select the "Optimal" setting. Your monitor manual should include information on which refresh rates are supported.*

6. Click on OK to exit the Display Properties dialog box. You may need to reboot your computer to complete the process of changing the refresh rate.

Changing Your Display Font

Windows 98 allows you to specify the size of the standard font used in dialog boxes (often referred to as your *display* or *system font*). If you find a larger font easier to read, Windows 98 will adjust your desktop whenever possible to allow the use of a larger display font. To select the size of your display font, follow these steps:

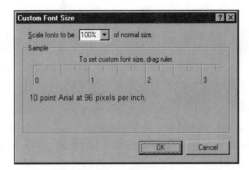

Figure 4.2 **You can specify a custom display font size by making changes in the Custom Font Size dialog box.**

1. Click on Start|Control Panel.

2. Click on Display on the Control Panel menu to open the Display Properties dialog box.

3. Click on the Settings tab.

4. Click on the Advanced button and then click on the General tab.

5. Click on the Font Size drop-down list to display the three choices for display font size: Small Fonts (the default), Large Fonts, and Other. Select Small Fonts for the standard 96-dpi font. Select Large Fonts for the 120-dpi font. If you select Other, Windows 98 displays the Custom Font Size dialog box, shown in Figure 4.2. You can select a percentage of normal size from the drop-down list or you can click on and drag the ruler control to set a custom font size. Click on OK to save your changes.

6. Click on OK to exit the Properties dialog box for your video card.

7. Click on OK to exit the Display Properties dialog box. You may need to reboot your computer to change the size of your default font.

Configuring Hardware Acceleration

As mentioned at the beginning of this chapter, most video adapter cards on the market today offer some kind of Windows *acceleration* support through hardware. If you have an accelerated video card, some of the hardware on your card is dedicated to speeding up the display of menus, dialog boxes, and graphics within Windows 98. Because the video card's acceleration feature reduces the amount of graphics work that your CPU would normally do, your entire Windows 98 system will run faster with hardware acceleration.

However, some video cards exhibit problems if all of the hardware acceleration functions are turned on. Symptoms of this problem can include:

- Portions of your desktop not being properly redrawn after a dialog box is moved or closed

- Exceptionally slow display of menus within applications

- Lockups or very slow motion within programs that display animated graphics

- A "disappearing" mouse pointer, or a pointer that appears at irregular moments

If you experience these kinds of problems, you can selectively reduce the amount of hardware acceleration by turning off functions. To do so, follow these steps:

1. Click on Start|Control Panel.

2. Click on Display on the Control Panel menu to open the Display Properties dialog box.

3. Click on the Settings tab.

4. Click on the Advanced button and then click on the Performance tab.

5. Click on and drag the slider control from the minimum setting on the left (no accelerator functions at all) to the maximum on the right (all functions are enabled). Experiment with each setting, and after you find the proper level of hardware acceleration, click on OK to save your changes.

6. Click on OK to exit the Properties dialog box for your video card.

7. Click on OK to exit the Display Properties dialog box. You may need to reboot your computer to change the amount of hardware acceleration.

Disabling Restart For Video Changes

If you change screen resolution or color depth often, you'll find that Windows 98 will force you to restart after each change so that your new video settings can take effect. Be aware that only a small number of programs actually require this restart—virtually all Windows applications can automatically handle a change in screen resolution or color depth. To eliminate the restart step (and the wait that accompanies it), follow these steps:

1. Click on Start|Control Panel.

2. Click on Display on the Control Panel menu to open the Display Properties dialog box.

3. Click on the Settings tab.

4. Click on the Advanced button and then click on the General tab.

5. Click on the Apply The New Color Settings Without Restarting field.

6. Click on OK to exit the Properties dialog box for your video card.

7. Click on OK to exit the Display Properties dialog box.

Displaying Video Full Screen

Today's faster Pentium and Pentium II PCs have the raw speed and enhanced video adapter cards necessary to display digital video full screen, without the dropped frames and jerky speeds that computer owners have dealt with in recent years. Even if your system doesn't have a DVD drive, it might have hardware or software support for MPEG-2 compressed video (the standard video format on the Web and many CD-ROM games and entertainment titles). DVD drives are discussed in greater detail in Chapter 3. To display digital video full screen, follow these steps:

1. Click on Start|Control Panel.

2. Click on Multimedia on the Control Panel menu to open the Multimedia Properties dialog box, as shown in Figure 4.3.

3. Click on the Video tab.

Figure 4.3 *The Multimedia Properties dialog box determines how digital video will appear within Windows 98.*

4. Click on the Full Screen option. (If you elect to view digital video in a window, you can select the size of the window in the drop-down list.)

5. Click on OK to exit the Multimedia Properties dialog box.

Related solution:	Found in:
Using DVD Under Windows 98	Chapter 3

Adjusting System Colors And Fonts

Windows 98 comes with a number of desktop and application color schemes that you can choose from, so it's easy to personalize the colors and fonts in your system. You'll find the Appearance pane of the Display Properties dialog box especially useful if:

• You need a set of high-visibility colors and fonts throughout Windows 98 to make text, menus, and dialog boxes easier to see

• Your company wants a specific color scheme or a specific font for all workstations

- You need to alter the document window color for your word processor or another Windows 98 application
- You're taking screen shots on your PC that require specific colors for proper printing later on

Selecting An Existing Color And Font Scheme

You can change the appearance of all the standard colors and fonts within Windows 98 by selecting an existing scheme. To do so, follow these steps:

1. Click on Start|Control Panel.

2. Click on Display on the Control Panel menu to open the Display Properties dialog box.

3. Click on the Appearance tab to display the dialog box, shown in Figure 4.4.

4. Click on the Scheme drop-down list box and select one of the existing color schemes. The preview window at the top of the dialog box will change to reflect the new system colors, font family, and font size that make up the selected scheme. You can display as many schemes from the list as necessary.

5. After you find the scheme you want to use, click on OK to save your changes and exit the Display Properties dialog box.

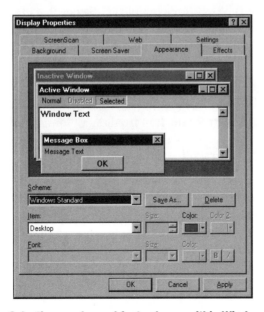

Figure 4.4   Selecting a color and font scheme within Windows 98.

Customizing Your Own Color And Font Scheme

If you want to create your own scheme to improve readability within Windows 98 (or just substitute your favorite colors for the defaults), follow these steps:

1. Click on Start|Control Panel.

2. Click on Display on the Control Panel menu to open the Display Properties dialog box.

3. Click on the Appearance tab to display the Appearance dialog box.

4. Select the item you want to change, using either of the following methods:

   • Click directly on the item in the preview window; for example, to change the inactive window title bar, you would click on the words "Inactive Window" in the preview window.

   • Click on the Item drop-down list and select the display item you want to modify.

5. If the selected item has a size (such as an icon), use the Size scrolling list box to change it if necessary. The value is in pixels.

6. If the selected item has at least one color associated with it, choose the color from the drop-down Color list. If the item has two colors—for example, a title bar that gradually changes color in the middle of the window—you can also specify the second color in the Color 2 drop-down color list.

7. If the selected item has a font associated with it (such as a title bar or menu), choose the font family name and the font size in the Font and Size fields, respectively.

8. Select a color for the font from the Color drop-down list. To toggle bold and italic attributes for the font, click on the bold "B" character and the italic slash.

9. If you want to save your new scheme under a new name, click on the Save As button, enter a new scheme name, and then click on OK.

10. Click on OK to save your changes and exit the Display Properties dialog box.

Configuring Color Management

Windows 98 includes a new feature called *color management.* This system allows you to load a "monitor profile" that essentially defines the characteristics of each color displayed on your screen.

Note that it's certainly not necessary to change your default color profile—however, graphics professionals and desktop publishing professionals will use this feature to adjust the colors displayed on their monitors to match specific color palettes. For example, a profile might adjust the default color spectrum from a monitor to match the Pantone color system widely used in publishing.

TIP: Not for the adventurous—Monitor profiles are generally distributed by a monitor manufacturer or created with a separate application; I recommend that you avoid experimenting with different profiles unless you know that a specific monitor profile will work with your hardware.

To select a default monitor profile with colors you specify, follow these steps:

1. Click on Start|Control Panel.

2. Click on Display on the Control Panel menu to open the Display Properties dialog box.

3. Click on the Settings tab.

4. Click on the Advanced button and then click on the Color Management tab, as shown in Figure 4.5.

5. The list box displays all monitor profiles that Windows 98 specifically recognizes for your monitor. To select one of these files as your default color profile, click on the entry to highlight it and then click on the Set As Default button.

6. To add a new color profile to your list box, click on the Add button. By default, Windows 98 displays the contents of your \Windows\System\Color folder, but you can also load a color profile from another location on your hard drive, a floppy disk, or a removable drive. Highlight the desired file and then click on Add.

7. To remove a color profile from the list box, highlight the entry and then click on Remove.

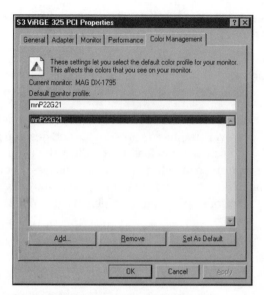

Figure 4.5   The Windows 98 Color Management pane.

8. After you select the right color profile, click on OK to exit the Properties dialog box for your video card.

9. Click on OK to exit the Display Properties dialog box.

Troubleshooting

Troubleshooting Graphics Problems

If you're troubleshooting a graphics problem, there's nothing more frustrating than a blank screen—and, unfortunately, that's one of the very real possibilities you might encounter! In this section, I discuss common video and graphics problems that you may encounter with Windows 98 and possible solutions.

Your Display Flickers Or Appears Fuzzy

Your Display Flickers Or Appears Fuzzy

If your monitor flickers noticeably, seems to pulse, or appears fuzzy, it may be the result of a hardware problem—or you may need to make a simple setting change. Check these possible problems:

- *Improper refresh rate*—This problem is a prime candidate for eyestrain, especially if you move your PC from one location with one type of lighting to another. Follow the instructions in this chapter's previous "Selecting A Refresh Rate" section, and set your refresh rate to the highest supported rate. Alternately, you can also select the Optimal refresh rate. (I recommend that you experiment with different refresh rate and screen resolution combinations until you get a display you can easily see.)

- *Magnetic interference*—There are two culprits in this case: your left and right stereo speakers, which are probably close to your monitor. Unshielded computer speakers are rare, but if you have a pair, they can cause your display to flicker or pulse.

- *Color depth/screen resolution mismatch*—This problem occurs often with laptop computers; setting your resolution too high on a liquid crystal display in 24-bit color may result in fonts that appear "weak" and distorted. If you must run high-resolution and 24-bit color on a system with a liquid crystal display, consider using a larger display font.

- *High dot pitch*—Unfortunately, you can't do much if your monitor has a dot pitch of .29 or above; this kind of a hardware limitation prevents your monitor from displaying fine detail at higher resolutions, which results in a fuzzy display.

Problems Setting Resolution Or Color Depth

If Windows 98 prevents you from setting a particular resolution or color depth, consider these problems:

- *Insufficient video RAM*—This problem causes a PC owner to utter the often-heard exclamation, "Why is it *doing* that?" when he or she is knee-deep in the Display Properties dialog box. (The cause? Every time you select more colors, the resolution slider automatically moves to a lower resolution.) As I mentioned previously in this chapter, you'll need a minimum of 4MB of video RAM to display 24-bit color at a resolution of 1024×768. With 2MB (or less) of video RAM, you'll probably have to decide on the best possible trade-off between higher resolution and more colors.

- *Dot pitch*—If Windows 98 recognizes your specific monitor, it will prevent you from setting a resolution or color depth beyond the range of your hardware. A monitor with a dot pitch of .29, for example, may not be able to display more than 1024×768, no matter how much video RAM you have.

- *Safe mode*—If you're running Windows 98 in Safe mode, you can't select either a higher resolution or more colors. You're stuck at 16 colors in 640×480; if possible, start Windows 98 normally.

No Display At All

Have you just been greeted with a blank screen? Focus your troubleshooting on these areas:

- *Whoops!*—Check to make sure your monitor cable is securely connected to the VGA port on your PC. If it isn't, don't be embarrassed; it happens to everyone.

- *The resolution is too high*—If you're experimenting with screen resolutions and you just tried to set the maximum that Windows 98 will allow, you may have exceeded the scan range of your monitor. (Windows 98 probably wasn't able to determine the exact model of monitor, so you were able to exceed the recommended limits.) Luckily, Windows 98 will restore your original video settings if you don't respond to the confirmation prompt, so your PC should reset itself after a few moments.

- *The startup sequence did not complete*—It's possible for Windows 98 to stall during the startup sequence at a point before it displays the desktop; in this case, your video settings or hardware are probably not causing the problem. Try booting in Safe mode, or generate a boot logfile to see what's causing the problem. (For complete information on the boot process, see Chapter 1.)

- *One of your video drivers is incompatible*—If you just upgraded or switched video drivers, you should immediately reload the driver you were using before—boot Windows 98 in Safe mode so that you can restore your original settings.

- *The DirectX drivers were not installed properly*—Many computer games written for Windows 98 require DirectX drivers, and these games will stubbornly refuse to load (and often lock up) if those drivers are not correctly installed. If you lose your video (if your screen blanks or displays multi-colored "garbage") directly after installing a computer game or you lose your video each time you try to run the game, re-install DirectX from the CD-ROM.

Related solutions:	Found in:
Troubleshooting Startup Errors	Chapter 1

Font And Color Problems

If you're having trouble with system fonts or colors, consider these possible problems:

- *Fonts are truncated*—Some programs have "hard-coded" sizes for their dialog boxes and menus. If the text within these programs is truncated, reduce the size of your system font, or select the Windows Standard scheme within the Appearance pane of the Display Properties dialog box.

- *Colors look grainy*—This is a common effect called *dithering*, where Windows 98 is trying to display a 16- or 24-bit color image on a system set for 256 colors. If your video adapter has the necessary video RAM, I definitely recommend that you use either 16- or 24-bit color on your system.

- *Colors shift or blink*—This is another example of dithering; also, some older 16-bit programs that were written for Windows 3.1 might not be compatible with the Active Desktop. If this effect happens each time you run a specific 16-bit program, upgrade the program to a 32-bit version if possible.

Chapter 5

Sound And Music

In Brief

Sound And Music

With Windows 3.0 on the PC desktop came sound and music as well as enhanced graphics and video. Before Windows—in the days of MS-DOS—only computer games dared to require audio!

Today, most of us can never imagine buying a computer without speakers and a stereo sound card. In fact, those PC owners who are dead-set against computer games still seem fascinated by the various beeps, bells, and whistles of a typical Windows 98 desktop. Another feature of Windows 98 is *Musical Instrument Digital Interface (MIDI)*, which allows musicians to record music directly in electronic format.

Today's PCs aren't limited to simply playing sound and music. With the multimedia hardware and software available for Windows 98, you can use your computer to capture sounds from television, radio, or videotape. You also can add your voice to your email, edit recorded sounds with sophisticated effects, or send your voice across the Internet to friends and family—literally anywhere around the world!

With the right software, you can even control Windows 98 with your voice alone—but this technology is still in development. Seamless voice control of your PC is still a few years away, but no one doubts any longer that you will be able to talk to your computer in the coming years. Soon, your computer will act on your spoken commands and reply to questions in a normal speaking voice.

In this chapter, you will learn how configure your PC's audio hardware to provide the best recording and playback quality. You'll select (or create) a *sound scheme* (an entire collection of related sounds) that both pleases the ear and draws attention to important system events. You'll record audio from your PC's microphone and an external line-in source—and, as usual, I'll provide a number of troubleshooting tips to help you track down audio problems within Windows 98.

Immediate Solutions

Adjusting Audio Settings

In this section, I'll demonstrate how you can configure several audio settings within Windows 98. Everyone who has a stereo system is already familiar with some of these settings; other settings, however, are unique to your computer.

Setting The System Audio Volume

Let's start with the most basic audio setting: volume. If you want to change the volume of all the kinds of sound that your PC can produce, follow these steps:

1. Left-click on the speaker icon in the *system tray* (the area at the right side of your Taskbar).

2. Windows 98 displays the standard system Volume Control. To move the slider, click on and drag it to the desired direction. Moving the slider up increases the volume, whereas moving the slider down decreases the volume.

3. If you want to mute (disable) all sound, enable the Mute checkbox. This option is perfect for that lunchtime game you play on the office network, or for when you are Web surfing multimedia sites late at night. To restore your audio, disable the Mute checkbox.

4. After you are done, click on the Windows 98 background to hide the Volume Control.

Setting The Audio Volume For Individual Sources

Windows 98 also allows you to customize the sound levels for each individual sound source on your PC (or mute an individual source, if necessary). To change the volume settings for each sound source, follow these steps:

1. Right-click on the speaker icon in the system tray and select Open Volume Controls from the pop-up menu.

2. Windows 98 displays the complete Volume Control dialog box, shown in Figure 5.1 (this dialog box is different from the simple Volume Control you displayed previously from the Taskbar, so I'll refer to it as a dialog box). The specific

controls on your Volume Control dialog box will vary according to the audio hardware and manufacturer-specific drivers installed on your PC and the display mode (recording or playback). For example, the WaveSynth shown in Figure 5.1 was added by my Creative Labs AWE sound card. Most systems will include the following controls:

- *Volume Control*—This control is the master volume, and it corresponds to the simple system volume control covered in this chapter's preceding section, "Setting The System Audio Volume." This control determines the combined volume of all your sound sources.

- *Wave*—This control sets the volume for WAV-format digital sounds, which are used by games and as sound effects for Windows 98 system events.

- *MIDI*—This control sets the volume for MIDI music. *MIDI music* is electronic music either created on the computer or recorded in a MIDI-format song file for playback.

- *CD Audio*—If your system has a CD-ROM drive, you can use it to play standard audio compact discs. This control sets the volume for audio CDs.

- *Line-In*—As with the traditional stereo system line-in, most sound cards can accept audio from another source, and this control sets the volume for the incoming signal. Line-in is most often connected to your home stereo system—which enables you to record sound from cassettes and vinyl albums—or a VCR, which enables you to capture sound from TV shows and movies.

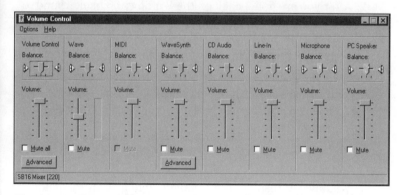

Figure 5.1   The complete system Windows 98 Volume Control dialog box shows all your sound sources.

- *Microphone*—If you have a microphone to record your voice for email, videoconferencing, or an Internet telephone program, this control sets the volume for your voice.

- *PC Speaker*—The last (and certainly least) control involves the humble PC speaker. If you run DOS programs, you can set the volume of the PC speaker with this control.

3. For each volume level that you want to change, click on the slider and drag it in the desired direction.

4. If you want to mute all sound from a particular source, enable the corresponding Mute checkbox. To restore the audio from that source, disable the Mute checkbox.

5. You can also adjust the left-to-right stereo balance for each of your audio sources. For example, if your left speaker is farther away from your PC than your right speaker, click on the Balance slider and move it to the left to increase the volume of the left channel. Doing so decreases the volume of the right channel, thereby restoring the stereo balance for your system.

6. To exit the Volume Control dialog box, click on OptionsIExit. Windows 98 saves your current volume and balance settings.

Setting Advanced Controls

Some sound card drivers also allow you to set advanced properties on the Volume Control dialog box. Depending on your card, you may have advanced controls for the master volume, Wave, MIDI, or Line-In sources. To display or change the advanced settings for a sound source, follow these steps:

1. Right-click on the speaker icon in the system tray and select Open Volume Controls from the pop-up menu.

2. Windows 98 displays the complete system Volume Control dialog box.

3. Click on the Advanced button to display the Advanced Controls dialog box for the corresponding audio source. Figure 5.2 shows the Advanced Controls dialog box for the master volume on a PC that uses a common sound card. Depending on the specific sound card you have installed, these advanced controls may include the following:

Figure 5.2 **Many sound cards provide advanced controls that you can adjust in the Advanced Controls For Volume Control dialog box.**

- *Bass/Treble*—These controls are just like their counterparts on your home stereo system; the Bass control adjusts the volume of low notes in music and speech, whereas the Treble control adjusts the volume of the high notes.

- *3D Stereo Enhancement*—The 3D stereo (sometimes called *spatial*) feature that some sound cards offer creates an audio illusion of movement in three dimensions; for example, sounds in a computer game might seem to come from behind you.

- *Reverb*—Many advanced sound cards offer a *reverb* function, which simulates the audio environment of a concert hall.

4. After you finish making any changes to the Advanced Controls dialog box, click on Close to save your changes and exit.

5. Click on Options|Exit to close the Volume Control dialog box. Windows 98 saves your current volume and balance settings.

Customizing The Volume Control Dialog Box

It's easy to customize the appearance of your Volume Control dialog box by changing its display properties. To do so, follow these steps:

1. Right-click on the speaker icon in the system tray and select Open Volume Controls from the pop-up menu to display the Volume Control dialog box.

2. Click on Options|Properties to display the Volume Control Properties dialog box, shown in Figure 5.3.

3. If you have more than one sound card on your PC, you can select which card to control by selecting it in the Mixer Device drop-down list. Most PC owners have only one sound card, so this value usually will not change.

4. The Volume Control dialog box can control either the Playback or Recording volume levels; by default, the Playback levels are displayed. If you select the Recording option, only those audio sources capable of recording are displayed—the master volume control is also automatically renamed to the master recording volume. You may also select from a custom display for a special application (like voice commands) by selecting Other.

5. If you decide to hide one of the volume controls to reduce the size of the dialog box (or eliminate the possibility of that control being changed), click on the corresponding checkbox within the scrolling list box. Clicking on this checkbox disables the control. You can redisplay the control at any time by enabling the checkbox.

6. After you make all your changes to the Volume Control's Properties dialog box, click on OK to save your changes and exit.

7. Click on Options|Exit. Windows 98 saves your current volume and balance settings.

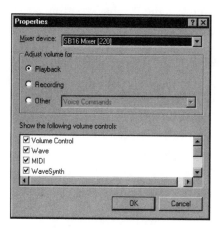

Figure 5.3 *You can customize the appearance of your Volume Control dialog box from the Volume Control Properties dialog box.*

Selecting Playback And Recording Devices

As mentioned previously in this chapter, many musicians and audiophiles have more than one sound card in their PCs, and Windows 98 provides a number of settings that allow multiple sound cards to share recording and playback tasks.

However, many of today's standard multimedia PCs also feature more than one way to record and play back audio—for example, both a sound card and a fax/modem with voice answering and speakerphone options. So even if you're not a musician, the material in this section may come in handy.

Selecting A Playback Device

Windows 98 uses the sound card you specify as the playback device to play all the electronically generated sounds that your computer produces, including digital sound in WAV format and MIDI music. If you have more than one sound card or audio device, however, you can select which device to be used for playback—typically, the highest-quality sound card. To select the playback device, follow these steps:

1. Click on Start|Settings.

2. Click on Control Panel to open the Control Panel window and then double-click on the Multimedia icon to open the Multimedia Properties dialog box, shown in Figure 5.4.

3. To select the playback device, click on the Preferred Device drop-down list in the Playback section and then click on the desired device. To display the Volume Control dialog box for the selected device, click on the square icon next to the drop-down list.

4. Click on OK to close the Multimedia Properties dialog box and save your changes.

Selecting A Recording Device

The recording device you specify is used within Windows 98 to record all audio signals—for example, the sound of your voice, a signal fed through the line-in jack on your sound card, or even music from an audio CD. If you have more than one sound card or audio device, follow these steps to select the device to use for recording:

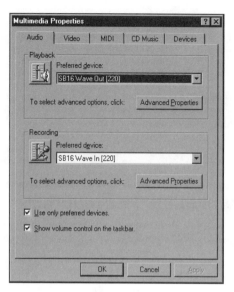

Figure 5.4   Windows 98 can use separate audio devices for both playback and recording.

1. Click on Start|Settings.

2. Click on Control Panel to open the Control Panel window and then double-click on the Multimedia icon to open the Multimedia Properties dialog.

3. Click on the Preferred Device drop-down list in the Recording section and then click on the desired device. To display the Volume Control dialog box for the selected device, click on the square icon next to the drop-down list.

4. Click on OK to close the Multimedia Properties dialog box and save your changes.

TIP: *How do I know which device to use? —If Windows 98 recognizes your playback and recording hardware, the device names are automatically added to the proper drop-down list within the Multimedia Properties dialog box—generally, with the words "Wave Out" for playback and "Wave In" for recording. By default, these preferred devices will be the only ones available for use in Windows 98 applications. You can select from any audio device within your applications by disabling the Use Only Preferred Devices checkbox at the bottom of the Multimedia Properties dialog box.*

However, a device will often identify itself with a different name to Windows 98. For example, some versions of the Creative Labs SoundBlaster AWE-32 card call themselves "SB16" (short for SoundBlaster 16-bit). If you have more than one audio device on your PC, look for a brand identifier or model number that may help determine which device you're selecting. If more than one audio device has the same driver, the number in brackets next to the name is the hardware base address for that device (you'll learn more about device addressing in Chapter 13).

Related solution:	Found in:
Configuring Hardware Resources	Chapter 13

Adjusting Multimedia Properties

As you may expect, Windows 98 supports a number of advanced configuration settings available on today's audio hardware for both recording and playback. In this section, you learn how to customize these advanced features for your PC.

Displaying The Taskbar Volume Control

By default, Windows 98 displays the volume control icon on your Taskbar. If your Taskbar is rapidly expanding and you want to remove the volume control icon, follow these steps:

1. Click on Start|Settings.

2. Click on Control Panel to open the Control Panel window and then double-click on the Multimedia icon to open the Multimedia Properties dialog box.

3. Click on the Show Volume Control On The Taskbar checkbox to disable it.

4. Click on OK to close the Multimedia Properties dialog box and save your changes.

Customizing Advanced Playback Properties

It's easy to fine-tune the operation of your audio playback device to achieve the best possible sound from your PC. To reach the advanced playback settings, follow these steps:

1. Click on Start|Settings.

2. Click on Control Panel to open the Control Panel window and then double-click on the Multimedia icon to open the Multimedia Properties dialog box.

3. Click on the Advanced Properties button in the Playback section of the dialog box to display the Advanced Audio Properties dialog box, shown in Figure 5.5.

***Figure 5.5   The Advanced Audio Properties dialog box for your
playback device.***

4. On the Speakers pane, click on the Speaker Setup drop-
    down list and select the speaker placement configuration
    that most closely matches the location of the speakers on
    your system. The example placement graphic in the middle
    of the Speakers pane changes to match your selection. Your
    choices are:

    *   *Desktop*—If your PC has free-standing speakers sitting
        alongside the monitor, Desktop Stereo Speakers (the
        default choice) is right for you.

    *   *Monitor*—If your monitor has built-in speakers, select
        Monitor Stereo Speakers. If your monitor has speakers
        mounted on the sides, select Monitor Mounted Stereo
        Speakers. If your monitor stand has built-in speakers,
        select Monitor Stand Stereo Speakers.

    *   *Laptop*—If your laptop or notebook computer has a single
        built-in speaker, select Laptop Mono Speakers. If your laptop
        has stereo built-in speakers, select Laptop Stereo Speakers.

    *   *Keyboard*—If your PC keyboard has stereo built-in
        speakers, select Keyboard Stereo Speakers.

    *   *Audiophile*—If your PC is equipped with four speakers
        and a sound card with quadraphonic support, select
        Quadraphonic Speakers. If you're watching DVD movies
        or playing DVD games with Dolby Digital Surround Sound,
        select Surround Sound Speakers. (For more details on
        DVD within Windows 98, refer to Chapter 3.)

- *Headphones*—Finally, if you're using a set of headphones with your PC or laptop computer, select
Stereo Headphones.

5. Click on the Performance tab to customize the quality and
acceleration of your audio playback hardware; Windows 98
displays the dialog box, as shown in Figure 5.6.

6. If you have a 16-bit sound card that provides hardware
acceleration for audio playback, click on and drag the
Hardware Acceleration slider to the Full setting. (If you
experience problems with Windows 98 DirectSound when
playing games, you need to decrease the level of hardware
acceleration to Standard or Basic.) If your sound card or
audio device doesn't support hardware acceleration, this
slider is disabled at the None position.

7. Most Pentium PCs and all Pentium II PCs should have the
highest possible quality for digital sound enabled. To enable
this setting, click on and drag the Sample Rate Conversion
Quality slider to the Best setting. (If you have a PC slower
than a Pentium 100 and it drags noticeably while playing
WAV-format digital sound files or digital sound effects in
applications, the current setting for this option is probably
too high. Decrease the conversion quality level until your PC
no longer slows down while playing digital sounds.)

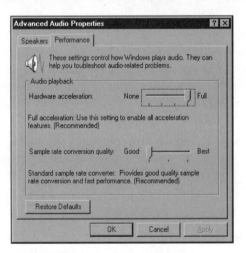

**Figure 5.6   Configuring the performance settings for your audio
playback device.**

8. Click on OK to close the Advanced Audio Properties dialog box and save your changes. Click on OK again to exit the Multimedia Properties dialog box and return to the Control Panel window.

Related solution:	Found in:
Using DVD Under Windows 98	Chapter 3

Customizing Advanced Recording Properties

You can also tailor the performance and quality settings for your audio recording device from the Advanced Audio Properties dialog box. To do so, take the following steps:

1. Click on Start|Settings.

2. Click on Control Panel to open the Control Panel window and then double-click on the Multimedia icon to open the Multimedia Properties dialog box.

3. Click on the Advanced Properties button in the Recording section of the dialog box to display the Advanced Audio Properties dialog box.

4. If your sound card offers hardware acceleration for audio recording, click on and drag the Hardware Acceleration slider to the Full setting. (If you experience problems with Windows 98 DirectSound when recording audio, decrease the level of hardware acceleration to Standard or Basic.) If Windows 98 doesn't recognize hardware acceleration as an option on your sound card, this slider is disabled at the None position.

5. Most Pentium PCs and all Pentium II PCs should have the highest possible quality for digital sound enabled. To do so, click on and drag the Sample Rate Conversion Quality slider to the Best setting. (If you have a PC slower than a Pentium 100 and it drags noticeably while recording audio in applications, the current setting for this option is probably too high. Decrease the conversion quality level until your PC no longer slows down while recording.)

6. Click on OK to close the Advanced Audio Properties dialog box. Click on OK again to exit the Multimedia Properties dialog box.

Creating A Single-Instrument MIDI Configuration

With the right hardware, a musician can actually play music from a MIDI synthesizer keyboard directly into electronic form on a PC, or the PC can "play" the instrument all by itself.

TIP: *The sweet sound of wavetable—Today's advanced wavetable sound cards are especially suited to playing MIDI music, as the wavetable feature allows your PC to use sound samples taken from actual instruments (instead of approximating their sound using traditional FM synthesis). In other words, if a MIDI song file calls for an acoustic guitar, a sound card with wavetable support can recreate the sound of a guitar much more realistically than older sound cards could.*

Windows 98 allows you to select a single MIDI configuration. Typically, your sound card's installation software sets this output configuration as the default. However, if your PC has multiple audio devices with MIDI capability, you can select the best configuration by following these steps:

1. Click on Start|Settings.

2. Click on Control Panel to open the Control Panel window and then double-click on the Multimedia icon to open the Multimedia Properties dialog box.

3. Click on the MIDI tab.

4. Windows 98 displays all the MIDI output configurations available on your PC in the Single Instrument scrolling list, including any external ports for connecting to MIDI instruments. Click on the desired MIDI output configuration to select it.

5. Click on OK to save your changes and return to the Control Panel window.

Creating A Custom MIDI Configuration

If your sound card allows you to make changes to your MIDI output configuration, you can create a custom configuration with instruments that you choose. To do so, follow these steps:

1. Click on Start|Settings.

2. Click on Control Panel to open the Control Panel window and then double-click on the Multimedia icon to open the Multimedia Properties dialog box.

3. Click on the MIDI tab.

4. Click on Custom Configuration. Windows 98 provides a single default custom configuration named (appropriately enough) "Default", but if you already created a custom configuration, you can select it from the MIDI Scheme drop-down list.

5. Click on the Configure button to open the MIDI Configuration dialog box, shown in Figure 5.7.

6. The Channel scrolling list displays each of the MIDI hardware channels that the audio device supports. To change a specific instrument, click on the desired channel and then click on the Change button; to change more than one instrument, press and hold the Ctrl key and then click on each desired instrument. Windows 98 displays the Change MIDI Instrument dialog box.

7. Click on the Instrument drop-down list and select the desired output instrument for this channel (or, if you selected multiple instruments, channels). Click on OK to accept the change and return to the MIDI Configuration dialog box.

8. Repeat Steps 6 and 7 for each instrument you need to change.

9. When you're satisfied with your new custom configuration, you can either save it under the existing name ("Default") or save it under another name. To use a new name, click on Save As, enter a new scheme name, and click on OK. Finally,

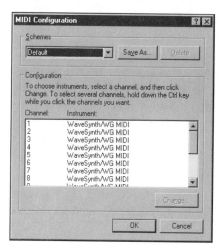

Figure 5.7   The MIDI Configuration dialog box.

click on OK on the MIDI Configuration dialog box to accept the change and return to the Multimedia Properties dialog box.

10. Click on OK to save your changes and return to the Control Panel window.

Adding A New MIDI Instrument

If you need to add a new MIDI instrument definition to your MIDI configuration, you're in luck: Windows 98 provides a Wizard to help automate the process. You can add an external MIDI instrument—or, if you have a wavetable sound card that can be loaded with new instrument sound samples, a new "software" instrument.

TIP: *First things first—if you're adding an external musical instrument, make sure that it's powered on and connected to your PC's external MIDI port before you start this process.*

To add a new MIDI instrument, follow these steps:

1. Click on Start|Settings.

2. Click on Control Panel to open the Control Panel window and then double-click on the Multimedia icon to open the Multimedia Properties dialog box.

3. Click on the MIDI tab.

4. Click on Add New Instrument to display the MIDI Instrument Installation Wizard, shown in Figure 5.8.

5. In the MIDI ports scrolling list, click on the port that is connected to the instrument and then click on Next.

6. Select the proper definition for your new instrument. If you're installing an external MIDI instrument, you probably can find the definition (in IDF format) on disk or from the manufacturer's Web site; click on Browse to load it from any drive on your system. (If you're unsure which definition to use or you're installing a new sound sample, click on General MIDI Instrument.) Click on Next to continue to the next Wizard page.

7. Enter a new identifying name in the Instrument Name field and then click on Finish to complete the process.

8. Click on OK to return to the Control Panel window.

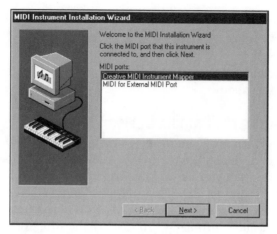

Figure 5.8 *You can add a new MIDI instrument with this Windows 98 Wizard.*

Customizing CD Audio Properties

If you're like me, you enjoy playing audio CDs in your CD-ROM drive while you work; Windows 98 can also use CD audio in games and educational programs. To configure the audio properties for your PC's CD-ROM drive, follow these steps:

1. Click on Start|Settings.

2. Click on Control Panel to open the Control Panel window and then double-click on the Multimedia icon to open the Multimedia Properties dialog box.

3. Click on the CD Music tab.

4. If you have more than one CD-ROM drive installed in your PC. For example, if you have both a CD-ROM drive and a CD recorder, you can specify the drive to be used for playing audio CDs. Select the drive in the Default CD-ROM driver for playing CD music drop-down list.

TIP: *CD variations—The ability to select the CD-ROM drive to use for audio CDs is especially handy. If one of your drives has front-mounted audio controls for next/previous track and pause, you can use these controls without displaying the Windows 98 CD Player application.*

---

5. Click on and drag the CD Music Volume slider to the desired level for CD audio.

6. If the CD-ROM drive you're using supports digital playback, enable the checkbox labeled Whenever Possible, Use Digital Playback On This Device.

7. Click on OK to save your changes and return to the Control Panel window.

Displaying Multimedia Device Properties

Windows 98 allows you to access the properties for your multimedia devices and drivers from the Multimedia Properties dialog box. Although this same information is available from the System Properties dialog box, it's much more convenient to access when you're customizing multimedia properties or troubleshooting audio problems. To display the properties for your multimedia hardware, follow these steps:

1. Click on Start|Settings.

2. Click on Control Panel to open the Control Panel window and then double-click on the Multimedia icon to open the Multimedia Properties dialog box.

3. Click on the Devices tab to display the major multimedia components installed in your system.

4. Click on the plus sign to the left of the entry you want to display or change to expand the branch and display the devices and drivers for that component.

5. Highlight the desired device or driver and then click on Properties to display its Properties dialog box.

6. Done? Click on OK to apply any changes and exit the Properties dialog box.

7. Click on OK to exit the Multimedia Properties dialog box.

Customizing Your Sound Scheme

OK, I admit it: I'm one of those adults who's really a kid at heart, and I really get a kick out of the multimedia sound effects on my Windows 98 desktop. Somehow, the right set of sounds can help relieve the tension of a busy workday, remind you of that great vacation you took a few years ago, or even turn your computer into a famous personality.

In this section, I'll show you how to create and select your own sound scheme, and you can transform your computer into a virtual rainforest or a robot!

Selecting A Sound Scheme

Windows 95 included a number of default sound schemes that you also can use within Windows 98. To select a sound scheme, follow these steps:

1. Click on Start|Settings.

2. Click on Control Panel to open the Control Panel window and then double-click on the Sounds icon to open the Sounds Properties dialog box, shown in Figure 5.9. You can assign each major event within Windows 98 a digital sound file in WAV format.

3. Click on the Schemes drop-down list and then click on the desired scheme.

4. You can preview any sound in the current scheme by clicking on the desired event in the Events scrolling list. Windows 98 automatically displays the full path and file name of the sound file associated with that event. To play the sound, click on the button with the triangular play icon; to stop the playback, click on the button with the square stop icon.

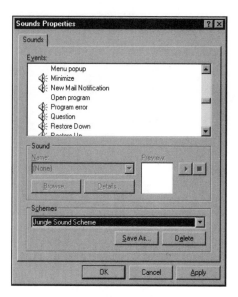

Figure 5.9   Selecting a sound scheme within Windows 98.

5. Click on the Details button to display the Properties dialog box for that sound file, as shown in Figure 5.10. This screen includes the copyright, the length of the sound in seconds, the audio format, and information like the sound's creator and the audio application used to create the sound.

TIP: *The content of these fields depends on how the recording was made, so some of the fields may be empty. Even if some fields are empty, the sound should still play fine.*

---

6. After you select a scheme, click on OK to close the Sounds Properties dialog box and save your changes.

Creating A New Sound Scheme

You can also create your own sound scheme using sounds that you recorded or downloaded from the Internet, or sounds from existing schemes. Follow these steps to create a new custom sound scheme:

1. Click on Start|Settings.

2. Click on Control Panel to open the Control Panel window and then double-click on the Sounds icon to open the Sounds Properties dialog box.

3. If you want to use an existing scheme as the basis for a new scheme, click on the Schemes drop-down list and then click

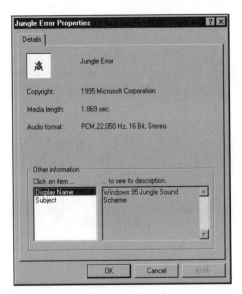

Figure 5.10   You can display information about any sound file in the current scheme.

on the desired scheme. To start a brand-new scheme, select No Sounds from the Schemes drop-down list.

4. Next, click on the event you want to assign in the Events scrolling list. To select the corresponding sound file, click on Browse to navigate through your system and open any WAV-format file. To preview the sound, click on the button with the triangular play icon; to stop the playback, click on the button with the square stop icon. To view the details on the current sound file, click on the Details button.

5. Repeat Step 4 until you have assigned sounds to all the events you like.

6. Click on Save As to save your new sound scheme with a unique name.

7. Click on OK to close the Sounds Properties dialog box.

Recording Audio By Using Sound Recorder

Although a sound recording program probably came with your sound card, Windows 98 offers an application that allows you to record digital audio. You can use the Windows 98 Sound Recorder, for example, to record your voice as a sound file to attach with your email.

TIP: *A recording precheck—By default, most sound cards use a "boom" or "clip-on" microphone connected to the card's microphone jack; many multimedia computer monitors have built-in microphones, and the connector for the monitor's microphone goes to the sound card's microphone jack. Before you attempt to record digital audio with Sound Recorder, make sure that your microphone is properly connected. Also, make sure that the Microphone Volume on your Volume Control dialog box is centered about halfway, and that the Microphone Mute checkbox is disabled.*

To record audio by using Sound Recorder and your microphone, take the following steps:

1. Click on Start|Programs.

2. Click on Accessories|Entertainment|Sound Recorder. Windows 98 runs the Sound Recorder, shown in Figure 5.11. The box with the green line at the center of the dialog box displays the audio waveform as you record your sound file. Using the slider, you can navigate quickly from one end of

Figure 5.11   The Windows 98 Sound Recorder application.

the sound file to the other. The buttons at the bottom of the application window are (in order): Seek To Beginning, Seek To End, Play, Stop, and Record. The Sound Recorder also displays the current position of the slider and the total length of the current sound file in seconds.

3. Click on the Record button (which has a circular icon) to begin recording. To stop recording, click on the Stop button (which has a square icon).

TIP: *Make a test—Always record a test sound first to make sure that you have the correct recording volume.*

---

4. Click on Play to listen to the sound you just recorded.

5. You can add a special effect to your sound file if you like. Sound Recorder includes these settings under the Effects menu:

   • *Volume*—Increases or decreases the volume of the sound file.

   • *Speed*—Increases or decreases the playback speed.

   • *Add Echo*—Adds an echo special effect to the sound file.

   • *Reverse*—Reverses the entire sound file so that it plays backwards.

6. Sound Recorder also allows you to edit your file by removing portions from the beginning or end of the file (perfect for "cropping" a sound file to eliminate unnecessary length). Click on and drag the slider until you reach the desired point—or play the sound file and then click on Stop at the desired point—and then select either Delete Before Current Position or Delete After Current Position from the Edit menu.

7. When your sound file is perfect, click on File|Save As, enter a unique name, and save your new audio creation to disk.

8. Click on File|Exit to close Sound Recorder and return to the Windows 98 desktop.

Playing Audio CDs With CD Player

Another Windows 98 sound application, CD Player, allows you to listen to audio CDs, offering the same functionality as your stereo CD player—using your PC CD-ROM drive. To play an audio CD, follow these steps:

1. Load the audio CD into your CD-ROM drive. If you have Auto Insert Notification turned on within the properties for the drive, Windows 98 automatically recognizes the audio CD, launches CD Player, and starts playing the disc.

2. If Auto Insert Notification is turned off (it's turned on by default), click on Start|Programs|Accessories| Entertainment|CD Recorder. Windows 98 runs the CD Player, shown in Figure 5.12.

3. Click on the large Play button (which has a triangular icon) to begin playing the CD. To stop playing the CD, click on the Stop button (which has a square icon).

4. Click on Disc|Exit to close CD Player and return to the Windows 98 desktop.

Figure 5.12   The Windows 98 CD Player application.

Troubleshooting

Troubleshooting Audio Problems

If you like the audio you hear from an expensive wavetable sound card, you'll be just as disappointed if you don't hear anything at all. In this section, I will cover a number of potential audio problems under Windows 98 and how you can correct them.

No Audio At All

If your PC has a sound card and Windows 98 recognizes it—but you're not hearing any audio at all—check these possible problem areas:

*   *Hardware conflict*—Sound cards are prime targets for DMA and IRQ conflicts with other adapter cards and devices within your PC. (Usually, plug-and-play adapter cards eliminate this problem, but many sound cards still use jumpers to set DMA and IRQ.) To check for hardware conflicts, take the following steps:

    1. Right-click on My Computer to display the System Properties dialog box and then click on the Device Manager tab.

    2. Click on the plus sign next to the entry for sound, video, and game controllers to expand the branch and display your multimedia devices.

    3. If your sound card appears in the Device Manager list with a yellow exclamation point or a red checkmark, you may have a conflict with another device. The other device may also have a yellow exclamation point next to it.

    4. Click on Properties to display the Adapter Card Properties dialog box and then click on the General tab.

    5. Click on Update Driver to check for newer drivers for your sound card. Windows 98 launches the Update Device Drivers Wizard.

    6. If updating the driver doesn't work, follow the instructions in your sound card manual for resolving resource conflicts.

    7. Click on OK to exit the Adapter Card Properties dialog box and then click on OK to exit the System Properties

dialog box. If you made any changes, you will need to reboot your computer.

- *Volume control is muted or too low*—Display the Volume Control dialog box (as described at the beginning of this chapter) and check to make sure that the Mute checkbox on the main volume control is disabled. Move the Volume Control slider to at least at the mid-point.

- *Bad connection*—Check your speaker cables to make sure that they're connected to the proper jack on your sound card.

- *No power to the speakers*—If your speakers are powered, make sure that they have batteries or AC power. Also, don't forget to make sure that they're turned on and their volume control is set at least at mid-point.

Audio From
Only One
Speaker

Audio From Only One Speaker

If you're hearing audio from only one speaker, one of the following problems may be the culprit:

- *Balance is set incorrectly*—Display the Volume Control dialog box and make sure that all the balance sliders are positioned in the middle.

- *One of your cables has shorted*—To determine if you have a short in either your speaker cables or your speaker jack, look for a common symptom. If wiggling the plug from your speaker inside the speaker jack sometimes produces sound from both speakers, replace the cable or plug for your speaker wire.

No CD Audio

No CD Audio

If you can't hear CD audio through your sound card, check these problem areas:

- *Your CD cable is not connected*—In order to play CD audio, your CD-ROM drive must be connected by a cable to your sound card; this cable should have come with either your sound card or your CD-ROM drive. Check to make sure that this cable is connected.

- *You are playing audio CD in the wrong drive*—If you have more than one CD-ROM drive on your system, make sure that you're playing the audio CD in the drive designated in the Multimedia Properties dialog box.

- *The CD audio or drive volume control is too low*—Check the Volume Control dialog box and make sure that the Audio CD slider is at its mid-point and the Mute checkbox is disabled. Also, check the volume control on the CD-ROM drive itself and make sure that it's turned to at least mid-point.

Audio Applications Return Display Driver Errors

Audio Applications Return Display Driver Errors

If a game or application that uses digital audio or MIDI returns an MCI driver error, check these possible problems:

- *An improperly set playback device*—You need to display the current playback device and make sure that your system is using the correct audio device for playback.

- *A corrupted or missing driver*—You need to reinstall the software that accompanied your sound card to replace the multimedia MCI driver.

- *A corrupted or missing IDF MIDI definition file*—You need to reinstall the software that accompanied your sound card to replace the IDF file, or recreate the custom MIDI configuration you were originally using to reload any missing instruments.

CHECK SPEAKER CONNECTIONS — WIRES TO SPEAKER MAYBE PLUGGED IN WRONG!

Your Keyboard And Mouse

In Brief

Your Keyboard And Mouse

Of all the peripherals connected to your computer, the keyboard and mouse are probably the two tools most of you deem the least important. At one time or another, you've probably glanced at your keyboard or mouse and said, "Every computer has one of each, they all work in the same way, and they're relatively inexpensive to buy or replace. Unlike with that expensive printer or flatbed scanner I bought last year, I don't have to set anything. How can I 'optimize' a keyboard or a mouse?"

Not so fast! In fact, the keyboard and mouse are the only input devices for most of us—probably your only connection to your computer at this time—and they're both *very* important and *very* customizable. Any computer power user or programmer will tell you that selecting just the right keyboard and pointing device can improve both your physical *and* mental condition at the end of a busy workday at the PC. Those professionals would probably fight like cats and dogs to keep their favorite input devices.

To illustrate the importance of your keyboard, consider the appearance of more and more "ergonomic" keyboards such as the Microsoft Natural. These keyboards are designed to support the wrist and allow users to type more quickly with a healthier angle to the keys. Windows 98 recognizes additional keys on newer keyboards; for example, with a single key, you can display the Start menu, application menus, or the Task List. Some keyboards even include their own pointing device, and others are specially designed with tactile response in mind (that satisfying "click" you probably remember from your first IBM keyboard).

As for pointing devices, you'll find an even wider range of personal choices. You can still use the traditional mouse if you like, but I personally recommend a *trackball*—a pointing device that resembles an upside-down mouse, where you move the ball with your thumb or finger. Other pointing devices include the *touchpad* (where you move your finger across the surface to move the mouse pointer), the *fingertip mouse* (where you push a small button in the desired direction), and the *drawing tablet* (where you use a plastic stylus to draw on the tablet's surface).

The days when everyone used the same input devices are long gone. In this chapter, you'll learn how to customize the operation of your keyboard and mouse within Windows 98 to save you time and trouble. You'll also configure your system for other languages and learn a number of troubleshooting techniques in case you encounter problems with your input devices.

Adjusting Keyboard Settings

As I have just mentioned, you can customize your keyboard properties in Windows 98. Although every PC owner prefers a keyboard that is "tuned," those who spend hours typing letters and documents or entering data into spreadsheets will especially appreciate the sections "Configuring Character Repeat Settings" and "Configuring Cursor Blink Rate."

Using Alternate Languages

Windows 98 allows your standard U.S. English keyboard to do double duty as one of many keyboards with international characters from other languages. You can create a separate keyboard layout for another language, and you can switch between English and other languages at any time with only one key combination. For example, you can type a letter in Japanese to a business associate and then work on a proposal in English.

You can find all these language options in the "Adding A New Language," "Removing A Language," and "Selecting A Switch Language Key Combination" sections.

Customizing Mouse Settings

Under Windows 98, you can specify everything from the speed and sensitivity of your pointing device to the shape of the various pointers. Whether you have a traditional mouse or a trackball, the sections "Selecting A Mouse Pointer Scheme," "Creating A Pointer Scheme," "Changing Individual Pointers," "Setting Button Assignments And Double-Click Speed," and "Configuring Pointer Settings" include all you will need to customize your pointing device.

Immediate Solutions

Configuring Character Repeat Settings

If you hold down a key for a specific length of time within Windows 98, it starts to *repeat*, and it continues as long as the key is held down. This feature can be a problem if you're entering data into a spreadsheet or a database program, or if you're a slow typist who tends to leave your fingers on the keys. If you'd like to adjust the repeat settings for your keyboard, follow these steps:

1. Click on Start|Settings.

2. Click on Control Panel to open the Control Panel window, and double-click on the Keyboard icon to open the Keyboard Properties dialog box shown in Figure 6.1.

3. The Repeat Delay slider controls the length of time you must hold down a key before the repeat function is activated. If you prefer a short delay before the key repeats, move the slider to the right; for a longer key repeat delay, move the slider to the left.

4. The other setting that controls the keyboard repeat function is the Repeat Rate. This setting determines how fast the key is repeated after the repeat function is activated. If you decide that you want the key to repeat faster, move the slider to the right; if you decide that you want the key to repeat more slowly, move the slider to the left.

5. For your convenience, the Keyboard Properties dialog box includes a test field where you can experiment with different combinations of values for repeat delay and repeat rate. To try out a combination, click your mouse within the Click Here And Hold Down A Key To Test Repeat Rate field and then press and hold down any alphanumeric key.

6. After you have selected the combination of delay and rate that will work best for you, click on OK to close the Keyboard Properties dialog box and save your changes.

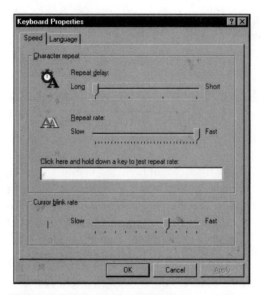

Figure 6.1   The Keyboard Properties dialog box.

Configuring Cursor Blink Rate

Windows 98 allows you to set the rate at which the insertion cursor blinks within all of your Windows 98 applications. Although some PC owners find it easier to locate a fast-blinking cursor, others find a fast blink rate distracting. To adjust the cursor blink rate, follow these steps:

1. Click on Start|Settings.

2. Click on Control Panel to open the Control Panel window and double-click on the Keyboard icon to open the Keyboard Properties dialog box.

3. The Cursor Blink Rate slider specifies how fast the position and text-insertion cursors blink. If you want the cursor to blink faster, you should move the slider to the right; move the slider to the left to slow the rate of blinking. The example text-position cursor to the left of the slider demonstrates your current cursor blink rate.

4. After you're satisfied with the cursor blink rate, click on OK to close the Keyboard Properties dialog box and save your changes.

Adding A New Language

TIP: *If you add one or more new languages, your system asks for your original Windows 98 CD-ROM; load it into your CD-ROM drive when prompted.*

To add a new language layout to your keyboard, take the following steps:

1. Click on Start|Settings.

2. Click on Control Panel to open the Control Panel window and double-click on the Keyboard icon to open the Keyboard Properties dialog box.

3. Click on the Language tab to display the pane shown in Figure 6.2.

4. By default, Windows 98 includes only the English language layout for a 101-key keyboard; click on Add to select another language.

5. Windows 98 displays the Add Language dialog box. Click on the Language drop-down list box and select the entry for the language you'd like to add. Click on OK to continue.

6. If you would like the new language you have selected to be the default at startup, highlight its entry in the Language drop-down list box and click on Set as Default.

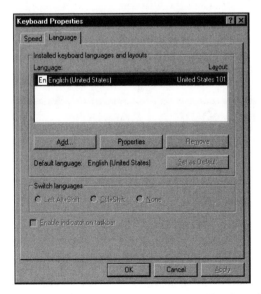

Figure 6.2   Displaying the available languages and keyboard layouts.

7. If you would like an indicator added to your Taskbar that displays which language you're using, click on the Enable Indicator On Taskbar checkbox to activate it.

8. After you have selected one or more desired languages as well as specified a new default language (if you would like to do so), click on OK to close the Keyboard Properties dialog box and save your changes.

Removing A Language

If you no longer need a language and you want to save disk space, you can remove the keyboard layout and language files. To remove the support for an existing language and keyboard layout, take the following steps:

1. Click on Start|Settings.

2. Click on Control Panel to open the Control Panel window and double-click on the Keyboard icon to open the Keyboard Properties dialog box.

3. Click on the Language tab.

4. Click on the Language drop-down list box and select the entry for the language you'd like to remove.

6. Click on the Remove button.

7. Click on OK to close the Keyboard Properties dialog box and save your change.

Selecting A Switch Language Key Combination

You can choose from two key combinations for switching between languages. Follow these steps to specify the combination:

1. Click on Start|Settings.

2. Click on Control Panel to open the Control Panel window and double-click on the Keyboard icon to open the Keyboard Properties dialog box.

3. Click on the Language tab.

4. Click on one of the following options to choose how to switch languages:

   - *Left Alt+Shift*—Holding down the left Alt key on your keyboard and pressing Shift switches languages.

   - *Ctrl+Shift*—Holding down the Ctrl key on your keyboard and pressing Shift switches languages.

   - *None*—Select this option if you would rather switch languages from the Keyboard Properties dialog box. (Doing so avoids an accidental language switch if other applications use the preceding two key combinations.)

5. Click on OK to close the Keyboard Properties dialog box and save your changes.

Selecting A Mouse Pointer Scheme

Selecting a different *mouse pointer scheme* (a group of pointers designed to work together) can make your work easier by making your pointers more visible. To select an existing pointer scheme, follow these steps:

1. Click on Start|Settings.

2. Click on Control Panel to open the Control Panel window and double-click on the Mouse icon to open the Mouse Properties dialog box.

3. Click on the Pointers tab to display the pane shown in Figure 6.3.

4. To load an existing pointer scheme, click on the Scheme drop-down list box and select one of the entries. The preview window automatically updates to display the pointers for the selected scheme.

TIP: *If you have a notebook or a laptop computer, try one of the schemes with Large or Extra-Large pointers. With one of these schemes, you won't "lose" your pointer on your desktop.*

---

5. Click on OK to close the Mouse Properties dialog box and save your changes.

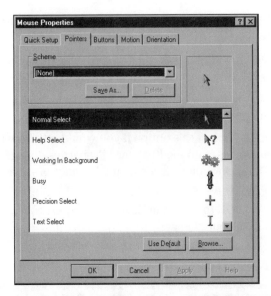

Figure 6.3   Selecting a mouse pointer scheme within Windows 98.

Creating A Pointer Scheme

To create a new pointer scheme, follow these steps:

1. Click on Start|Settings.

2. Click on Control Panel to open the Control Panel window and double-click on the Mouse icon to open the Mouse Properties dialog box.

3. Click on the Pointers tab.

4. To change a specific pointer, click on it within the preview window and click on the Browse button. Windows 98 enables you to navigate your system and select any ANI or CUR cursor file (two file formats recognized by Windows 98 that may contain either static or animated cursors); click on Open to load the pointer.

5. Repeat Step 4 as many times as necessary until you've loaded all the pointers you need for your new scheme.

6. Click on Save As; enter a new, unique name for your pointer scheme; and then click on OK.

7. Click on OK to close the Mouse Properties dialog box and save your changes.

Changing Individual Pointers

To change individual pointers within your current pointer scheme, take the following steps:

1. Click on Start|Settings.

2. Click on Control Panel to open the Control Panel window and double-click on the Mouse icon to open the Mouse Properties dialog box.

3. Click on the Pointers tab.

4. To change a specific pointer, click on it within the preview window and click on the Browse button. Windows 98 allows you to navigate your system and select any ANI or CUR cursor file; click on Open to load the pointer.

5. Repeat Step 4 as many times as necessary.

6. Click on OK. This action closes the Mouse Properties dialog box and saves your changes.

Setting Button Assignments And Double-Click Speed

PC mice typically have either two or three buttons, and Windows 98 allows you to set your mouse as left- or right-handed. You can also fine-tune the double-click speed to your preferences. To change these two settings (controlled in the same dialog box), follow these steps:

1. Click on Start|Settings.

2. Click on Control Panel to open the Control Panel window and double-click on the Mouse icon to open the Mouse Properties dialog box.

3. Click on the Buttons tab.

4. By default, Windows 98 assumes you're right-handed; if you're left-handed, click on Left-handed to swap button assignments.

5. The Double-Click Speed slider bar determines how fast you must press your Click button to register as a double-click within Windows 98. If you'd like a faster double-click speed,

move the slider to the right; for a slower double-click speed, move the slider to the left.

6. You can try out your double-click speed setting by double-clicking within the Test area.

7. Click on OK to close the Mouse Properties dialog box and save your changes.

Configuring Pointer Settings

Another setting that can make a significant difference in your productivity is the speed of your mouse pointer. To set cursor options, follow these steps:

1. Click on Start|Settings.

2. Click on Control Panel to open the Control Panel window and double-click on the Mouse icon to open the Mouse Properties dialog box.

3. Click on the Motion tab.

4. The Pointer Speed slider bar determines how fast your mouse pointer moves across the desktop. To speed up mouse movement, move the slider to the right; for a slower mouse, move the slider to the left.

5. If you enable Pointer Trails, your mouse cursor leaves a "shadow" outline as it moves across your screen—this setting is often very helpful for PC owners with less-than-perfect eyesight. You can also specify the length of the trail. Move the slider to the right to lengthen the trails. To shorten the trails, move the slider to the left.

TIP: *Got a notebook or laptop computer? If so, I highly recommend that you enable Pointer Trails; trails make it much easier to locate your cursor on an LCD screen.*

6. Click on OK to close the Mouse Properties dialog box and save your changes.

Troubleshooting

Troubleshooting Keyboard And Mouse Problems

A keyboard or mouse problem can make it very hard to use your PC at all. This section provides a number of troubleshooting tips to help you figure out what's wrong with your mouse or keyboard and fix it *quickly*.

Mouse Doesn't Move Or Locks Up Your PC

Does your PC lock up when you move your mouse, or does it simply not move your pointer? Check these possible problems:

- *There is a hardware conflict.* Mouse operations can conflict with other devices in your PC, especially your modem. Follow these steps to check for hardware conflicts:

    1. Right-click on My Computer to display the System Properties dialog box and then click on the Device Manager tab.

    2. Click on the plus sign next to the entry for Mouse to expand the branch and display your pointing device.

    3. If your mouse appears in the Device Manager list with a yellow exclamation point or a red check, you may have a conflict with another device. The other device may also have a yellow exclamation point next to it.

    4. Click on Properties to display the Mouse Properties dialog box and then click on the Driver tab.

    5. Click on Update Driver to check for newer drivers for your sound card. Windows 98 launches the Update Device Drivers Wizard.

    6. If updating the driver doesn't work, follow the instructions in your mouse manual for resolving resource conflicts.

    7. Click on OK to exit the Mouse Properties dialog box and then click on OK to exit the System Properties dialog box. If you made any changes, you will have to reboot your computer.

Mouse Doesn't Move Or Locks Up Your PC

- *The mouse ball is jammed.* Your mouse uses a rubber or plastic ball to pick up the movement of your hand. Turn your mouse over and make sure that the ball turns freely. If it doesn't, twist the retaining ring in the specified direction, remove the ball, and clean both the ball and the internal rollers with a good dose of alcohol on a Q-tip. (It's a good idea to clean your mouse—and keyboard as well—at least once a month, especially if you like to snack at the PC.)

- *Mouse connected to the wrong port.* The keyboard port on most PCs today can also accept a PS/2 connector, so you may have your mouse connected to the wrong port.

Mouse Buttons Switched

If you're left-handed and you have set your button assignments—but your buttons aren't reversed—check these possible problem areas:

- *You recently reinstalled Windows 98.* If you recently reinstalled Windows 98 to correct another problem, your mouse properties probably also were reset to their right-handed defaults. To set your mouse as left-handed, follow the instructions in the "Setting Button Assignments And Double-Click Speed" section previously in this chapter.

- *Your application options have not been configured.* Many games and multimedia programs require you to set left-handed operation within the application's Options menu. In other words, although Windows 98 knows you're left-handed, your favorite game may need to be reconfigured before it realizes your buttons need to be switched.

No Keyboard Activity

If your keyboard is frozen, one of the following problems may be the culprit:

- *The current application is locked up.* Typically, Windows 98 will not respond to keyboard input if the current application is locked up. Try pressing the Ctrl+Alt+Del keyboard combination to display the Task Manager dialog box; and follow the instructions there. If doing this doesn't work, you may have to reboot your PC completely.

- *The cursor is in a non-alphanumeric field.* If your cursor is currently resting on an option button, a checkbox, or some other field that doesn't require alphanumeric input, your PC may either beep when you try to type something or play the default system sound.

- *The application does not recognize "unnecessary" keys.* Check the application's Options menu; many games and educational programs disable much of the keyboard to prevent input from any keys not used by the application. For example, a child's painting program may disable the Escape key to prevent the child from exiting the program by accident.

- *The keyboard connector has been pulled out.* If you've just moved your PC or keyboard, check to make sure that the keyboard connector is still plugged in.

Printing

In Brief

Printing

On the surface, printing under Windows 98 seems very simple; you select File|Print in your application (or, if the application has a toolbar, click on the Print icon) and everything is sent to your printer automatically. You can choose between color or black-and-white output with one click, and even switch from portrait to landscape mode for those long spreadsheet pages. Although printing under Windows 98 really can be that easy—and usually is—keep in mind that the "one-click" approach uses all of the default settings that your printer's manufacturer specified.

Suppose that, however, you want to change an option or two. Suddenly you will find yourself lost in a forest of dialog boxes, and you will realize that your printer has more confusing settings than just about any other peripheral you can add to your PC! Additionally, every printer has different features and options, so that nifty settings that work on your PC at the office may not even be available on your PC at home.

Windows 98 actually makes printing easier by hiding most of these options, but wading through all those different dialog boxes can be very frustrating if you're trying to fine-tune your printer's performance.

In this chapter, you will learn how to navigate those nested dialog boxes as well as configure Windows 98 to operate faster and print better. You will also learn how to add TrueType and OpenType printing fonts to your system. Finally, this chapter ends with a number of troubleshooting tips that may help you fix a misbehaving printer and get it back online.

Installing A New Printer

Do you need to add a new printer to your system? Many printers include easy-to-use software that automatically performs the necessary steps under Windows 98. If your new printer has such software, you probably will save time and trouble if you use it and skip to the "Configuring Printer Settings" section. (Plus, the software version on the driver provided with your printer may be more up to date than the driver that came with Windows 98.)

If, on the other hand, your printer didn't come with installation software, you need to know how to install a printer under Windows 98. You can do so by looking at both the automatic detection method (see "Installing A Printer Automatically") and the manual method (see "Installing A Printer Manually").

Configuring Printer Settings

Correct configuration of your printer's settings can often be a complex task. In the sections "Changing Settings From The Print Dialog Box" and "Changing Settings From Printer Properties," you will learn more about how to change printer options and settings within Windows 98.

Optimizing Your Printing Under Windows 98

The 32-bit printer drivers used within Windows 95 and Windows 98 offer much faster printing than with any 16-bit operating system like DOS or Windows 3.11, but there's always room for improvement. In the printing optimization sections, I will show you how to speed up the printing process ("Spooling Printer Output," "Disabling Printer Port Polling," and "Defragmenting Your Hard Drive"), prepare print projects when you're offline ("Working Offline"), and use draft mode to print faster ("Selecting A Print Quality").

Using TrueType And OpenType Fonts

Although you may not be familiar with the various types of fonts used within Windows 98, you're probably well versed in using different fonts within your word processing, desktop publishing, and graphics applications. Everyone has their own favorite fonts, and those who make a living by creating printed media on a PC consider a large collection of fonts to be a necessary and important tool.

Here's a quick introduction to the two major font types used within Windows 98:

- *TrueType*—TrueType fonts have been a popular standard within Windows for some time now. You can fully scale and rotate these outline fonts, and they will not lose their shape.

You can use TrueType fonts for both screen display and printed material.

- *OpenType*—OpenType is a new Microsoft font standard, making its debut in Windows 98. Although very similar to TrueType, OpenType fonts also include sophisticated typography positioning and outline information that advanced applications can use to produce character derivatives and multilingual documents.

The Immediate Solutions sections in this chapter, "Installing Fonts In Windows 98—The Drag-And-Drop Method" and "Installing Fonts In Windows 98—The Font List Method" sections cover both available methods of how you install fonts within Windows 98.

Immediate Solutions

Installing A Printer Automatically

One of the features of both Windows 95 and Windows 98 that I appreciate the most—and always recommend using—is known as *automatic device detection*. During the Windows 98 startup sequence, the operating system "polls" the various ports, nooks, and crannies within your PC to determine exactly what hardware you've connected since your last session.

For example, if you added a printer, Windows 98 can determine that a new device was added to your parallel port. Your PC can recognize most current and older printers by name, and you don't even need a driver disk from the manufacturer if Windows 98 recognizes your printer. (Windows 98 maintains a database of drivers, and it may ask for specific drivers to be loaded from your Windows 98 CD-ROM.) If the automatic detection method doesn't work, you can always add the printer manually; I will cover doing so shortly.

TIP: *If you don't have the installation software for your printer, you may still be able to download it from the manufacturer's Web site. Luckily, most manufacturers tend to archive their drivers and installation software, so you also may be able to find information on older printers.*

To add a printer automatically, follow these steps:

1. Shut down Windows 98 and turn off your PC.

2. Connect the end of your printer cable with 25 holes to the port on your PC labeled "Printer" or "LPT." Connect the other end to your printer.

3. Make sure that your printer is plugged into the wall socket and turned on.

TIP: *You may be wondering why your printer must be turned on and connected before you turn on your PC: Doing so allows Windows 98 to automatically detect devices. If your printer is not turned on and connected during the startup sequence, Windows 98 may not be able to print (even if you turn your printer on later). Because of this problem, I recommend that you use a powerstrip for your system; it allows you to start the entire system at one time, including your monitor and printer.*

---

4. Turn on your PC and allow Windows 98 to boot normally.

5. Windows 98 should automatically detect your new printer. It halts during the startup sequence and displays a dialog box announcing that a new device has been added to your PC. One of the following happens, depending on whether Windows 98 recognizes your specific printer:

    *   *The printer is recognized.* If the dialog box identifies the exact brand and model of your printer, you're in luck: Windows 98 was able to recognize your hardware, and it has a driver for your printer. After Windows 98 uses this driver and automatically configures your new printer, the startup sequence will finish. Note that you may be asked to load your original Windows 98 CD-ROM so that the driver can be copied. At this point, your printer has been success-fully installed, and you can skip to the next section.

    *   *The printer is not recognized.* Windows 98 can detect the addition of a printer, but doesn't have a driver for your specific make and model. Continue to the next step in this section.

6. If Windows 98 doesn't recognize your printer, it displays a scrolling list box of all the printer manufacturers and models within its driver database, as shown in Figure 7.1. At this point, your action depends on whether or not you have a software driver for your printer:

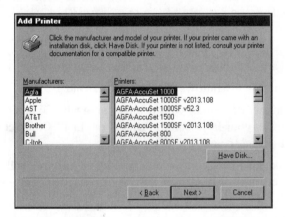

Figure 7.1   Windows 98 displays a list of all the printers it recognizes.

- *You have a driver.* If the printer is a brand-new model, the manufacturer should include a driver compatible with Windows 98. If you have a Windows 3.1 or Windows 95 driver on disk, you can also try the older driver. Click on the Have Disk button to browse your system and load the driver.

- *You don't have a driver.* If you have no driver software at all, pick the correct manufacturer and select the closest model to yours. For example, if you're installing a model 670 and it doesn't have a driver entry, try the model 650 or 680 instead. Click on OK to continue.

7. After Windows 98 loads the driver you selected and automatically configures your new printer, the startup sequence will finish. (You may be asked to load your original Windows 98 CD-ROM so that the driver can be copied.)

TIP: *Most of today's advanced inkjet and laser printers will install their own dialog boxes and user interface "on top" of the standard Windows 98 Printer Properties dialog box. Therefore, the printer properties that you see on your PC may differ from those in the illustrations and descriptions in this chapter. Wherever possible, I have listed alternate names that may identify the same settings within your printer driver; you may also have to consult your printer manual from time to time.*

Installing A Printer Manually

You can also install a printer manually at any time, with or without a driver. This technique comes in handy if Windows 98 doesn't automatically detect your printer as a new device, which can happen with some older printers. To install a printer manually, follow these steps:

1. First, follow Steps 1 through 4 in the "Installing A Printer Automatically" section previously in this chapter to connect your printer.

2. Click on Start|Settings.

3. Click on Printers to open the Printers dialog box, as shown in Figure 7.2. (Your Printers dialog box probably won't look like it does in the figure because it contains the printers and printer drivers you've installed on your PC. However, it will at least contain the Add Printer icon.)

Figure 7.2   Windows 98 groups both printers and printer drivers within the Printers dialog box.

4. Click on the Add Printer icon to run the Add Printer Wizard. Click on Next to continue.

5. The Wizard displays a scrolling list box of all the printer manufacturers and models within its driver database. The direction you take now depends upon whether you have a software driver for your printer:

   • *I have a driver.* If the printer is a brand-new model, the manufacturer should include a driver compatible with Windows 98. If you have a Windows 3.1 or Windows 95 driver on disk, you can also try the older driver. Click on Have Disk to browse your system and load the driver.

   • *I don't have a driver.* If you have no driver software at all, pick the correct manufacturer and select the closest model to yours. For example, if you're installing a model 670 and it doesn't have a driver entry, try the model 650 or 680 instead. Click on Next to continue.

6. Next, the Wizard asks you to specify the port that will be connected to your new printer, as shown in Figure 7.3. In almost every case, this is LPT1; however, if you're using a serial printer (a rare beast indeed), select either COM1 or COM2, depending on which port will be active. Click on Next to continue.

7. The next Wizard screen has two fields:

   • *Printer name*—You can assign a unique name to the printer you're setting up. Doing so is a good idea if

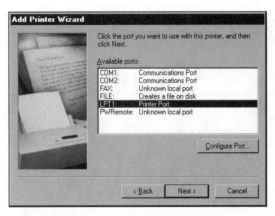

Figure 7.3   Identifying the port on your PC that will connect to your printer.

multiple printers of the same type are connected to your PC or if your printer will be available as a server for other users on a network.

- *Default toggle*—If you want your Windows 98 applications to use this printer as the system default, click on Yes. (Doing so is a convenient way to use a single printer for most of your documents; you can always select another printer right before you start your print job.) Click on the Next button to continue.

8. The Wizard asks you if you would like to print a test page to make sure that the printer is operating correctly. Click on Yes|Finish to complete the process.

Changing Settings From The Print Dialog Box

The Print dialog box allows you to select a printer or change settings for the current printer from within a Windows application, typically right before Windows 98 actually sends the print job to your printer. To change settings from the Print dialog box, take the following steps:

1. Select File|Print from your Windows application. Windows 98 displays the Print dialog box; as an example, Figure 7.4 shows the Print dialog box from Microsoft Word 7.

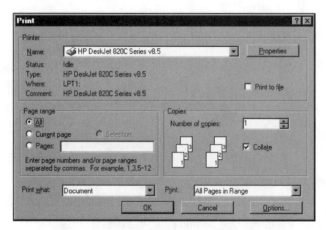

Figure 7.4   The Microsoft Word 7 Print dialog box.

Depending on your specific printer driver and the Windows 98 application you're running, the Print dialog box may look somewhat different, but the following settings are generally included:

• *Printer*—This drop-down list allows you to select any printer as the target for your print job. The target printer must be currently connected and correctly installed under Windows 98.

• *Print To File*—Enable this checkbox to save the contents of the document as a formatted ASCII or Rich Text Format file in the folder you specify.

• *Page Range*—Click on All to print the entire document. Click on Current Page to print just the page where the cursor is currently located. Click on Pages and enter a range of page numbers in the text field to print specific pages.

• *Copies*—Click on the up or down arrows at the top and bottom of this scrolling box to select the number of copies you need from this print job. If your printer and printer driver support collating, you can enable this feature to arrange your printed pages in the proper order.

2. To print your document with the current settings, click on OK; to cancel printing, exit the Print dialog box by clicking on Cancel.

Changing Settings From Printer Properties

To change the settings for a specific printer through the printer's
Properties dialog box, follow these steps:

1. Click on Start|Settings|Printers to open the Printers dialog box.

2. Right-click on the desired printer icon and select Properties
   from the menu. Figure 7.5 illustrates the Properties dialog
   box for a Hewlett-Packard DeskJet 820C printer.

   Depending on your specific printer, the Properties dialog
   box will be considerably different, and the settings listed
   below may be on different panes, but the following settings
   are generally included:

   - *Port Selection*—This drop-down list box allows you to
     select the port to which your printer is currently con-
     nected. (Remember that different printer drivers display
     unique dialog boxes, so your version may contain differ-
     ent selections.)

   - *Bi-Directional Control*—Older printers are unable to
     communicate with the PC (unlike today's printers, which
     take advantage of *bi-directional* communications). Older
     printers are only able to receive data and cannot send

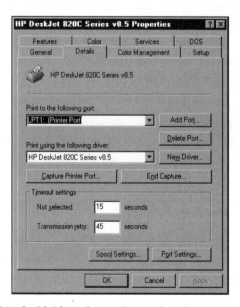

*Figure 7.5   A typical inkjet printer's Properties dialog box, showing the
Details pane.*

data to the computer, and you may need to turn off bi-directional communications to make your printer work.

- *Paper Size*—This setting identifies the dimensions of the paper currently loaded onto the printer.

- *Paper Orientation*—This setting identifies in which direction the document will flow. *Portrait* documents have their longest dimensions at the left and right sides of the page. *Landscape* documents have their largest dimensions at the top and bottom of the page.

- *Paper Type*—Most printers can be set to accept plain paper, transparency sheets, and glossy photo paper.

- *Print Quality*—Your printer may allow you to select from different levels of print quality for the finished document. The higher the quality, the longer it takes to print and the more ink you will use.

- *Two-Sided Printing*—Advanced inkjet and laser printers can print on both sides of a sheet of paper; if your printer offers this feature, you can probably select an orientation as well.

- *DOS Printing*—Although most of us do our printing under Windows 98 now, your printer may allow you to select the font and paper size for documents printed in a DOS box or in DOS mode.

TIP: *The changes you can make within the Print dialog box usually affect only the current print job, whereas any changes you make within the printer's Properties dialog box are global and permanent.*

---

3. Click on OK to accept any changes that you have made and then click on OK to exit the Properties dialog box.

Spooling Printer Output

One way to significantly speed up printing within Windows 98 is to use a *print spooler*—essentially, a portion of memory set aside under Windows 98 that holds your print data until your printer is ready for it. With a print spooler, you don't have to sit and wait while your PC prints—rather, your PC returns to your control, and you can resume using your application. (The printing process itself doesn't actually speed up, but it sure seems like it.)

Large documents with dozens of pages will benefit the most from a print spooler, because your PC doesn't have to wait until the entire document prints before you can continue using your application.

If your printer supports spooling, follow these steps to enable it under Windows 98:

1. Click on Start|Settings|Printers to open the Printers dialog box.

2. Right-click on the desired printer icon and select Properties from the menu.

3. Check each pane within your printer's Properties dialog box for a feature called "Printer Spooling," "Printer Queue Buffer," or "Printer Buffer." Enable the option.

4. Click on OK to accept any changes you've made and then click on OK to exit.

Disabling Printer Port Polling

By default, Windows 98 always checks your LPT port (and through it, your printer) to make sure that it's ready to receive data; this process is known as *polling*. Depending on the manufacturer and model of your printer, polling can take from one or two seconds to five or six seconds before your PC can begin sending data— and this polling step occurs each time you send a print job.

If you share a printer with other users, if you have a notebook computer, or if you are accessing your printer through the network, polling is a good idea. On the other hand, if your printer is always connected to your PC, you don't share your printer, and you send only one print job to your printer at a time, this polling step is essentially a waste of time. If your printer driver supports the disabling of this function, these few seconds can really add up. Follow these steps to disable polling under Windows 98:

1. Click on Start|Settings|Printers to open the Printers dialog box.

2. Right-click on the desired printer icon and select Properties from the menu.

3. Check each pane within your printer's Properties dialog box for a feature called "Port Polling," "Check Port State Before Printing," or "Port Checking." Disable the option.

4. Click on OK to accept any changes that you have made and then click on OK to exit.

Working Offline

If you're using a notebook PC or you work on an office network, you may not always have access to your printer. However, you can still prepare a file under Windows 98 so that it's ready to print at a moment's notice. This deferred printing feature allows you to store print documents on your hard drive for any printer currently installed on your system.

Follow these steps to enable deferred printing under Windows 98:

1. Click on Start|Settings|Printers to open the Printers dialog box.

2. Right-click on the desired printer icon and select Use Printer Offline from the menu.

3. Click on OK to accept all the changes that you have made and then click on OK to exit.

You will notice that the printer icon is dimmed to indicate that you're working offline. After your printer has been reconnected, follow the steps above and disable the offline mode to begin printing any files you've queued.

Selecting A Print Quality

Most inkjet and laser printers provide at least two levels of quality: fine (the best possible, although the slowest, printing for finished projects) and draft (a lower quality print mode that's usually much faster). It's always better to print in draft mode for test pages, rough drafts, and sometimes even proof pages; you're likely to save a great deal of time and a considerable amount of toner or ink as well.

To set draft or fine mode for a system printer, follow these steps:

1. Click on Start|Settings|Printers to open the Printers dialog box.

2. Right-click on the desired printer icon and select Properties from the menu.

3. Check each pane within your printer's Properties dialog box for a feature called "Print Quality" or "Print Mode" (often found on the Setup pane). To save time and toner (or ink), select "Low Quality" or "Draft Mode." For finished documents with the best possible reproduction of color and the sharpest appearance, select "High Quality" or "Fine Mode."

4. Click on OK to accept any changes you've made and then click on OK to exit.

Defragmenting Your Hard Drive

Because Windows 98 uses your hard drive to temporarily store print jobs, a heavily fragmented drive slows down the entire printing process.

Related solution:	Found in:
Defragmenting Your Drives	Chapter 3

Installing Fonts In Windows 98— The Drag-And-Drop Method

If you've bought a commercial font, it probably came with an installation program that will automate the entire installation process. However, many TrueType freeware and shareware fonts are now available on the Internet and on CD-ROM, and these font families often do not have installation software.

In this section, you will learn how to install fonts the easy way under Windows 98—by using drag and drop. To use the drag-and-drop method, follow these steps:

1. Click on Start|Settings.

2. Click on Control Panel to open the Control Panel window and then double-click on the Fonts icon to open the Fonts dialog box, as shown in Figure 7.6.

3. Using Windows Explorer or the My Computer window, open the drive that contains the fonts you want to add to your system.

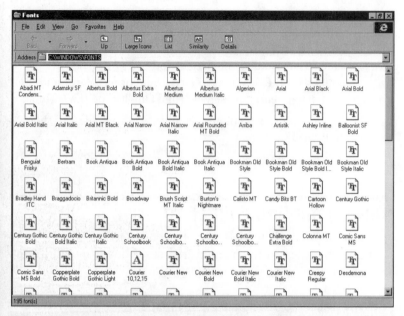

Figure 7.6 Viewing your collection of fonts from the Fonts dialog box.

4. Drag the font icons for the desired fonts from the drive to your Fonts dialog box and release the button.

5. Click on File|Close to close the Fonts dialog box, and then close the Control Panel dialog box in the same fashion to return to your desktop.

Installing Fonts In Windows 98—The Font List Method

You can also install fonts using the Install New Font menu item in the Fonts dialog box. To do so, follow these steps:

1. Click on Start|Settings|Control Panel|Fonts to open the Fonts dialog box.

2. Click on File|Install New Font to display the Add Fonts dialog box, shown in Figure 7.7.

3. Use the Drives and Folders controls to navigate through your system to the location of the new fonts, which should appear in the List Of Fonts scrolling list.

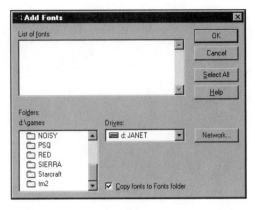

Figure 7.7   Adding fonts the old-fashioned way.

4. From the List Of Fonts scrolling list, highlight one or more fonts that you want to install on your system and then click on OK to add them.

5. Click on File|Close to close the Fonts dialog box, and then close the Control Panel dialog box in the same fashion to return to your desktop.

Troubleshooting

Troubleshooting Printer Problems

Having problems with printing? In this section, I will give you the details on possible hardware and software trouble spots that can affect printing under Windows 98.

Nothing Prints

If your printer simply sits there like Sleeping Beauty when you send it a print job, check for the following possible problems:

- *Your cable is connected incorrectly.* Make sure that your printer cable is properly connected to the LPT port on the back of your PC, and make sure that your PC is plugged in and turned on.

- *Something is wrong with the printer cartridge or paper.* Many printers simply blink an error indicator light if the cartridges are incorrectly installed or out of ink/toner—no beeps, buzzers, or other indications that something is wrong. The same is true for paper; fill the printer's paper tray and check for small pieces of paper jammed in the machine.

- *The wrong printer is selected.* Check your application: Have you selected the right printer in the Print dialog box? Some fax and HTML conversion drivers "look" like printers themselves, but selecting one of these drivers does not send a print job to your printer.

- *The printer is set for offline work.* If your printer is set for offline work (as mentioned in the "Working Offline" section previously in this chapter), toggle it online again.

- *You have an application-based printing problem.* Try printing to the same printer from another application, or try to print a test page using the printer's software. If your printer works with other programs, check the options within the Print dialog box for the application that's giving you trouble.

TIP: *If you think your printing problem may be related to Windows 98 or your printer driver, you can always try to send a simple ASCII text file directly to your printer through DOS. Doing so is a good way to test your printer. To do so, use the following command:*

```
copy filename lpt1:
```

As an example, the following command sends the file TEST.TXT (in your current directory) to your system printer:

```
copy TEST.TXT lpt1:
```

If your printer works and prints the text file, you're probably using the wrong Windows 98 printer driver, or a problem exists with your printer's properties.

Printer Communication Errors

If your printer recognizes that you're sending it a print job but returns an error, one of these problems may be the reason:

- *You need a bi-directional cable.* Most printers manufactured these days require a bi-directional printer cable that meets the IEEE-1284 standard specification for printer communications; if you use an older cable that doesn't meet this specification, your printer cannot communicate with Windows 98. Check your cable and make sure that it meets this specification— look for lettering on the cable or the specification printed on one of the connectors—and run any communication test that may be included with your printer's driver software.

- *There is a problem with the network protocol or your printer access.* If a printer server on your network reports a communications error when you attempt to use it, you may not have the proper access to the printer, or your workstation may not have the required network protocols and drivers installed.

Only Part Of The Document Prints

If your printer only produces part of the text or graphics that should be on the printed page, check these potential problems:

- *Your printer requires more RAM.* This kind of problem typically occurs only with laser printers that have their own on-board memory, especially with documents that contain large or detailed graphics. Try either printing the same document without the graphic or substituting a smaller graphic.

- *There is insufficient hard drive space.* Windows 98 uses your hard drive to temporarily store print data during the printing process, so make sure that you have sufficient free space on the drive where your Windows 98 directory is located.

- *Your printer cartridge is misaligned.* If your printer's driver or software includes a utility to help align your ink/toner cartridge, run it. Doing so may correct streaks or lines within text and graphics.

- *You are trying to use a corrupted or nonexistent font.* If some of your text is printing but material in another font is not, you may be trying to use a corrupted font. Check to see if all of the text in your document will print if you use another font.

Fonts Do Not Print Correctly

If your fonts do not print correctly, check these problem areas:

- *You are trying to use a corrupted or nonexistent font.* Re-install the font from the original media and try printing a short page with a full range of uppercase and lowercase characters.

- *The fonts were not downloaded correctly.* If you're using a laser printer, it may actually download the font before printing, and some older laser printers stubbornly refuse to recognize TrueType fonts. To enable TrueType fonts, follow these steps:

  1. Click on Start|Settings|Printers to open the Printers dialog box.

  2. Right-click on the icon of the printer that you want to check and select Properties from the menu.

  3. Check each pane within your printer's Properties dialog box for a feature called "Download TrueType Fonts as Bitmap Soft Fonts" and then enable it.

  4. Click on OK to accept all changes you have made and then click on OK to exit.

Fonts Do Not Print Correctly

Chapter 8

Communications, Faxing, And The Internet

In Brief

Communications, Faxing, And The Internet

Today's PC is tied closer to data communications than ever before—but the modem has not been a featured performer among PC peripherals for very long. As recently as five years ago, the Internet was unknown. People used modems chiefly to connect to online services, such as CompuServe and America Online, as well as to thousands of local bulletin board systems (called BBSes for short) run by hobbyists. In fact, most PC owners had either never used or never heard of a modem. Fax modems were more expensive than regular data-only modems, and the software to send and receive faxes cost several hundred dollars.

Of course, the simultaneous growth of both Windows and the Internet has changed all that ancient history. These days, the Internet is a well-traveled communications pathway in most countries, virtually every modem manufactured today has fax capability built in, and the software you need to send and receive faxes is included with Windows 98.

However, communications under Windows 98—as with printing—can still present a huge number of settings and options. Modem technology can be quite confusing by itself, but adding all of the numbers and settings necessary to configure an Internet connection can confuse even the most experienced PC owner.

Before you swear off computers in general and the Internet in particular, *do not panic*! This chapter contains both the basics (such as connecting a new modem, creating a new Internet dial-up account, and configuring faxes) and advanced topics (how to speed up your data communications and change specific TCP/IP settings). You'll also find a troubleshooting guide at the end of the chapter that will help you deal with data-communications and faxing problems.

Immediate Solutions

Adding A New Modem

Under Windows 98, you can add a new modem in the following three ways:

- *Run the modem's installation software*—If your modem arrived complete with an installation program, running that program is probably the easiest method of ensuring that your modem is correctly installed under Windows 98.

- *Install it automatically*—If Windows 98 recognizes your modem, it has a default driver that should allow automatic installation. (Keep in mind, however, that the modem driver that shipped with your modem may be more recent than the driver included with Windows 98.)

- *Install it manually*—If Windows 98 doesn't recognize your modem and it didn't come with installation software, you can install it manually.

If your modem came with installation software and instructions, I recommend following them; after you have your new modem up and running, skip to the section titled, "Changing Modem Settings." For those of you whose modem didn't come with these items, read on; I cover automatic and manual installations next.

TIP: *If you don't have the installation software for your modem, you may still be able to borrow a friend's modem and download it from the manufacturer's Web site.*

Installing A Modem Automatically

As with printers (covered in Chapter 7), Windows 98 automatically recognizes when you've added a modem—but only if it's included in the modem database. Follow these steps to install your modem:

1. Shut down Windows 98 and turn off your PC.

2. If your modem is an external model, connect the end of your modem cable to the serial port on your PC. Connect the other end to your modem. Also, make sure the modem's power supply is plugged in.

TIP: *If you're using an external modem, it must be turned on and connected during the startup sequence for Windows 98; if it isn't, Windows 98 does not recognize it for automatic installation.*

---

3. If your modem is an internal model, follow the manual's instructions to install it within your PC's case.

4. Connect the telephone cable from the wall socket to the correct jack—which is typically marked "Wall" or "Tel"—on your modem.

5. Turn on your PC and allow Windows 98 to boot normally.

6. Windows 98 should automatically detect your new modem; it interrupts the startup sequence and displays a dialog box announcing that a new device has been added to your PC. One of the following happens:

   • *Your specific modem is recognized.* If the dialog box identifies the exact brand and model of your modem, you're in luck: Windows 98 recognized your hardware and has a driver for your modem. Windows 98 uses this driver and automatically configures your new modem; then the startup sequence finishes (you may be asked to load your original Windows 98 CD-ROM so that the driver can be copied). At this point, your modem has been successfully installed, and you can skip to the section titled, "Changing Modem Settings."

   • *Your specific modem is not recognized.* Windows 98 can detect the addition of a modem, but doesn't have a driver for your specific make and model. Proceed to Step 7.

7. If Windows 98 doesn't recognize your modem, it displays a scrolling list of all the modem manufacturers and models within its driver database. One of the following occurs:

   • *You have a driver.* If you have an older Windows 95 driver on disk, you can try it. Click on Have Disk to browse your system and load the driver.

   • *You don't have a driver.* If you have no driver software at all, pick the correct manufacturer and select the closest model to yours. For example, if you're installing a Hayes modem and it doesn't have a driver entry, try the model with the most similar name instead. Click on OK to continue.

8. Windows 98 loads the driver you selected and automatically configures your new modem; then the startup sequence finishes (you may be asked to load your original Windows 98 CD-ROM so that the driver can be copied).

Installing A Modem Manually

If Windows 98 doesn't automatically recognize your new modem as a new device, you can choose to install it manually (with or without a driver). To do so, follow these steps:

1. Follow the instructions in Steps 1 through 5 in the previous section, "Installing A Modem Automatically," to prepare your modem.

2. Click on Start|Settings.

3. Click on Control Panel to open the Control Panel and then double-click on the Modems icon to display the Modems Properties dialog box, shown in Figure 8.1.

4. Click on Add to run the Install New Modem Wizard, shown in Figure 8.2. Click on the Next button to continue.

5. Windows 98 did not recognize your modem earlier, so the autodetect feature does not work here either; therefore, save yourself some time and enable the Don't Detect My Modem; I Will Select It From A List checkbox. Click on Next to continue.

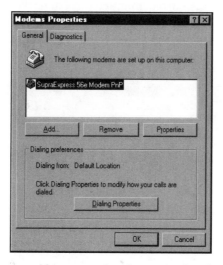

Figure 8.1   You can add a new modem to your system from the Modems Properties dialog box.

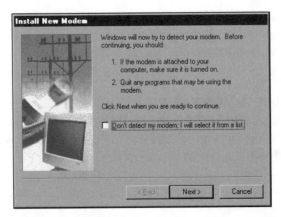

Figure 8.2   The welcome screen when you run the Install New Modem Wizard.

6. The Wizard displays a scrolling list of all the modem manufacturers and models within its driver database, as shown in
Figure 8.3. One of the following happens:

  • *You have a driver.* If the modem is a brand new model,
    the manufacturer should include a driver that is compat-
    ible with Windows 98. If you have an older Windows 95
    driver on disk, you can try it. Click on Have Disk to
    browse your system and load the driver.

  • *You don't have a driver.* If you have no driver software at
    all, pick the correct manufacturer and select the closest
    model to yours. If you can't find a model that's anywhere
    close to yours, select one of the Standard Modem Types;
    when you choose one of them, Windows 98 tries to

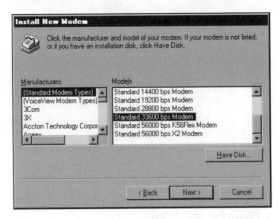

Figure 8.3   Selecting a standard 33.6Kbps modem from the Wizard's list.

provide the most generic, vanilla configuration possible. Click on Next to continue.

7. Next, the Wizard asks you to specify the port that will be connected to your new modem, as shown in Figure 8.4. In almost every case, the port is COM1 through COM4—one of the four standard serial ports, depending on which port will be active. If you're using an external modem, pick the port connected to the modem; if you're using an internal modem, pick the port that you selected before you installed the modem. Click on the Next button to continue.

8. The Wizard completes the process, and the new modem appears within the Modems Properties scrolling list.

Removing A Modem From Your System

If you've bought a new modem to replace an aging 14.4Kbps dinosaur, you should remove all traces of that old modem from Windows 98 after you've physically switched modems and successfully installed the new model. To remove a modem from Windows 98 after you've disconnected it from your PC, follow these steps:

1. Click on Start|Settings.

2. Click on Control Panel to open the Control Panel window and then double-click on the Modems icon to open the Modems Properties dialog box.

3. Click on the modem you wish to remove from the system to highlight it and then click on Remove. Windows 98

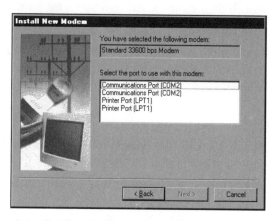

Figure 8.4   Selecting the port for a new modem.

prompts you for confirmation before removing the modem from the list.

4. Click on OK to close the Modems Properties dialog box and save your changes.

Changing Modem Settings

The previous sections helped you install your modem with a number of default settings that the good folks at Microsoft feel are the proper settings—and, in almost every case, they're right. The vast majority of Windows 98 users with modems will never have to touch their modem settings.

However, if you travel often, you want the modem's speaker turned off when you dial, or you want to disable call waiting while you're connected to the Internet, it's time to get knee-deep in modem settings. This section shows you how.

Configuring Modem Properties

As with other peripherals on your PC, each modem installed within Windows 98 has its own set of properties. This section describes each setting, the effect it has on your modem, and how to change its value.

Setting Speaker Volume—The Speaker Volume slider determines the volume of all sound that your modem produces. Although some PC owners like to hear the dialing and modem negotiation when connecting, others prefer the modem to be completely silent. To change the speaker volume, follow these steps:

1. Click on Start|Settings.

2. Click on Control Panel to open the Control Panel window and then double-click on the Modems icon to open the Modems Properties dialog box.

3. Click on the modem you want to configure in the scrolling list and then click on Properties.

4. Windows 98 displays the Properties dialog box for the modem you selected.

5. To move the slider, click on and drag it to the desired direction. Moving the slider to the right increases the volume; moving it to the left decreases the volume.

6. Click on OK to close the Modems Properties dialog box and save your changes.

Setting Maximum Speed—The Maximum Speed drop-down list allows you to specify the maximum transfer speed between your PC and your modem (this speed is also called "locked baud rate" or "locked rate"). Today's high-speed modems generally use 115200 for this setting, but older modems can't achieve those speeds. Typically, Windows 98 automatically sets the maximum speed during installation. To choose another speed, follow these steps:

1. Click on Start|Settings.

2. Click on Control Panel to open the Control Panel window and then double-click on the Modems icon to open the Modems Properties dialog box.

3. Click on the modem you want to configure in the scrolling list box and then click on Properties.

4. Click on the Maximum Speed drop-down list and then select the desired transfer speed. For 56Kbps modems, choose 115200. For 33.6 and 28.8Kbps modems, use 57600. For most 14.4Kbps modems, the proper setting is 19200. If your modem is slower than 14.4Kbps, use the same maximum speed as the maximum rated speed of your modem.

TIP: *If your modem's manual suggests a specific "locked baud rate" or a specific speed "between computer and modem," use that value in this field.*

---

5. Enable the Only Connect At This Speed checkbox if you want Windows 98 to drop any connection that is made at a speed less than the maximum speed you've selected. It's generally a good idea to leave this checkbox disabled, especially if you'll be calling a wide range of online systems; it's rare for any modem to connect at its maximum speed during every call.

6. Click on OK to close the Modems Properties dialog box and save your changes.

Setting Connection Preferences—If you're an old-timer in the online world, you'll recognize the Data Bits, Parity, and Stop Bits fields in the Connection Preferences section as the standard communications parameters you used to set for BBSes and online services. These three settings have been around since the days

of the first modems. To set your Connection preferences, follow
these steps:

1. Click on Start|Settings.

2. Click on Control Panel to open the Control Panel window
   and then double-click on the Modems icon to open the
   Modems Properties dialog box.

3. Click on the modem you want to configure in the scrolling
   list and then click on Properties.

4. Click on the Connection tab to display the pane shown in
   Figure 8.5.

5. Click on the Data Bits drop-down list and then select the
   number that the host computer (another word for the
   service you're accessing) requires. The universal setting
   today tends to be 8 data bits; however, some older mini and
   mainframe computers or online services may still require 7
   data bits.

6. The standard setting for the Parity field is None, but older
   mini and mainframe computers may require Even or Odd. If
   you need to change the parity value to match an older
   computer, click on the parity drop-down list and then select
   the required parity.

7. Click on the Stop Bits drop-down list to specify the number
   of stop bits used during connections with this modem. The
   value you'll see most often these days is 1 stop bit. If you

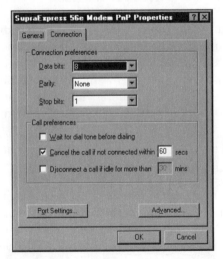

Figure 8.5   Setting modem connection preferences in Windows 98.

need to change the number of stop bits (for example, for a connection with an older minicomputer), click on the Stop Bits drop-down list and then specify the required number.

8. Click on OK to close the Modems Properties dialog box and save your changes.

Setting Call Preferences—The Call Preferences section contains fields that apply globally to every outgoing call you make with this modem. Follow these steps to configure your Call Preferences settings:

1. Click on Start|Settings.

2. Click on Control Panel to open the Control Panel window and then double-click on the Modems icon to open the Modems Properties dialog box.

3. Click on the modem you want to configure in the scrolling list and then click on Properties.

4. Click on the Connection tab to display the pane shown in Figure 8.5.

5. The Wait For Dial Tone Before Dialing checkbox determines whether your modem delays the dialing process until it recognizes an actual dial tone. The modem probably receives a dial tone immediately if it's connected to a typical home telephone line. If you hear a dial tone the moment you pick up your phone, disable this checkbox and save yourself a bit of time with each outgoing call you make. If your telephone line requires a second or two before you receive a dial tone, enable this checkbox to prevent your modem from dialing before it receives a dial tone.

6. The next combination checkbox/text field, Cancel The Call If Not Connected Within *nn* Secs, allows you to specify the amount of time the modem will remain off-hook as it tries to make a connection. Some of today's high-speed modems can take between 5 and 10 seconds to negotiate a connection, so don't set this field to less than 15 seconds. To allow your modem to remain off-hook indefinitely until a connection is made, disable the checkbox.

7. The third Call Preferences field, Disconnect A Call If Idle For More Than *xx* Mins, determines how long your modem maintains the connection if it's idle (not sending or receiving any data). This field can be very important for those connecting long-distance, or those whose

Internet Service Provider (ISP) or online service bills them by the minute for access. If you wish your modem to remain connected if it's idle, disable this field's associated checkbox.

8. Click on OK to close the Modems Properties dialog box and save your changes.

Setting Advanced Connection Properties—Depending on your modem's age and speed, Windows 98 may allow you to configure several advanced features that globally affect every connection. To set these Advanced Connection properties, follow these steps:

1. Click on Start|Settings.

2. Click on Control Panel to open the Control Panel window and then double-click on the Modems icon to open the Modems Properties dialog box.

3. Click on the modem you want to configure in the scrolling list and then click on Properties.

4. Click on the Connection tab and then click on Advanced to display the Advanced Connection Settings dialog box, shown in Figure 8.6.

5. If your modem can reach speeds of 14.4Kbps or higher, you should enable the Use Error Control checkbox; doing so will provide error checking between the sending and the receiving modems. You can enable or disable the following three checkboxes that appear below this checkbox only if the Use Error Control checkbox is enabled:

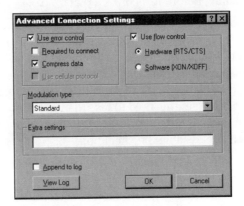

Figure 8.6   *These connection properties can be set on most high-speed modems.*

- *Required To Connect*—Enable this checkbox to force your modem to require error control to connect. If the other modem does not support error control, the call will be disconnected. Unless error control is an absolute requirement, leave this field disabled so that your modem can connect to a wider range of modems.

- *Compress Data*—All high-speed modems feature compression algorithms that allow you to send more data in the same time period than with a modem that doesn't have data compression. For the best possible performance, leave this feature enabled unless you're specifically advised to turn compression off by the host computer administrator.

- *Use Cellular Protocol*—If Windows 98 recognizes that your modem has cellular support, you can enable cellular protocols for use with portable telephones. If your modem is not recognized as cellular-capable, this field is grayed and cannot be enabled.

6. All modems can use some kind of *flow control* (a system of regulating the flow of data in a connection that prevents your PC from being "overloaded" with incoming data). High-speed modems typically use hardware flow control, whereas older, slower 300 and 1200bps modems usually use software flow control. You can specify either form of flow control as long as the Use Flow Control checkbox is enabled.

7. Both modems in a connection must use the same modulation type to successfully communicate, and you can select which type to use from the Modulation Type drop-down list. Standard modulation should work in almost every case.

8. The Extra Settings text field allows you to enter additional, modem-specific commands and switches to enable or disable other special functions or features of your modem. Refer to the modem's manual and enter the command in the field as instructed. (The Extra Settings field can accept any modem-initialization commands that would normally be entered into a communications program's Initialize Modem field.)

TIP: The Extra Settings commands are sent to the modem after Windows 98 completes its initialization, so any of these commands override other fields in the Advanced Connection Settings dialog box.

9. If you prefer, Windows 98 can maintain a modem activity Log that records all connections and connection attempts; the Log file is named MODEMLOG.TXT, and it's saved in the directory where Windows 98 was installed (typically C:\WINDOWS). To turn on the logging function, enable the Append To Log checkbox; to turn off activity logging, disable the checkbox. You can view the contents of MODEMLOG.TXT with the Windows 98 Notepad by clicking on the View Log button.

TIP: *You can delete the MODEMLOG.TXT file within Windows Explorer if it becomes too large, or you can archive the modem log by saving the file to another drive on your system.*

---

10. Click on OK to close the Advanced Connection Settings dialog and save your changes, then click on OK again to exit the Properties dialog box.

Configuring Advanced Port Settings

To achieve optimum performance from your high-speed modem, it is critical that you configure your serial port properly. If you don't have the right serial port hardware or that hardware isn't configured correctly, you may not be able to connect at all! To make changes to your Advanced Port Settings, follow these steps:

1. Click on Start|Settings.

2. Click on Control Panel to open the Control Panel window and then double-click on the Modems icon to open the Modems Properties dialog box.

3. Click on the modem you want to configure in the scrolling list and then click on Properties.

4. Click on the Connection tab and then click on Port Settings to display the Advanced Port Settings dialog box, shown in Figure 8.7.

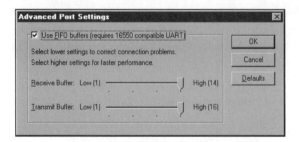

Figure 8.7   The Windows 98 Advanced Port Settings dialog box.

5. If you're running a 14.4Kbps modem or faster, your PC should be equipped with *16550-series UART* chips (fancy words for a high-speed serial port, which most PCs made in the last two or three years already have). If your PC does have a high-speed serial port, the Use FIFO Buffers checkbox should *always* be enabled; if you disable this checkbox, you will substantially reduce your modem's throughput.

TIP: *If your PC is an older model without high-speed serial ports and this checkbox is grayed so you can't enable it, head directly to your local computer store and buy a new serial/parallel I/O card. Without a high-speed serial port, you'll find it nearly impossible to use a 14.4Kbps or faster modem.*

---

6. The Receive Buffer slider determines the size of the receive buffer (used to store incoming data from your modem until your PC can process it). Generally, the higher the setting, the better the modem's performance; however, you may find that setting this buffer too high results in a large number of retries while downloading files, or problems connecting with other modems. The default setting for your modem is the optimum setting in most cases, but you can experiment to determine if your PC benefits from the highest setting. Moving the slider to the right increases the buffer's size to provide better performance; moving it to the left makes the buffer smaller to correct retry problems.

7. The Transmit Buffer slider specifies the size of the buffer for outgoing data, which is stored until the modem is ready to send it. As with the receive buffer, most PCs benefit from the default optimum setting, but you can experiment with lower settings if you experience connection problems with other modems. Move the slider to the right or to the left as in Step 6 above.

8. Click on OK to close the Advanced Port Settings dialog box and then click on OK to close the Modems Properties dialog box and save your changes.

Configuring Dialing Properties

If you travel often with a portable computer, you probably spend at least several minutes a day retrieving email, sending and receiving faxes, or uploading and downloading information from your home office or the Internet. Before Windows 95, however, you first had to take the time to reconfigure your dialing directories within your applications for your current location; you had to change settings such as current area code, local versus long-distance calls, and calling cards.

Windows 95 (and now Windows 98) made this process much easier by defining *location entries* for your communications applications. After you add and set up a location entry, it will include all of the settings and information specific to that area of the world. When you are in that location in the future, you simply select that entry and Windows 98 automatically configures your dialing properties.

Selecting An Existing Location Entry—If you've already set up a location entry for the region you're in, follow these steps to load it:

1. Click on Start|Settings.

2. Click on Control Panel to open the Control Panel window and then double-click on the Modems icon to open the Modems Properties dialog box.

3. Click on Dialing Properties to display the Dialing Properties dialog box, shown in Figure 8.8.

4. Click on the I Am Dialing From drop-down list and then select the proper location entry.

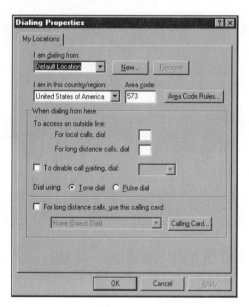

*Figure 8.8   You can set up different locations from the Dialing Properties
dialog box.*

5. Click on OK to close the Dialing Properties dialog box.

6. Click on OK again to close the Modems Properties dialog box and save your changes.

Removing An Existing Location Entry—"I'm not coming back *here* again!" If you know you won't return to a location, you can delete the corresponding location entry by following these steps:

1. Click on Start|Settings.

2. Click on Control Panel to open the Control Panel window and then double-click on the Modems icon to open the Modems Properties dialog box.

3. Click on Dialing Properties to display the Dialing Properties dialog box.

4. Click on the I Am Dialing From drop-down list and then select the location entry you want to delete.

5. Click on Remove.

6. Click on OK to close the Dialing Properties dialog box.

7. Click on OK again to close the Modems Properties dialog box and save your changes.

Creating A New Location Entry

Let's assume that you're in a new place and you'd like to create a new location entry for your data communications applications. Follow these steps to create a new entry:

1. Click on Start|Settings.

2. Click on Control Panel to open the Control Panel window and then double-click on the Modems icon to open the Modems Properties dialog box.

3. Click on Dialing Properties to display the Dialing Properties dialog box.

4. Click on New; Windows 98 creates a new location entry titled (appropriately enough) "New Location."

5. Highlight the words "New Location" in the I Am Dialing From drop-down list and then type the name you want to assign to this location.

6. Select the country or region for your current location in the I Am In This Country/Region drop-down list .

7. Type the area code for your current location in the Area Code field.

8. If you need to set up 10-digit dialing for the current area code or other area codes, click on Area Code Rules to display the Area Code Rules dialog box, shown in Figure 8.9. You have these two choices:

- *When Calling Within My Current Area Code*—If your modem should always dial the area code from this location, enable the Always Dial The Area Code (10-Digit Dialing) checkbox. If this checkbox is disabled, the area code is omitted by default; however, you can add numbers individually for 10-digit dialing by clicking on New. To remove numbers from the list, highlight the desired number and then click on Remove. Click on OK to return to the Dialing Properties dialog box.

- *When Calling To Other Area Codes*—If one or more numbers should not be prefixed with a 1 when dialing, you can add them here by clicking on New. To remove numbers from the list, highlight the desired number and then click on Remove. Click on OK to return to the Dialing Properties dialog box.

9. If you're dialing from within an office PBX system, you may have to dial an additional number to access either a local or long-distance outside line. If you must do so, enter the number in either the For Outside Calls, Dial Field or the For Long Distance Calls, Dial field.

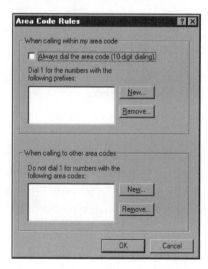

Figure 8.9   You can also set up area code rules from the Area Code Rules dialog box.

10. If your telephone line provides call waiting, you should disable this feature before connecting with your modem; the tone used to alert you to an incoming call typically hangs up most modems. To disable call waiting, enable the To Disable Call Waiting, Dial checkbox and select the correct disable prefix for your location.

11. Next, specify whether you'll be using tone or pulse dialing at this location by selecting the proper option in the Dial Using field.

12. If you'll be using a telephone calling card for long-distance calls at this location, enable the For Long Distance Calls, Use This Calling Card field, and select the proper card from the drop-down list. To add a new calling card, click on Calling Card and then follow the instructions on the Calling Card dialog box.

13. Click on OK to close the Dialing Properties dialog box.

14. Click on OK again to close the Modems Properties dialog box and save your changes.

Displaying Modem Diagnostics

If you're having problems with a modem, you can display more information about it; although you can't modify this information, it may help you when you are troubleshooting. Windows 98 provides a Diagnostics pane in the Modems Properties dialog box. Follow these steps to display this information:

1. Click on Start|Settings.

2. Click on Control Panel to open the Control Panel window and then double-click on the Modems icon to open the Modems Properties dialog box.

3. Click on the Diagnostics tab to display the Diagnostics pane, shown in Figure 8.10.

4. In the list box, Windows 98 displays each device and serial port on your system that it recognizes. To display the driver assigned to a specific COM port, click on the port to highlight it and then click on Driver; Windows 98 also includes the time and date stamp for the driver.

5. Select a COM port. Then click on More Info to display the port's interrupt number, base address value, UART type, and

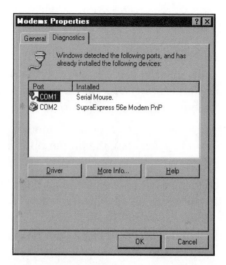

Figure 8.10   This diagnostic information can help you fix modem problems.

the highest speed that the port supports. The More Info dialog box also displays the model and identifying characteristics of the modem connected to the port.

6. Click on OK to close the More Info dialog box and then click on OK to close the Modems Properties dialog box.

Adding A
Dial-Up
Networking
Connection

Adding A Dial-Up Networking Connection

In the early days of Windows 3.0, the Internet started growing; now, it has become a major attraction for PC owners, and Windows 98 makes it very easy to add an Internet connection. Most PC owners access the Internet through their modems by calling an ISP using a *dial-up networking connection*—in effect, a dial-up connection makes your PC a part of the Internet network by transferring data through your modem to the ISP.

Don't get the wrong idea—although an ISP's computer is the most common host for a dial-up networking connection, those connections are not limited to the Internet. For example, if your office network is configured to allow you to dial in, you can log on at work and access data from your office on your home PC, just as if you were sitting at your office desk.

Although the process of creating a dial-up networking connection is still somewhat complicated—and you must make some changes manually—the Make New Connection Wizard has made it easier. If you need to add a new dial-up networking connection, follow these steps:

1. Click on My Computer to open the My Computer window.

2. Click on the Dial-Up Networking icon to open the Dial-Up Networking folder and then click on Make New Connection to run the Wizard, as shown in Figure 8.11.

3. Enter a unique name that will help you to recognize this connection in the Type A Name For The Computer You Are Dialing field.

4. Click on the Select a device drop-down list and then choose one of the modems on your system. If you need to configure the selected modem, click on Configure and then follow the instructions in the "Configuring Modem Properties" section previously in this chapter. Click on Next to continue.

5. Next, enter the number that your modem should dial to make this connection. Type the area code and telephone number of the host; if you're connecting to an ISP, it should tell you the access number you call to connect. Select the proper country code for the host in the Country Code drop-down list . For example, if the host you're dialing is in the United Kingdom, you would choose "United Kingdom" and the country code 44 would automatically be added to the telephone number. Click on the Next button to continue.

Figure 8.11   Creating a new dial-up connection with the Make New Connection Wizard.

6. Windows 98 displays a final screen identifying your new connection; click on Finish to complete the process and click on File|Close from the menu to close the Dial-Up Networking folder.

Dialing A Dial-Up Networking Connection

At this point, Windows 98 has created a new dial-up networking connection icon with the name you specified in the Dial-Up Networking folder. For some dial-up networking connections, this is all the information you need, and you can dial immediately— for example, if you're calling another user's computer or your home PC.

TIP: *Those of you who connect to the Internet through an ISP should follow the instructions in the next section, "Configuring Settings For An Internet Dial-Up Connection," before you can connect.*

To dial, follow these steps:

1. Click on My Computer to open the My Computer window.

2. Click on the Dial-Up Networking icon to open the Dial-Up Networking folder.

3. Click on the connection icon you want to dial. Windows 98 displays the Connect To dialog box shown in Figure 8.12.

4. Enter the User Name and Password required by the host; note that asterisks mask the Password field to prevent others from seeing your password. If security isn't a concern—for example, if you're calling from home—you can save yourself the trouble of retyping your password each time you connect by enabling the Save Password checkbox.

5. Click on Connect to begin dialing.

Configuring Settings For An Internet Dial-Up Connection

If you're going to connect to the Internet using an ISP, you need to change somewhat the basic dial-up networking connection created by the Wizard in the "Adding A Dial-Up Networking Connec-

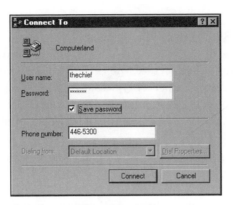

**Figure 8.12   Windows 98 displays this dialog box when you click on a
Dial-Up Networking icon.**

tion" section previously in this chapter. You must manually enter
additional information such as the network protocol to use and
your ISP's Internet address.

TIP: *After you've signed up for Internet service, your ISP should provide you with
documentation that contains the values you must enter in this section.*

To configure an ISP connection for the Internet, follow these steps:

1. Click on the My Computer icon to open the My Computer
   window.

2. Click on the Dial-Up Networking icon to open the Dial-Up
   Networking folder.

3. Right-click on the connection icon that you want to configure and then select Properties from the menu.

4. Windows 98 displays the Properties dialog box for this
   connection.

5. If you used the Make New Connection Wizard to create your
   basic connection (as described in the "Adding A Dial-Up
   Networking Connection" section previously in this chapter),
   everything on the General pane of the Properties dialog box
   should be correct. If you must add an area code or use the
   dialing properties for this modem, enable the Use Area
   Code And Dialing Properties checkbox. If you need to
   configure the selected modem, click on the Configure
   button and then follow the instructions in the "Configuring
   Modem Properties" section previously in this chapter.

6. Click on the Server Types tab to display the pane shown in Figure 8.13. Your ISP should tell you whether you connect with PPP or SLIP. (If you're unsure, PPP is more common, so try it first.) Click on the Type Of Dial-Up Server drop-down list and select the server type that your ISP uses. If it uses PPP, choose the PPP: Internet, Windows NT Server, Windows 98 entry; if it uses SLIP, choose SLIP: Unix Connection.

TIP: *The Advanced Options and Network Protocols you're allowed to use change when you select different types of dial-up servers.*

---

7. Your ISP should tell you whether or not you need to log on to the network using your Windows 98 name and password; if you do, enable the Log On To Network checkbox. By default, this field is enabled, but it should be disabled for most Internet dial-up networking connections.

8. If your ISP supports software compression, you should enable it on your end as well for faster performance; click on the Enable Software Compression checkbox.

9. Some ISPs require an encrypted password for greater security. If your Internet provider uses password encryption, enable the Require Encrypted Password checkbox.

10. Next, you need to specify the network protocols that this connection should support. Windows 98 supports the following three protocols:

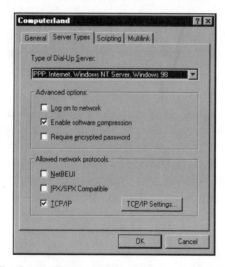

Figure 8.13   The Server Types portion of the connection Properties dialog box.

- *NetBEUI*—This protocol is used to connect to Windows NT computers, Windows for Workgroups networks, and LAN Manager. If you will not be connecting to any of these hosts, I recommend disabling this checkbox.

- *IPX/SPX Compatible*—This protocol is used to connect to NetWare networks, Windows NT servers, and other PCs running Windows 98; however, it is not typically required for an Internet connection, so it's best to disable the checkbox.

- *TCP/IP*—TCP/IP is the foundation of Internet communications, so make sure this checkbox is enabled!

11. Now you must provide Windows 98 with specific values that identify your ISP on the Internet. Click on the TCP/IP Settings button to display the dialog box shown in Figure 8.14.

12. Your ISP server can assign you a dynamic *IP address* (essentially, your "street address" for the current Internet connection), and most ISPs use this technique; your IP address will be different each time you connect. To allow your ISP to assign a dynamic IP address, click on the Server Assigned IP Address field. If your ISP provides you with a dedicated IP address that you use each time you call (often called a *static address*), click on Specify An IP Address and then enter the value in the IP address field.

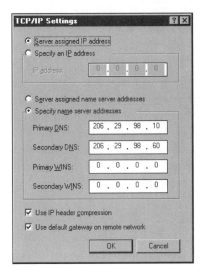

Figure 8.14   Configuring TCP/IP settings within Windows 98.

13. As with your IP address, your ISP offers you two choices: You can either assign your PC a dynamic *domain name server (DNS)* address for each connection, or you can use the same DNS address for every call. To accept a dynamic DNS address, click on the Server Assigned Name Server Addresses field. To specify one or more static DNS addresses, click on the Specify Name Server Addresses Field and then enter the values that your ISP gave you.

14. Most ISPs support *header compression*, which allows faster throughput for your connection. The Use IP Header Compression field is enabled by default; you should disable this field only if your ISP specifically tells you to do so.

15. The Use Default Gateway On Remote Network field is enabled by default. Again, you should disable this field only if your ISP specifically tells you to do so.

16. Click on OK to close the TCP/IP Settings dialog box and then click on OK to close this connection's Properties dialog box and click on File|Close from the menu to close the Dial-Up Networking folder.

Optimizing Data Transfer Rates

In this section, I'll discuss four tips within Windows 98 that will help you optimize the speed of your modem connections.

Increasing The Maximum Speed Of Your Modem

Setting Maximum speed too low can dramatically slow your modem's transfer rate. For example, if you're using a 56Kbps v.90 modem and your PC is equipped with high-speed serial ports, there's no reason why you should set the maximum speed level to lower than its maximum of 115200. To change this setting, refer to and then follow the steps outlined in the "Setting Maximum Speed" section in this chapter.

Enabling Data Compression

To increase the transfer rate of your modem, you should enable data compression—with compression, your modem can move more data across the connection in a shorter time. To change this setting, refer to and then follow the steps outlined in the "Setting Advanced Connection Properties" section in this chapter.

Increasing The Transmit And Receive Buffers

By selecting the highest settings for your receive and transmit buffers, you can increase the efficiency of your modem and improve its performance. To change these settings, refer to and then follow the steps outlined in the "Configuring Advanced Port Settings" section in this chapter.

Transferring Files From Your Hard Drive

Whenever possible, avoid transferring files to or from a floppy disk; instead, copy the file to your hard drive before uploading it, or download the file to your hard drive instead of directly to a floppy disk. The time it takes for your PC to read and write data to and from a floppy disk can dramatically slow down a transfer.

Configuring Fax Send And Receive

*Configuring
Fax Send
And Receive*

Windows 98 provides basic send and receive fax functionality—nothing fancy, but certainly enough for most of us with personal and small-business applications. If you're looking for a fax package with all the bells and whistles, invest in a commercial fax application.

In this section, you'll learn more about the process of sending and receiving faxes under Windows 98, and how you can configure your PC to send scheduled faxes during off-peak hours to save money for long-distance calls.

TIP: *If you've installed Windows 98 without upgrading from Windows 95, you won't be able to send and receive faxes because fax support is not installed along with Windows 98. However, if you've upgraded to Windows 98 from Windows 95 and you installed fax support under Windows 95, your new Windows 98 installation retains the fax commands.*

Composing A Fax

To send a fax within Windows 98, follow these steps:

1. Click on Start|Programs|Accessories|Fax and then choose Compose New Fax.

TIP: *If you've already set up Microsoft Fax, skip to Step 5.*

---

2. (Steps 2 through 4 apply if you are running Microsoft Fax for the first time.) Windows 98 displays the Inbox Setup Wizard. Click on the modem to be used for fax functions from the scrolling list. (You can also display the Properties dialog box for the selected modem from this Wizard dialog box by clicking on Properties.) If the modem you want to use for faxing does not appear in the list, click on Add to run the Install New Modem Wizard. After you've selected the proper modem for fax operations, click on Next to continue.

3. Windows 98 also needs to know whether the fax modem you selected should answer every incoming call. Click on No to prevent your fax modem from answering calls. If you do want your modem to autoanswer, click on Yes and then specify how many rings the fax modem should wait before answering a call.

4. The next Inbox Setup Wizard screen prompts you to enter your name, country, and fax number. Type the information, click on Next to continue, and then click on Finish to close the Inbox Setup Wizard and run the Compose New Fax Wizard.

5. As illustrated in Figure 8.15, you must first specify a location entry to use for this fax session. To select a different location entry (or build a new location entry), click on Dialing Properties. After you've selected the proper location entry, click on Next to continue.

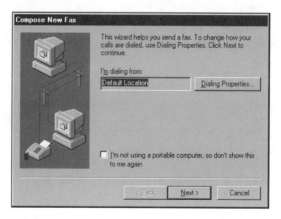

Figure 8.15   Selecting a location entry in the Compose New Fax Wizard.

TIP: *If you're sending a fax from your desktop computer, don't forget to enable the I'm Not Using A Portable Computer, So Don't Show This To Me Again checkbox. You're not using a portable computer, so your location won't change in the future and you can skip this screen.*

6. On the next Compose New Fax Wizard screen, you'll select the recipient for this fax. You have two choices:

   • If the recipient is not currently entered in your Address Book, enter the recipient's name, country, and fax number. (Note that by enabling the Dial Area Code checkbox, you can have Windows 98 dial the area code.) After you've entered the information, click on Add To List to add the name to the recipient list . Click on Next to continue.

   • If the recipient is already in your Address Book, click on the Address Book button to display the Address Book dialog box. After you've selected an entry and clicked on OK, click on Add To List to add the name to the Recipient. Click on Next to continue.

7. Next, Windows 98 offers a number of standard fax cover pages that you can add to your fax; to do so, click on the Yes. Send This One field and then click on one of the page descriptions to send that page, as shown in Figure 8.16. Click on Next to continue.

TIP: *Need to set the delivery time for your fax? Click on the Options button and then follow the instructions in the "Configuring Fax Options" section later in this chapter.*

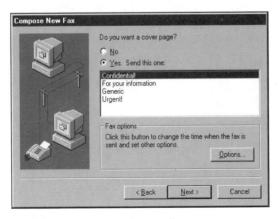

Figure 8.16   Adding a cover page to your fax.

8. The Wizard now allows you to enter a subject description line and a short text note that will be sent along with your fax. If you want the note text to appear on your cover page, enable the Start Note On Cover Page checkbox. After you've entered the subject and note for this fax, click on Next.

9. Fax modems can send binary files along with standard fax documents. To send a file with your fax message, click on Add File and within the Open A File To Attach dialog box, select the file(s) you want to send. After doing so, click on Next to continue.

10. For instructions on setting a delivery time, see the section in this chapter titled "Configuring Fax Options." To send your file at the time specified in the Fax Options dialog box, click on Finish.

Requesting A Fax

Your PC can call a fax machine or fax information service and receive fax documents and files. To request a fax, follow these steps:

1. Click on Start|Programs|Accessories|Fax and then choose Request A Fax.

2. Windows 98 displays the Request A Fax Wizard, as shown in Figure 8.17. You have the following two options:

   • To retrieve whatever documents are available for your fax modem to receive, click on the Retrieve Whatever Is Available field. Click on Next to continue.

   • To retrieve a specific document, click on the Retrieve A Specific Document field and enter the title of the

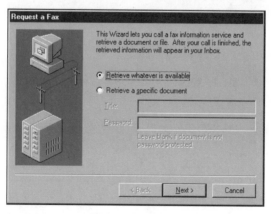

Figure 8.17   The Windows 98 Request A Fax Wizard.

document. If the document is password-protected, you should enter the required password as well. Click on Next to continue.

3. On the next Wizard screen, you will select the fax machine or information service to call. You have the following two options:

   • If the host is not currently entered in your Address Book, enter the host's name, country, and fax number. (Note that by enabling the Dial Area Code checkbox, you can have Windows 98 dial the area code.) After you've entered the information, click on Add to complete the request. Click on Next to continue.

   • If the host is already in your Address Book, click on the Address Book button to display the Address Book dialog box. After you've selected an entry and clicked on OK, click on Add to complete the request. Click on Next to continue.

4. Select a time for the call. If you select the A Specific Time field, click on the arrows to select the time. Click on Next to continue.

5. To send your file at the time you specified, click on Finish.

Configuring Fax Options

From the Fax Options dialog box, you can set fax options that apply only to the current fax session. To configure your fax options while composing a fax, follow these steps:

1. Follow Steps 1 through 6 in the previous section, "Composing A Fax," in this chapter.

2. At the cover-page selection screen, click on the Options button to display the Fax Options dialog box, shown in Figure 8.18.

3. Select the delivery time for this fax session. Click on the As Soon As Possible field if you want the fax to be sent as soon as your fax modem is idle. Select the Discount Rates field if you want your fax sent during off-peak hours for long-distance carriers. Finally, click on the A Specific Time field and then click on Set to schedule a date and time in the future for the fax to be sent.

TIP: *Remember that if you set a specific time at a certain date and time in the future, your PC must be on at the specified time in order for the fax to be sent successfully.*

Figure 8.18   The Fax Options dialog box.

4. Microsoft Fax can send documents as editable files or
   standard Group 3 fax documents; however, the fax machine
   or fax modem on the receiving end of the connection limits
   your choice of message format. If you select the Editable, If
   Possible Radio Button, Microsoft Fax attempts to send the
   document as an editable file (but only if the hardware on
   the receiving end supports this format). If you select the
   Editable Only Radio Button, Microsoft Fax disconnects if it
   can't send an editable format to the receiver. Select the Not
   Editable Radio Button to send a standard fax document;
   with this option, you can also specify the quality of the fax
   document by clicking on the Paper button.

5. If you'd like to select a cover page you've created yourself,
   enable the Send Cover Page checkbox and then click on
   Browse to navigate through your system to locate the
   desired cover-page file.

6. Click on OK to return to the Wizard and continue composing your fax.

Using A Dial-Up Script

Most ISPs that offer a PPP connection now allow your PC to automatically log on with your user name and password, so you don't
have to manually type that information in at a prompt. However, if
your ISP does still require you to log on manually, it can provide
you with a *dial-up script* to automate the entire logon process.

TIP: *Uh-oh—if that sounds like programming, it is (at least sort of). Luckily, most ISPs provide standard logon scripts as part of their new member documentation.*

A script is a file that contains a series of simple text commands that Windows 98 executes upon a successful connection. The following commands can appear in a dial-up script:

```
delay nSeconds
getip value
goto label
halt
if condition then commands endif
set port databits 5 | 6 | 7 | 8
set port parity none | odd | even | mark | space
set port stopbits 1 | 2
set screen keyboard on | off
set ipaddr string
transmit string [ , raw ]
waitfor string [ , matchcase ] [ then label] [ until time ]
while condition do commands endwhile
```

TIP: *It's beyond the scope of this book to teach dial-up scripting; however, if you've upgraded to Windows 98 from Windows 95, a basic scripting tutorial is already on your system. The file SCRIPT.DOC is located in the directory where you installed Windows; you can either load it within WordPad and print it out, or you can read it on screen.*

After your ISP has provided you with a script file or you've written your own, follow these steps to install it:

1. Click on the My Computer icon to open the My Computer window.

2. Click on the Dial-Up Networking icon to open the Dial-Up Networking folder.

3. Right-click on the connection icon that uses the script file and select Properties from the menu.

4. Click on the Scripting tab and then click on Browse to select the script file (it should end with the .SCP extension). When you've selected the file from the Open dialog box, it should be displayed in the File Name field.

5. Enable the Start Terminal Screen Minimized checkbox.

6. Click on OK to close the Properties dialog box and click on File|Close from the menu to close the Dial-Up Networking folder.

Configuring Multilink Connections

If your ISP supports *multilink* PPP connections, you're really in luck: A multilink connection uses two modems to double the throughput of a single dial-up session. For example, if you have a multilink connection with two 56Kbps v.90 modems, your connection could reach as high as 112Kbps in total throughput; both modems carry some of the data, and the entire connection speed is doubled.

Many modems are already supporting this new Windows 98 feature—but remember, you'll need two modems of the same speed and two separate telephone lines; also, it's generally easier to use two modems of the same brand from the same manufacturer. To configure a multilink connection, follow these steps:

1. Click on the My Computer icon to open the My Computer window.

2. Click on the Dial-Up Networking icon to open the Dial-Up Networking folder.

3. Right-click on the desired connection icon and select Properties from the menu.

4. Click on the Multilink tab.

5. Click on Use Additional Devices and then click on Add to select the first device name and telephone number. Click on OK; the device name and telephone number appear in the list box.

6. Repeat Step 5 and then select the second modem to use for your multilink connection.

7. Click on OK to close the Properties dialog box and click on OK again to close the Modems Properties dialog box and save your changes.

Troubleshooting

Troubleshooting Modem Problems

Although Windows 98 can automatically detect modems, which makes it easier to install a modem, you can still run into trouble around practically every corner when it comes to data communications. In this section, I'll offer you a number of solutions for common communications problems.

PC Locks Up

If your PC locks up when you try to access your modem, you're probably experiencing a hardware conflict—your modem is "arguing" with your mouse or some other device that's trying to use the same settings. To check for a hardware conflict, follow these steps:

1. Right-click on My Computer to display the System Properties dialog box and then click on the Device Manager tab.

2. Click on the plus sign next to the entry for modems to expand the branch and display the modems that Windows 98 recognizes.

3. If your modem appears in the Device Manager list with a yellow exclamation point or a red check mark, you probably have a conflict with another device. The other device may also have a yellow exclamation point next to it.

4. Click on Properties to display your modem's Properties dialog box and then click on the General tab.

5. Click on Update Driver to check for newer drivers for your modem. Windows 98 launches the Update Device Drivers Wizard.

6. If updating the driver doesn't work, follow the instructions in your modem's manual for resolving resource conflicts.

7. Click on OK to exit the modem's Properties dialog box and then click on OK to exit the System Properties dialog box. If you made any changes, you must reboot your computer.

TIP: COM1 and COM3 share the same IRQ settings, so never configure a modem to use COM3 if you use a serial mouse or other device connected to your COM1 serial port. The same potential conflict exists between COM2 and COM4.

No Modem Response

No Modem Response

If your modem is on but Windows 98 fails to recognize that you have a modem within any Windows 98 applications or system dialog boxes, consider the following possible problems:

- *The modem was installed improperly.* Display the modem's Diagnostic pane in the Modems Properties dialog box and see if Windows 98 can at least detect if your modem is connected. If your modem's manufacturer supplied any diagnostic software, run that as well. You may need to re-install your modem.

- *You are using an incorrect or corrupted modem driver.* If you used the modem driver that the manufacturer supplied, use a friend's computer to visit the manufacturer's Web site or call its technical support department and request the newest driver for your model. If you used a driver that came with Windows 98, delete the modem from the Modems Properties dialog box and re-install it; this time, however, select a different driver or use the driver that the manufacturer supplied.

- *There are problems with the connection or the power.* Check the connection to an external modem and make sure that the modem is turned on before you boot Windows 98; if you turn your modem on after Windows 98 is already running, it may not recognize that the modem is online.

- *Your modem is malfunctioning.* Try using your modem on another computer and see whether it responds correctly; if not, bring the modem to a local computer shop and ask them to test it.

No Dial Tone

No Dial Tone

If your modem attempts to dial but reports that it didn't receive a dial tone, check these possible problems:

- *The cable is connected incorrectly.* Most modems have two jacks, one for a connection to your telephone line through the wall jack, and one for a standard telephone that you can use for voice calls. If you've connected your cable from the wall socket to the wrong jack on your modem, however, your modem reports "no dial tone". Make sure that you've connected the telephone cable from the wall socket to the correct jack—which is typically marked "Wall" or "Tel"—on your modem (your modem's manual will help you determine which jack is which).

- *The outside-line prefix is missing.* Do you need to dial a "9" or some other number to reach an outside line? If so, add this information to your location entry; your modem must dial that outside-line prefix in order to receive a dial tone.

Modem Dials But Doesn't Connect

If your modem attempts to dial but cannot successfully connect, these are the likely problems:

- *Your connection preferences are set incorrectly.* In order for your modem to successfully connect, both your computer and the host computer must be using the same settings for data bits, parity, and stop bits. Check with the host computer's administrator to see what settings it is using for the following fields.

- *The Error Control Required To Connect checkbox is on.* Check the Advanced Connection Settings dialog box for the modem that is experiencing the dialing problems; if the Error Control Required To Connect checkbox is enabled, the computer you're calling must support error control or Windows 98 automatically disconnects. I recommend disabling this option.

- *The modulation type is incorrect.* Again, check the Advanced Connection Settings dialog box and see if the modem is set for the standard modulation type. If it is and you're experiencing problems with only one host computer, change the modulation type to non-standard (but remember to set the modulation type back to standard for other connections).

- *The server computer is down.* Contact the host administrator to verify that the host computer is running and answering calls.

Modem Disconnects Unexpectedly

If your modem connects correctly but often disconnects without warning, these are possible trouble areas:

- *Call waiting is interfering.* If your telephone service includes call waiting, be aware that the call-waiting tone

Modem Dials But Doesn't Connect

Modem Disconnects Unexpectedly

disconnects most modems. Find out from your telephone company the prefix that disables it and then add it to all of your location entries.

- *The telephone cable is shorted or is improperly connected.* Check the telephone cable between the modem and the wall jack for breaks or possible shorts—if a friend has a spare telephone cable, connect it to your modem and see if the problem clears up. Make sure the cable is firmly connected to both the modem and the wall jack.

Modem Consistently Connects At Lower Speeds

Modem Consistently Connects At Lower Speeds

If your modem successfully connects but always at a significantly lower speed than it should, consider these possible problems:

- *The Maximum Speed is set too low.* Make sure that the maximum speed you've selected on the modem's Properties dialog box is set correctly for the specific speed of your modem. Modems running at 28.8, 33.6, or 56Kbps should use 57600 or 115200 as a maximum speed.

- *The host computer is using a slower modem than you are.* Your modem cannot connect at a speed faster than the maximum speed of the host modem. Therefore, make sure that the host is using a modem at least as fast as yours. (A good way to help you settle on an ISP in your area is to see if its modems support at least the same top speed as your modem.)

- *Data compression is turned off.* Check the Advanced Connection Settings dialog box and make sure that the Compress Data checkbox is enabled.

Dial-Up Networking Cannot Access Your Modem

Dial-Up Networking Cannot Access Your Modem

If a dial-up connection you've created cannot access your modem, check for these possible problems:

- *The wrong modem is specified in the connection.* If you have more than one modem on your PC, make sure that your connection is using the correct modem.

- *The modem is currently in use.* If another Windows application has accessed your modem, that application may not have released the modem. For example, if you're running a terminal program minimized, it doesn't allow any other application or a dial-up connection to use the modem. You must close the application that's currently using the modem.

- *There are connection or power problems.* Check the connection to an external modem and make sure that the modem is turned on before you boot Windows 98. If you turn your modem on after Windows 98 is already running, it may not recognize that the modem is online.

Your PC Cannot Connect To Your ISP

*Your PC
Cannot
Connect
To Your ISP*

If your PC is unable to connect to your ISP, consider these possible problems:

- *Your user name or password is incorrect.* Contact your ISP and make sure that your user name and password are spelled correctly. Also, remember that case is important for many server computers: "THIS" and "This" are not the same.

- *The server type is incorrect.* You must be using the proper server type to match that of your ISP. In most cases, PPP is correct, but some ISPs use SLIP.

- *TCP/IP is not allowed.* Check the Server Types pane of the Properties dialog box for your Internet connection and make sure that TCP/IP is enabled as one of the "allowed network" protocols.

- *TCP/IP is not configured correctly.* You must configure TCP/IP as described in this chapter with the correct values before you can successfully connect—check with your ISP to obtain the correct values for these TCP/IP settings.

- *You are using the wrong access number.* Contact your ISP and make sure you're calling the correct access number to connect to the server's modem.

- *There is a script error.* Ask your ISP for a working script that you can use on your system (or one that you can use as an example for your own programming).

Your PC Cannot Send Faxes

*Your PC
Cannot Send
Faxes*

If your fax modem is having difficulty sending fax documents, these are the likely problems:

- *Microsoft Fax is forcing editable documents.* If you've set a fax to be in editable only format and the receiving fax machine or fax modem doesn't support editable documents, the connection is automatically dropped. Select another format.

- *Your connection speed has been forced too high.* If you've enabled the Only Connect At This Speed checkbox for a fax modem, remember that the maximum connection speed for any fax device is currently 14.4Kbps. Disable this checkbox and try faxing again.

- *Error control has been forced on.* Check the Advanced Connection Settings dialog box for the fax modem that is experiencing the problems; if the Required To Connect checkbox is enabled, the fax device you're calling must support error control or Windows 98 automatically disconnects. Disable this checkbox to solve the problem.

- *The fax functions have been disabled.* If you selected a driver manually while installing your modem, check your modem's manual for the commands required to enable fax support and to properly configure your modem for sending and receiving faxes. (Of course, it's much easier to install a fax modem with the correct driver, so I strongly recommend obtaining from the manufacturer the proper driver for your modem.)

Automating Windows 98

In Brief

Automating Windows

Windows 98 is largely a self-maintaining operating system; however, you should regularly perform the following tasks in order to keep your PC running at optimum speed:

- Scan for file errors and viruses
- Defragment your hard drives
- Check free space on your hard drives
- Back up your hard drives
- Delete temporary files

TIP: All of these tasks can be automated from the Task Scheduler—in fact, most of them are already configured for you!

Another issue you need to monitor has to do with programs you've installed that need to run automatically, such as a fax application or a personal information manager. Some need a specific schedule, whereas others should run every time you boot your computer.

Of course, you can write down what needs to be done on a piece of paper and tape it to your monitor. However, do you really want to track all those events and when they should begin and end? After all, making things easier is what your computer is supposed to do in the first place!

In this chapter, I show you how to run any application automatically under Windows 98—on any schedule you choose—using several different methods. Thanks to our good friends at Microsoft, you don't have to buy any additional software—the utilities discussed in this chapter are built into Windows 98. After you become familiar with Task Scheduler and how to use it to configure events, your PC will maintain itself. This automation leaves you free to concentrate on your work.

TIP: You can also schedule many optimization tasks through the Tune-Up Wizard, which I discuss in full in Chapter 14.

Using Scheduled Tasks

If you need to automate an application with a regular, repeating timetable or an application that needs to run only once at a specific time, Windows 98 provides *scheduled tasks*, system events that Task Scheduler—a Taskbar program that runs constantly in the background as a part of Windows 98—launches. Figure 9.1 shows the Scheduled Tasks folder, which allows you to add, delete, and edit individual tasks in your schedule.

TIP: *Notice that I wrote, "runs constantly in the background as a part of Windows 98." Naturally, your PC must be turned on and Windows 98 must be running for any scheduled tasks to be performed. Some computers can also run scheduled tasks in Suspend mode— check your computer or motherboard's manual to see if it offers Advanced Power Management version 1.2 support (or above), which allows tasks to run in Suspend mode.*

Using StartUp Folder Programs

Scheduled tasks are the right solution for just about any system event—but there is an easier method of running a program or application when you start Windows 98. Here's the trick: Any application with a shortcut in the StartUp folder automatically runs during the last part of the Windows 98 startup sequence.

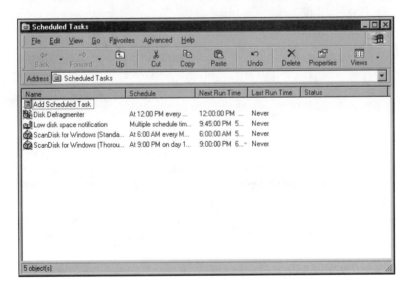

Figure 9.1   A typical list of scheduled tasks under Windows 98.

Startup programs are not as flexible or powerful as scheduled tasks because you don't set any schedules or properties. However, Startup programs are perfect for launching Taskbar programs or applications that run in the background.

Configuring A Network Server Backup Agent

With the right software, Windows 98 also supports automatic server backup for individual workstations across an entire network, eliminating the need for each employee to spend time backing up to tape or disk. *Agent programs* for two different manufacturers of backup software (Seagate and Cheyenne Software) are included free with Windows 98. The agent software specifies which files are to be backed up. Then it communicates any user-specific settings to the backup server program. The agent is configured on the local workstation and runs as a background task; however, you must load onto the network server a commercial backup program from one of the two manufacturers.

Although two different companies manufacture the two backup agents, you install and configure them using the same steps and settings.

***

TIP: *For more information on the Seagate and Cheyenne Software server programs required for network backup, visit these two company Web sites:* **www.seagate.com** *and* **www.cheyenne.com**.

Immediate Solutions

Scheduling A Task

Windows 98 provides yet another Wizard to simplify the task of...well, creating a task. To do so, follow these steps:

1. Click on the My Computer icon and then click on the Scheduled Tasks folder to open it.

2. Double-click on Add Scheduled Task in the scrolling list to run the Scheduled Task Wizard. Click on Next to move to the next Wizard screen.

TIP: *You can expect a delay and quite a bit of disk activity before the next Wizard screen appears because Windows 98 must first build a list of all available applications on your PC.*

---

3. As shown in Figure 9.2, the Wizard displays a scrolling list of all the programs located throughout your system that it can execute. Click on the program you want to schedule and then click on Next.

4. On the next Wizard screen, shown in Figure 9.3, you perform two actions. First, you assign a unique name to the new task; it can be identical to the name of the program you're scheduling. Next, you select a schedule based on time by clicking on the appropriate period; you have the

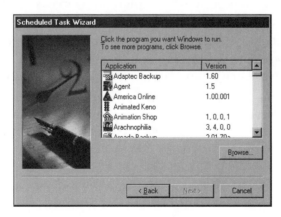

Figure 9.2   The Scheduled Task Wizard displays a list of applications.

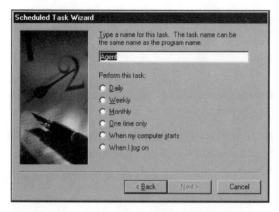

Figure 9.3   Selecting a name and schedule for your task.

following choices: Daily, Weekly, Monthly, One Time Only, When My Computer Starts, or When I Log On. After you're done, click on the Next button to continue.

5. If you selected a schedule based on time—including One Time Only—the Wizard displays a screen prompting you to enter the start time. If you indicated that the task will repeat, the Wizard also asks for more information dependent on the time period you selected:

    *   *Daily*—You can specify that the task should run Every Day, Weekdays Only, or Every *n* Days. Click on Next to continue.

    *   *Weekly*—The task will run on the days of the week that you select (enable one or more checkboxes next to each day). You can also specify how many weeks should pass before the task runs. Click on Next.

    *   *Monthly*—Monthly tasks can run on any day within selected months; once again, you can enable checkboxes to pick the appropriate months. Click on Next.

6. On the final screen, the Wizard displays the program and the schedule you specified for your confirmation. To leave the Wizard at this time, click on Finish. To make changes to the properties for the task you just created, enable the Open Advanced Properties For This Task When I Click Finish checkbox.

TIP: *The Wizard isn't doing anything that fancy here—if you enable the checkbox, it simply opens the Properties dialog box for the task you just created. You can show the Advanced Properties dialog box for any task whenever you want by right-clicking on the task in the Scheduled Tasks folder and then selecting Properties.*

7. If you elect to view the advanced properties for your task, the Wizard displays the dialog box shown in Figure 9.4. The Task pane shows the application path. You can also enable or disable the task from this pane. If you disable the En-abled (Scheduled Task Runs At Specified Time) checkbox, the task is not deleted from the Scheduled Tasks folder; however, it's not active and will not run at the specified time. To reactivate the task so that it will run, display the advanced properties for this task and then click on the Enabled checkbox again.

8. Click on the Schedule tab to change the schedule for this task or to create multiple schedules. If you enable the Show Multiple Schedules checkbox, a new drop-down list and two new buttons appear at the top of the dialog box. Click on New to create a new schedule with the date and time information currently displayed. Each new schedule you create is listed as an entry in the list box—this is handy for

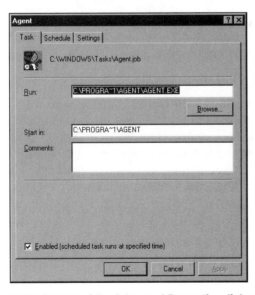

Figure 9.4   The Task pane of the Advanced Properties dialog box for a scheduled task.

those tasks that can run under more than one schedule. After you finish creating your schedules, select the one to use at this time from the drop-down list.

9. Click on the Settings tab to specify a number of advanced features for this task:

- *Completion*—If you want the Task Scheduler to delete this task after it completes, enable the Delete The Scheduled Task When Finished checkbox. If the task's application does not shut itself down, enable the Stop The Scheduled Task After *n* Hour(s) *n* Minute(s) checkbox and enter the desired number of hours and minutes you want the task to last.

- *Idle Time*—Does your task (such as a disk defragmentation program) run better if the PC is idle? If so, enable the Only Start The Scheduled Task If Computer Is Idle For *n* Minute(s) checkbox (specify the idle period in minutes).

  What happens if your PC has not been idle at the scheduled time for the number of minutes you specify? If you would like the Task Scheduler to retry the task—in effect, resetting the idle timer—specify the number of minutes for the retry in the second minute(s) field. If your application does not run well with other programs, enable the Stop The Scheduled Task If Computer Is In Use checkbox.

- *Power Management* (The two fields discussed in this section apply to laptops only)—If you're running an application that makes changes to your drive—once again, like a disk defragmenter—running out of battery power during the task might be a disaster. To prevent such an occurrence, enable the Don't Start Scheduled Task If Computer Is Running On Batteries checkbox. To prevent a task that's already running from continuing under battery power, enable the Stop The Scheduled Task If Battery Mode Begins checkbox.

10. Click on OK to save any changes you made to the task's advanced properties and return to the Scheduled Tasks folder.

TIP: *Windows 98 stores all scheduled tasks to be performed in a JOB file within the \WINDOWS\TASKS directory.*

Changing Task Settings

To edit the schedule or properties for an existing task, follow these steps:

1. Click on the My Computer icon and then click on the Scheduled Tasks folder to open it.

2. Right-click on the task you want to change and then select Properties from the menu.

3. Follow the instructions in Steps 7 through 10 in the preceding section, "Scheduling A Task."

4. After you finish, select File|Close to close the Scheduled Tasks folder.

Deleting A Task

If you no longer need a task, you can remove it from the Scheduled Tasks folder by following these steps:

1. Click on the My Computer icon and then click on the Scheduled Tasks folder to open it.

2. Click on the task you want to remove to highlight it.

3. Press the Delete key or click on the Delete button on the Scheduled Tasks toolbar.

4. Select File|Close to close the Scheduled Tasks folder.

Starting And Stopping Task Scheduler

By default, Windows 98 runs the Task Scheduler automatically after installation, and it appears in the right side of the Taskbar each time your computer boots. Task Scheduler is a small program and doesn't use many system resources; however, if you don't use any scheduled tasks, there's no reason to run it and you should turn off Task Scheduler permanently. To start or stop using Task Scheduler, follow these steps:

1. Click on the My Computer icon and then click on the Scheduled Tasks folder to open it.

2. If Task Scheduler is currently on, select Advanced|Stop Using Task Scheduler from the Scheduled Tasks folder menu. If Task Scheduler is currently off, select Advanced|Start Using Task Scheduler from the Scheduled Tasks folder menu.

3. Select File|Close to close the Scheduled Tasks folder.

TIP: *You can start and stop the Task Scheduler from this menu item (and I often do when I'm debugging an error that might be caused by a TS application).*

Pausing Task Scheduler

The Task Scheduler also provides a convenient pause feature. Pausing the Task Scheduler allows users to ensure that it doesn't launch an application for the moment—without having to disable it permanently by selecting Advanced|Stop Using Task Scheduler, as described in the preceding section.

TIP: *If you record your own CD-ROMs, you have probably already used the pause feature to avoid ruining the recording—by pausing Task Scheduler to prevent other applications from running while a CD-ROM is being recorded.*

To pause Task Scheduler, follow these steps:

1. Click on the My Computer icon and then click on the Scheduled Tasks folder to open it.

2. Select Advanced|Pause Task Scheduler from the Scheduled Tasks folder menu; a check mark will appear next to the menu item.

3. Select File|Close to close the Scheduled Tasks folder.

You can also right-click on the Scheduler Taskbar icon and select Pause Task Scheduler.

To activate Task Scheduler again, follow the preceding three steps; this time, however, clicking on the Pause Task Scheduler menu item will disable it.

TIP: *If you find yourself starting, stopping, and pausing the Task Scheduler often, it's a good idea to select Advanced|Notify Me Of Missed Tasks from the Task Scheduler menu to enable it. A check appears next to the menu item to indicate when this function is enabled. The Task Scheduler will now notify you of any tasks that didn't run because your PC was off or the Task Scheduler was stopped or paused.*

Adding A Startup Program

To automate a program through the StartUp folder, follow these steps:

1. Right-click on the Taskbar and then select Properties from the menu. Windows 98 displays the Taskbar Properties dialog box.

2. Click on the Start menu's Programs tab and then click on Advanced to open the Start menu within the Explorer window.

3. Click on the plus sign next to Programs to expand the directory tree and then click on the StartUp folder to open it. Figure 9.5 illustrates the contents of a StartUp folder in the Explorer window.

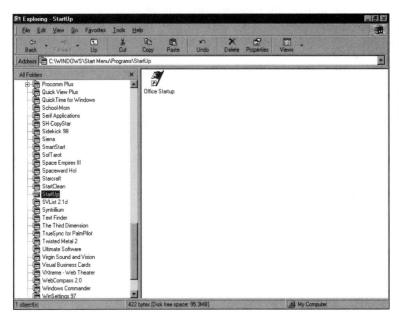

Figure 9.5   Preparing to add a program shortcut to the StartUp folder.

4. Select File|New|Shortcut. Windows 98 displays the Create Shortcut Wizard.

5. Click on Browse, navigate to the executable program that you want to load, and then double-click on it. Windows 98 displays the program with its full path in the command line field; if you need to add command line switches for the application, you can add them after the executable name. When the command line is correct, click on Next to continue.

6. Type a unique name for the shortcut and then click on Finish. The Wizard creates the shortcut icon in your StartUp folder.

7. Select File|Close to close the Explorer window and then click on OK to close the Taskbar Properties dialog box.

Deleting A Startup Program

To prevent an application shortcut in your StartUp folder from running automatically, you may need to remove it. Follow these steps to delete a startup shortcut:

1. Right-click on the Taskbar and then select Properties from the menu. Windows 98 displays the Taskbar Properties dialog box.

2. Click on the Start menu's Programs tab and then click on the Remove button to open the Remove Shortcuts/Folders dialog box, shown in Figure 9.6.

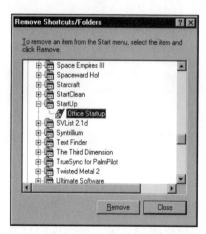

Figure 9.6   Removing a shortcut from the StartUp folder.

3. Click on the plus sign next to Programs to expand the Programs directory tree and then click on the plus sign next to the StartUp folder to display the contents.

4. Click on the shortcut icon you want to remove to highlight it and then click on Remove.

5. Select Close to close the Remove Shortcuts/Folders dialog box and then click on OK to close the Taskbar Properties dialog box.

Installing And Configuring A Backup Agent

If your network server is running the Seagate software, follow these steps to install and configure the Seagate backup agent on your workstation:

1. Click on Start|Settings|Control Panel to display the Control Panel and then click on Network to display the Network dialog box, shown in Figure 9.7.

2. Click on Add and then double-click on Service to display the Select Network Service dialog box.

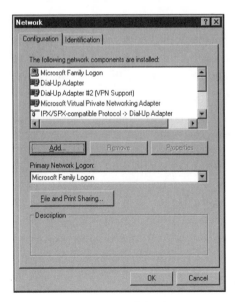

Figure 9.7   The Windows 98 Network dialog box.

3. In the Manufacturers list box, select Seagate Software; in the Network Services list box, select Backup Exec Agent. Click on OK to continue and load your Windows 98 CD-ROM when prompted.

4. Within the Network dialog box, double-click on Backup Exec Agent in the Network components scrolling list to display the Backup Exec Agent Properties dialog box.

5. Click on Enable Network Backup to activate the agent program.

6. If a password is required for security, enable the Password checkbox and then enter the password in the text field next to it. The network administrator must enter this password in order to access your workstation.

7. Click on Display Status Screen, which allows you to track the progress of the backup.

8. I recommend that you back up your Registry as well as your files; therefore, enable the Allow Registry To Be Restored checkbox.

9. Use the Add and Remove buttons to specify which drives and folders on your workstation will be backed up to the server. Click on Details to assign a password for certain directories.

10. Click on the Protocol tab and then enter the values your system administrator gave you.

11. Click on OK to close the Backup Exec Agent Properties screen and then click on OK to exit the Network dialog box.

Windows 98 runs the backup agent automatically as a background task, so you don't have to launch anything before the server begins the backup process.

Troubleshooting

Troubleshooting Automation Problems

In this section, I'll provide you with solutions to common problems that can affect Task Scheduler events and startup programs.

Task Or Program Does Not Launch

If you've scheduled a task or installed a startup program shortcut and the program did not run when it should have, check these possible problems:

- *Task Scheduler is turned off or paused.* Turning off or pausing the Task Scheduler prevents any scheduled tasks from running. Start the Task Scheduler, or deactivate pause mode.

- *The system clock is set incorrectly.* Check your system clock to make sure that your PC is set to the right time. To display the system date and time, click on Start|Settings|Control Panel to display the Control Panel and then click on Date/Time to display the Date/Time Properties dialog box. (Alternately, you can double-click on the Taskbar time display to open the same dialog box.)

- *The task entry was automatically deleted.* If your task was configured for automatic deletion after it ran the previous time, it cannot be run again. You must manually add the task again.

- *The system was not idle.* If you've set a minimum idle time for your PC before the task was to run, your system may not have met that minimum setting; consider reducing the required idle time and scheduling the event again.

- *The startup program has been moved or deleted.* If you've moved or deleted the program that corresponds to a StartUp folder shortcut, Windows 98 cannot locate the program and it will not run. Delete the StartUp folder shortcut and create a new startup program shortcut that points to the new location.

- *The system was started in Safe mode.* Windows 98 does not run any StartUp folder programs when it is started in Safe mode. Restart your system in Normal mode.

- *The system was suspended.* Many laptop and desktop computers cannot launch scheduled programs if your system is suspended (or in "sleep" mode). If you need scheduled tasks, you should either stop using your PC's suspend/sleep feature or schedule them at times when you know your PC will be on and active.

- *The JOB file was deleted.* Check your \WINDOWS\TASKS folder for a JOB file—without one, no scheduled tasks will run. If the JOB file has been deleted accidentally, you'll have to delete all of your scheduled tasks and add them again.

Task Or
Program
Does Not Run
Successfully

Task Or Program Does Not Run Successfully

If a scheduled task or startup program ran but did not finish successfully, check these possible problems:

- *The program required switches.* If the program you want to automate requires command line switches, make sure that you add them in the task Properties (or the StartUp folder shortcut Properties).

- *The program required an Internet connection.* If the program needs an active TCP/IP connection when it runs and it doesn't automatically launch a dial-up networking connection, it will fail. Make sure that your PC has an active TCP/IP connection at the time the scheduled task will run.

- *The program requires manual intervention.* If the program requires you to select menu choices or press buttons, it's probably not a suitable choice for use with Task Scheduler or your StartUp folder.

- *The program requires removable media.* Make sure that your program can access data on any CD-ROM or removable media drives before scheduling it.

Task Or
Program
Does Not
Quit

Task Or Program Does Not Quit

If your scheduled task or startup program ran successfully but didn't shut itself down, check these possible problems:

- *The program needs a forced shutdown.* If you're running the program through Task Scheduler and the program doesn't automatically exit, use the Stop The Scheduled Task After n Hour(s) n Minute(s) checkbox in the Advanced Properties dialog box for the task entry.

- *The program requires manual intervention.* If the program requires you to select menu choices or press buttons, it's probably not a suitable choice for use with Task Scheduler or your StartUp folder.

- *The program requires a reboot.* If the program you're running needs a reboot and does not do so automatically, you must perform the reboot manually.

Chapter 10

Optimizing Internet Explorer 4

In Brief

Optimizing Internet Explorer 4

In the space of a couple of years, Microsoft's Internet Explorer 4 (IE4)—in comparison to its earlier versions—has exploded in both features and popularity across the Internet. Now, millions of Windows owners around the world are choosing as their Web-surfing tool the browser that used to be called "The Ugly Duckling."

IE4's success is due in no small part to the following three strengths:

- *Extensive configuration options*—Users can alter or adjust virtually every aspect of the program.

- *Powerful security options*—IE4 offers encryption, secure transaction capability, and a number of features that help keep your data away from prying eyes. IE4 offers some of the most advanced security features of any browser available today, safeguarding both the data on your computer and the data you send to a Web site.

- *Expandability*—You can extend the features and capabilities of IE4 with both third-party plug-ins and additional plug-in components distributed by Microsoft.

With the arrival of Windows 98 and the Active Desktop, Microsoft has made it clear that this and future versions of the browser will be tightly integrated into tomorrow's desktop. Because of this integration, much of your information from the outside world will arrive via the Web.

Although the World Wide Web is a wondrous part of cyberspace, nearly everyone agrees that it suffers from one problem—for most of us, downloading pages, files, images, and information is as fast as the water evaporation rate at the South Pole. If you're lucky, you may be able to use your company's direct T1 connection, a satellite download system, an ISDN line, or even a cable modem. The vast majority of the connections made with IE4, however, will be through a modem with an average top speed of 33.6Kbps.

In this chapter, I'll show you how to fine-tune IE4: You will configure the interface colors, fonts, and features within the browser to match your personal taste. If you're interested in safeguarding your personal data, you'll learn how to take advantage of the various security options. Finally, I'll discuss the process of adding and using plug-ins within IE4 to expand your browsing adventures, as well as how to troubleshoot problems you may encounter while Web surfing.

Immediate Solutions

Configuring General Options For Speed

In this section, you learn more about how to optimize IE4 for the fastest possible access to the Web. You can set a number of options to improve the speed of IE4 from the Internet Options dialog box, shown in Figure 10.1. The projects in this section describe how to configure the options available from the General pane.

Setting A Blank Home Page

Have you defined a *home page*—the Web page that your browser displays when you start it up—within IE4? A home page is a good feature if you need to check a specific page each time you connect to the Web. If you like to check out new sites you see in books, magazines, and Internet newsgroups, however, it can be a pain to wait for your home page to load each time you launch.

If you'd like to avoid waiting for that page to load, I recommend setting a blank home page. You can immediately enter or paste

Figure 10.1   The General pane of the Internet Options dialog box within IE4.

the URL of the site you want to see in the Address field and start loading the page right away. To implement the blank home page setting, follow these steps:

1. Run IE4, select View|Internet Options, and then click on the General tab to display the General pane.

2. In the Home Page section, click on Use Blank.

3. Click on OK to close the Internet Options dialog box and save your changes.

TIP: The Explorer bars are a great convenience feature in IE4—see Chapter 2 for full details.

Optimizing Temporary Internet Files

One method of speeding up a Web session is to use *temporary files*—for example, image files and animation—that IE4 has loaded from previous visits; other browsers may call these temporary files a "cache." To set how IE4 uses temporary files, follow these steps:

1. Run IE4, select View|Internet Options, and then click on the General tab to display the General pane.

2. Click on Settings in the Temporary Internet Files section to display the Settings dialog box, shown in Figure 10.2.

3. To reduce the time that IE4 spends downloading pages you've already visited, you can adjust how often the program should check for a newer version of the page. You have these three choices:

Figure 10.2   You can speed up IE4 by using temporary files.

- *Every Visit To The Page*—This setting specifies that IE4 should check for a newer version of the page each time the page is accessed. Although you'll never miss information on an updated page with this setting, it also takes the longest time—often, IE4 has to re-download the entire page each time you access it. I recommend choosing this setting only if you'll be accessing Web pages that change quite often, such as ones that display stock quotes, news headlines, weather information, and so on.

- *Every Time You Start Internet Explorer*—This setting specifies that IE4 should check for a newer version of the page only once per browsing session, at the first point the page is accessed. This setting is generally the best selection for most users; the content on most pages doesn't change hourly, so IE4 can reload the same page from its temporary files in seconds.

- *Never*—This is the fastest setting; IE4 never checks for a new version of the page and always uses the page stored in its temporary files. Use the Never setting if the pages you access change only once or twice a year, such as a listing of Oscar winners from the Academy Awards, or if you want the fastest possible browsing session. Keep in mind, however, that you won't see any updates to the page without refreshing.

TIP: *If you decide to use the Every Time You Start Internet Explorer or the Never options, remember that you can always reload a fresh version of the page by clicking on Refresh in the IE4 toolbar (or by selecting View|Refresh or pressing F5). Refreshing ensures that you'll be seeing the latest information available on that page.*

---

4. Click on OK to close the Settings dialog box and then click on OK again to exit the Internet Options dialog box and return to the browser window.

Configuring Your Temporary Internet Files Folder

If you never check for newer versions of a page, you will need plenty of room to store those temporary files that IE4 reloads. You can adjust the maximum size of the Temporary Internet Files folder to allow more room (which, in turn, means that you can store more pages for longer). If the folder fills to the limit, IE4 automatically removes the oldest page files first (and you will have to reload those pages the next time you visit them). To set the size of your Temporary Internet Files folder, take the following steps:

1. Run IE4, select View|Internet Options, and then click on the General tab to display the General pane.

2. Click on Settings in the Temporary Internet Files section to display the Settings dialog box.

3. The Amount Of Disk Space To Use slider determines the size of the Temporary Internet Files folder. Generally, the higher the setting, the less IE4 has to download during your Web-browsing sessions (if you never check for newer versions of a page). Moving the slider to the right increases the folder's maximum size limit, which is also displayed to the right of the slider in both megabytes and a percentage of the drive's total space.

4. Click on OK to close the Settings dialog box and then click on OK again to exit the Internet Options dialog box and return to the browser window.

TIP: *Are you running out of space to expand your Temporary Internet Files folder? Consider moving the folder from its current drive (displayed as the Current Folder path above the slider control) to another drive on your system that has more free space. Click on Move Folder to specify the new location.*

Configuring Your History Folder

Another method of reducing your browsing time is to use your History folder. IE4 automatically keeps track of the Web pages you've visited in past sessions and lets you jump directly to any of these pages from the History window. It's a good idea to set a longer period for your History folder so that you can access with a single click more of the pages that you've visited recently (refer to Figure 10.1). To set the number of days that a Web page stays in your History folder, follow these steps:

1. Run IE4, select View|Internet Options, and then click on the General tab to display the General pane.

2. In the History section, click on the scroll buttons next to the Days To Keep Pages In History scroll box—I recommend selecting at least 30 to 45 days.

3. Click on OK to exit the Internet Options dialog box and return to the browser window.

TIP: *To access the History folder from within IE4, click on the History toolbar button. You will see every site you have visited recently.*

Configuring Advanced Options For Speed

You can also configure a number of options on the Advanced pane of the Internet Options dialog box, shown in Figure 10.3. The projects in this section describe how to set these global options to provide the fastest possible performance from IE4.

Setting Browsing Options

IE4 also includes a number of global options that can help you save time online. To speed up your browsing, follow these steps:

1. Run IE4, select View|Internet Options, and then click on the Advanced tab to display the Advanced pane.

2. In the Browsing section, enable (or disable) the following options:

   - *Use AutoComplete*—If this feature is enabled, IE4 automatically completes a partial URL address that you've typed in with the closest matching page that you've already visited. For example, if you type "www.yah" in the Address field and you've visited Yahoo! in the past, IE4 saves you time by automatically adding the rest of the address so that it reads "http://www.yahoo.com". Depending on the size of the address, this feature can save you a boatload of keystrokes!

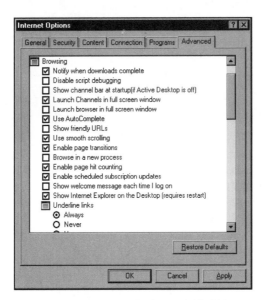

Figure 10.3   The Advanced Internet Options within IE4.

- *Enable Page Transitions*—With this setting on, IE4 gets fancy and fades out your current Web page while fading in the page you just selected. You'll save time by turning off this special effect.

- *Show Internet Explorer On The Desktop (Requires Restart)*—Enabling this option adds a shortcut icon to IE4 on your desktop, making it faster and more convenient to launch the program with a single click.

3. Click on OK to close the Internet Options dialog box and save your changes.

Setting Multimedia Options

One of the biggest bottlenecks for any page is the time it takes to display and play images and multimedia files. To speed up your Web sessions, follow these steps:

1. Run IE4, select View|Internet Options, and then click on the Advanced tab to display the Advanced pane.

2. In the Multimedia section, disable the following options:

- *Show Pictures*—Disabling this option forces IE4 to display only the text of a Web page—all images will be blank. (To see the image for a particular page, you can right-click on the image icon and then select Show Picture from the menu.)

- *Play Animations*—Java and GIF animations also take time to display; disabling this option prevents them from appearing on your pages.

- *Play Videos*—Disable this option to prevent video clips from displaying.

- *Play Sounds*—If you don't want sound files played, disable this option.

TIP: *"Hang on a second, Mark—what if a page includes an animation or video that I really want to see?" No need to enable any of these options: You can still see the animation or video file if you right-click on the multimedia file icon and then select Show Picture from the menu.*

---

3. Click on OK to close the Internet Options dialog box and save your changes.

Configuring Your Security Options

Figure 10.4 illustrates the Security pane of the Internet Options dialog box, where you can assign different security *zones*: Web sites grouped in each zone have different levels of security. The projects in this section describe how to configure the options available from this pane.

Understanding Security Zones

IE4 recognizes four distinct security zones. In order of least- to most required security, they are as follows:

- *Local Intranet Zone*—These are Web sites within your company's private intranet. Generally, these sites require few security measures.

- *Trusted Sites Zone*—These are Web sites that you have determined are trustworthy; you've accessed them before without security problems. If you assign a Web site within the Trusted Sites Zone, you believe that the site doesn't contain destructive Java applets or viruses. You can safely assign the Trusted Sites Zone to most Web sites from major corporations.

- *Internet Zone*—These are the vast majority of the sites you'll access—any site that you visit and you haven't assigned to another zone is automatically assigned to the Internet Zone.

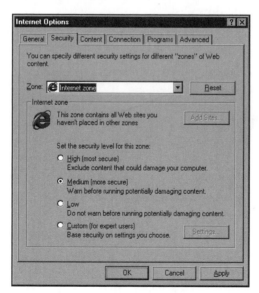

Figure 10.4   Specifying Security Internet Options within IE4.

- *Restricted Sites Zone*—These sites are suspected of offering content that could damage your PC's data. Naturally, Restricted sites require the highest level of security if you decide to access them.

You can set each of these four security zones to one of four security levels. In order of decreasing security, they are as follows:

- *High (Most Secure)*—IE4 filters out any content that could possibly destroy data on your PC.

- *Medium (More Secure)*—IE4 warns you with a message before running any script, program, or applet that could damage your PC.

- *Low*—IE4 does not warn you of possible harmful content.

- *Custom (For Expert Users)*—The custom security levels allow you to create your own security level by manually selecting security options. (Creating custom security levels is covered in the following section).

Configuring Security Zones

To select a specific security level for a zone, follow these steps:

1. Run IE4, select View|Internet Options, and then click on the Security tab to display the Security pane.

2. Select the zone you want to configure by clicking on the Zone drop-down list.

3. Click on the security level you want to set for this security zone.

4. Click on OK to close the Internet Options dialog box and save your changes.

Customizing A Security Level

If you like, you can select the custom security level and specify your own settings when you're configuring a security zone. To define a custom security level for a zone, follow these steps:

1. Run IE4, select View|Internet Options, and then click on the Security tab to display the Security pane.

2. Select the zone you want to configure by clicking on the Zone drop-down list.

3. Click on Custom|Settings to display the Security Settings dialog box, shown in Figure 10.5.

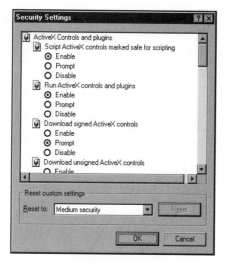

Figure 10.5   Creating a custom security level.

4. Scroll through the options and select those that you want to enable or disable.

5. After you have set all of the security options to your liking, click on OK to save them and return to the Security pane.

6. Click on OK to close the Internet Options dialog box and save your changes.

TIP: *If you like, you can choose high, medium, or low as a starting point for the custom security level. Placing a security level between high and medium—for example, to specifically guard against harmful signed ActiveX controls—is relatively easy. Click on the Reset button beside the drop-down list, choose Medium Security, and then click on Reset to reset all the values in the Security Settings box to Medium Security. You'll have to change fewer settings and you'll save time creating your custom security level.*

Adding A Web Site To A Security Zone

Once you've created a security zone, you can add Web sites to it. Each time you access a site assigned to a specific zone, IE4 uses the security options you've chosen for that zone. To add a Web site to a security zone, follow these steps:

1. Run IE4, select View|Internet Options, and then click on the Security tab to display the Security pane.

2. Select the zone you want to configure by clicking on the Zone drop-down list.

3. Click on Add Sites to display the list of sites that have been assigned to that zone. Type the full URL in the Address field and then click on Add; the site appears in the list.

4. Click on OK to save your addition and then click on OK again to close the Internet Options dialog box.

Removing A Web Site From A Security Zone

From time to time, you may want to reassign a Web site a higher or lower security level. To do so, you must first remove the site from its current zone. To remove a Web site from a security zone, follow these steps:

1. Run IE4, select View|Internet Options, and then click on the Security tab to display the Security pane.

2. Select the zone that contains the Web site you want to remove by clicking on the Zone drop-down list.

3. Click on Add Sites to display the list of sites that have been assigned to that zone. Click on the desired entry to highlight it in the list and then click on Remove to delete the entry.

4. Click on OK to save your changes and then click on OK again to close the Internet Options dialog box.

Configuring Advanced Options For Security

You can also set a number of security options on the Advanced pane of the Internet Options dialog box. The projects in this section describe how to make global adjustments that affect each site you access, regardless of its security level on the Security pane.

Setting Advanced Security Options

Enabling the global options improves the security of any connection made with Internet Explorer. Follow these steps:

1. Run IE4, select View|Internet Options, and then click on the Advanced tab to display the Advanced pane.

2. Scroll to the Security section. Enable the following global options:

   • *Enable Profile Assistant*—When this option is enabled, IE4 asks you for permission before providing any profile information that a site requests. You can elect to block all information or select which information is sent.

- *PCT 1.0, SSL 2.0, and SSL 3.0*—Web servers use these secure protocols to establish a secure connection with your browser. If you plan to transfer any sensitive information across the Web (including your credit-card number), the Web site probably uses one of these protocols, and you should enable all three.

- *Warn If Forms Submit Is Being Redirected*—Enabling this option allows IE4 to notify you if information from an online form you've filled out is being sent to another location besides the page you've accessed.

- *Warn If Changing Between Secure And Not Secure Mode*—If you enable this option, IE4 notifies you when you move to a secure connection (using PCT 1.0, SSL 2.0, or SSL 3.0). This option also warns you when you return to a connection that is not secure.

- *Prompt Before Accepting Cookies*—No, sorry, this setting has nothing to do with gingerbread men or chocolate chips—on the Internet, a *cookie* is a file that a Web site sends to your PC. This file typically contains your preferences and identifying information for that page, so that the next time you connect to that page, the Web server can retrieve the cookie and "recognize" you. Other Web sites retrieve cookies, so some Web surfers don't like cookies. The Security section of the Advanced pane offers three Cookie options. Generally, it's a good idea to enable either Prompt Before Accepting Cookies or Disable All Cookie Use.

TIP: *Disabling cookies can pose a problem for some Web servers that depend on them for tracking and identifying visitors. If you disable cookie use entirely, you probably cannot access these sites.*

---

3. Click on OK to close the Internet Options dialog box and save your changes.

Setting Advanced Java Options

The Java language has become a standard on the Internet for animation and simple programming tasks, and many sites now require the Java support within IE4. Follow these steps to set your advanced Java options:

1. Run IE4, select View|Internet Options, and then click on the Advanced tab to display the Advanced pane.

2. Scroll to the Java VM section. Enabling (or disabling) the following global options for Java language processing improves security under IE4:

   - *Java JIT Compiler Enabled*—Disabling this option prevents IE4 from automatically compiling and running Java applets, which could damage data on your PC.

   - *Java Logging Enabled*—With this option enabled, IE4 logs all Java program activity to a disk file; you can review this file at any time to check for Java activity that may jeopardize the security your data.

3. Click on OK to close the Internet Options dialog box and save your changes.

Changing Colors Within Internet Explorer 4

For a visual information medium like the World Wide Web, the color of screen elements such as text, your browser's background, and links is not just a preference—it can mean the difference between seeing a link or missing it. You can change colors within IE4 from the Colors dialog box, shown in Figure 10.6.

Selecting Text And Background Colors

Many Web pages define their own colors for text and background as part of the HTML file—if a page doesn't define its own colors, however, you can choose the default colors that IE4 uses. To select text and background colors, follow these steps:

1. Run IE4 and then select View|Internet Options.

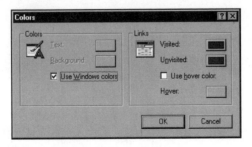

Figure 10.6   Changing color settings within IE4.

2. Click on the Colors button to display the Colors dialog box.

3. Disable the Use Windows Colors checkbox.

4. Click on the Text button to display a standard Windows 98 color palette (Figure 10.7 illustrates the entire Color palette dialog box, including the custom color selector). You can choose from one of the predefined Basic Colors by clicking on it—or if you like, you can create a custom color by clicking directly on a color in Custom Colors and then clicking on Add To Custom Colors. After you've selected the right color, click on OK. You'll notice that the color of the Text button changes.

5. Click on the Background button and follow the instructions in Step 4 to choose a background color.

6. Click on OK to close the Colors dialog box and then click on OK again to exit the Internet Options dialog box.

TIP: *If you enable the Use Windows Colors checkbox, IE4 uses the font and background colors you've specified within the Display Properties dialog box, and you cannot use the Text or Background buttons.*

Selecting Links Colors

If you want the hyperlinks on a page to stand out, the Colors dialog box is definitely the place to experiment! To select Links colors, follow these steps:

1. Run IE4 and then select View|Internet Options.

2. Click on the Colors button to display the Colors dialog box.

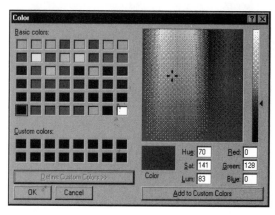

Figure 10.7   Selecting a text color.

3. Click on the Visited button to display a standard Windows 98 color palette; the color shown is the color for hyperlinks that you've already accessed. You can choose from one of the predefined Basic Colors by clicking on it—or, if you want, you can create a custom color by clicking directly on the color you like in Custom Colors and then clicking on Add To Custom Colors. After you select the right color, click on OK. You will notice that the color of the Visited button changes.

4. Click on the Unvisited button and then follow the instructions in Step 3 to choose a color for links you haven't followed yet.

5. IE4 can also change the color of a link if your mouse cursor "hovers" over it; this setting is a good test to determine whether your cursor is hovering over a true link or just underlined text. If you enable the Use Hover Color checkbox, you can choose the color of the link when your mouse pointer is hovering over it; follow the instructions in Step 3 to choose a hover color.

6. Click on OK to close the Colors dialog box and then click on OK again to exit the Internet Options dialog box.

Overriding Web Page Colors

Although it doesn't appear in the Colors dialog box, there is a setting that can totally override all color commands embedded in Web pages you receive. This setting specifies that Internet Explorer should always use either the text and background colors you've selected or your Windows colors (depending on whether the Use Windows Colors checkbox is enabled). To override all colors defined within Web pages you access, follow these steps:

1. Run IE4 and then select View|Internet Options.

2. Click on the Accessibility button to display the Accessibility dialog.

3. Enable the Ignore Colors Specified On Web Pages checkbox.

4. Click on OK to save your changes and then click on OK again to close the Internet Options dialog box.

Changing Fonts Within Internet Explorer 4

As anyone familiar with desktop publishing can tell you, you can drastically change the entire look and feel of a document by substituting a different font. Additionally, if your eyesight isn't perfect or you spend many hours staring at your browser screen, a larger font can prevent eyestrain and headaches. In this section, you will find projects to help you adjust your fonts within IE4 for the easiest reading; you will make these changes from the Fonts dialog box, shown in Figure 10.8.

Selecting Proportional And Fixed-Width Fonts

By default, IE4 uses Times New Roman and Courier New as the fonts for text information on your Web pages. To select your own fonts for Web text, follow these steps:

1. Run IE4 and then select View|Internet Options.

2. Click on the Fonts button to display the Fonts dialog box.

3. Click on the Proportional Font drop-down list to display a list of the proportional fonts you've installed that are compatible with IE4; click on the font that IE4 should use. Unlike fixed-width fonts such as Courier New, proportional fonts can be dynamically manipulated on screen to take up more or less space; proportional fonts typically look better than fixed-width fonts, and they're usually used for the text on most Web pages.

4. Click on the Fixed-Width Font drop-down list to display the compatible fixed-width fonts installed on your PC and then

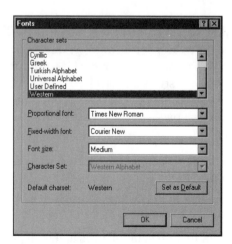

Figure 10.8   Changing font settings within IE4.

select the font that should be used within IE4. Fixed-width fonts are often used to display computer-language code, DOS commands, or HTML code (where precise spacing is required and letters of the alphabet must not be confused with numbers).

5. Click on OK to close the Fonts dialog box and then click on OK again to exit the Internet Options dialog box and save your changes.

Selecting Character Set And Font Size

Internet Explorer uses the *character set* (a standard group of letters, numbers, and symbols) and font size you choose on the Fonts dialog box for all Web pages that don't specify these values. To select a default character set and font size for Web text, follow these steps:

1. Run IE4 and then select View|Internet Options.

2. Click on the Fonts button to display the Fonts dialog box.

3. Click on the correct character set for your language within the Character Sets scrolling list and then click on Set As Default.

4. Click on the Font Size drop-down list to specify the default font size for Web pages that don't include an HTML font size instruction. You can choose from five sizes: Smallest, Small, Medium, Larger, and Largest.

5. Click on OK to close the Fonts dialog box and then click on OK again to exit the Internet Options dialog box and save your changes.

Overriding Web Page Font Styles And Font Sizes

You can force IE4 to override all font style and font size commands embedded in Web pages you receive. This setting ensures that IE4 always uses the font styles and sizes you've selected (which may be easier for you to read). To override the font characteristics defined within Web pages you access, follow these steps:

1. Run IE4 and then select View|Internet Options.

2. Click on the Accessibility button to display the Accessibility dialog box.

3. Enable the Ignore Font Styles Specified On Web Pages checkbox.

4. Click on OK to save your changes and then click on OK again to close the Internet Options dialog box.

Installing Plug-Ins

You can enhance IE4 with additional functionality by installing extra components (typically known as *plug-ins*). Microsoft distributes some of these components; third-party companies distribute others to support a specific file format or HTML function.

Examples of IE4 plug-ins include the following:

- *Viewers for multimedia files*—Although IE4 can view many types of images, animation, video, and sound files through internal support, dozens of proprietary file formats are in use around the Internet. These plug-ins allow you to view a specific multimedia file format, usually within a separate window displayed by the plug-in.

- *Archive managers*—Most files available for downloading on the Internet are compressed and archived in a format like ZIP or ARJ. These plug-ins can display the contents of an archive and uncompress the contents to a folder.

- *Encryption utilities*—For those who need the tightest possible security, a number of plug-ins can encrypt and decrypt the data you send and receive over the Web.

TIP: *For more information on IE4 plug-ins distributed by Microsoft, visit the IE4 Web site at www.microsoft.com/ie/ie40/.*

Many plug-ins operate automatically—for example, a ZIP archive manager probably displays its window immediately after you download a ZIP file. Others plug-ins may make changes to the IE4 menu system or run as a background task.

Adding Plug-Ins Through The Control Panel

If a particular plug-in that you want to use does not have its own setup program, its documentation probably will tell you to use the Add/Remove Programs function within the Windows 98 Control Panel for installation. To install a plug-in with the Add/Remove Programs function, follow these steps:

1. Click on Start|Settings|Control Panel to open the Control Panel window.

2. Click on Add/Remove Programs to display the Add/Remove Programs Properties dialog box (shown in Figure 10.9) and then click on Install.

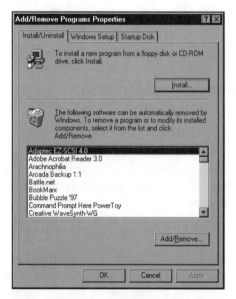

Figure 10.9   Adding a plug-in program through the Add/Remove Programs Properties dialog box.

3. Click on Next to continue. If the plug-in is stored on a floppy disk or a CD-ROM, Windows 98 displays the plug-in program; if the plug-in is stored on your hard drive, Windows 98 displays a field for a command line. (Alternately, you can click on Browse and locate the program anywhere on your system.)

4. After you've located the plug-in, click on Finish to complete the installation.

5. Click on OK to close the Add/Remove Programs Properties dialog box and then click on File|Close to close the Control Panel window.

Removing Plug-Ins

You can also remove most plug-ins from the Add/Remove Programs dialog box located in the Control Panel. To remove a plug-in, follow these steps:

1. Click on Start|Settings|Control Panel to open the Control Panel window.

2. Click on Add/Remove Programs to display the Add/Remove Programs Properties dialog box.

3. Scroll through the list and click on the entry for the plug-in you want to remove. Click on Add/Remove.

4. Confirm that you do indeed want to remove the plug-in.

5. After you have removed the plug-in, click on OK to close the Add/Remove Programs Properties dialog box and then click on File|Close to close the Control Panel window.

Troubleshooting

Troubleshooting Internet Explorer 4 Problems

As you might imagine, most of the problems you encounter with IE4 stem from two sources: your modem connection and your dial-up networking connection settings. In this section, I will provide you with some possible solutions to a number of Web and browser problems.

No Modem Response Or No Connection

No Modem Response Or No Connection

If you're using a dial-up connection to the Internet, your modem is on and recognized by Windows 98 but it won't dial out for an IE4 session or won't connect, consider the following possible problems:

- *You have specified an incorrect or nonexistent connection*—You must identify which type of connection you'll be using to access the Internet: a dial-up modem connection or a LAN connection. Within IE4, you specify the correct connection from the Connection pane of the Internet Options dialog box, shown in Figure 10.10. Make sure that you've selected the proper connection type; if you're using an existing dial-up networking connection, click on Settings and then check the connection you've already specified.

TIP: *If you haven't created a dial-up networking connection yet, click on Connect to run the Dial-Up Networking Connection Wizard.*

- *The location is wrong*—Check your Dialing Properties for the connection you're trying to use and see whether the current location is correct, including any prefixes necessary to dial an outside line. (For more information on setting dialing properties and location entries, see Chapter 8.)

- *Your Internet Service Provider's equipment has failed*— If your modem has been able to connect before this attempt, call your ISP's technical support and check to see whether or not its server computer is experiencing a problem.

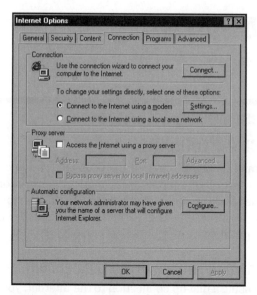

Figure 10.10   Specifying an Internet dial-up or LAN connection within IE4.

Logon Is Refused

If your modem makes the connection but eventually disconnects with an error message, one of these problems may be the culprit:

- *You are using incorrect user/password information*—Again, check the Connection pane of the Internet Options dialog box. Make sure that you've entered the correct user and password that your ISP gave you. Remember that asterisks always mask the password for security purposes. (For more information on dial-up networking, see Chapter 8.)

- *The wrong network protocol is specified*—Display the properties for the dial-up connection you're using and then click on the Server Types tab to display the network protocols you've assigned—make sure that TCP/IP is checked. (For more information on setting network protocols, see Chapter 8.)

- *An encrypted password is required/not required*—Display the properties for the dial-up connection you're using and then click on the Server Types tab to display the Advanced options for this connection. If your ISP doesn't require an encrypted password, make sure the Require Encrypted Password checkbox is disabled; enable it if an encrypted password is requested. (For more information on setting network protocols, see Chapter 8.)

Internet Explorer 4 Reports DNS Failure

**Internet
Explorer 4
Reports DNS
Failure**

If IE4 runs but cannot access any Web sites, check these possible problems:

- *The TCP/IP settings are incorrect*—Display the properties for the dial-up connection you're using, click on the Server Types tab, and then click on the TCP/IP Settings button. If your ISP provided you with primary and secondary DNS numbers, make sure that they're entered into the correct fields. (For more information on configuring TCP/IP settings, see Chapter 8.)

- *Your ISP's equipment has failed*—If you have previously been able to access sites with IE4 (using the same settings) but you cannot connect now, call your ISP's technical support and check to see whether or not its server computer is experiencing a problem.

- *You have typed in an incorrect or incomplete URL*—If IE4 can display a common page like **www.yahoo.com** but can't display the URL you're typing in, the address is probably wrong (or the target Web server is experiencing problems). Try to access the URL again later.

Related solutions:	Found in:
Configuring Dialing Properties	Chapter 8
Adding A Dial-Up Networking Connection	Chapter 8
Dialing A Dial-Up Networking Connection	Chapter 8
Configuring Settings For An Internet Dial-Up Connection	Chapter 8
Using A Dial-Up Script	Chapter 8

Internet Explorer 4 Does Not Load Graphics Or Multimedia

**Internet
Explorer 4
Does Not
Load
Graphics Or
Multimedia**

If IE4 loads a page but doesn't display graphics or play multimedia files, one of these problems may be to blame:

- *Graphics and multimedia are turned off*—Check the Advanced pane of the Internet Options dialog box to see if one or all of the multimedia options have been disabled.

- *The image file is corrupted or nonexistent*—If the image or multimedia file called by the Web page doesn't exist on the Web server (or if it's corrupted and won't load properly), IE4 cannot display/play it.

- *You need a plug-in*—You may need to install a proprietary plug-in to view or hear certain multimedia file formats.

- *The server is heavily loaded*—If you're connected to a particularly popular Web server, it may be sluggish and take longer to load files. Your only alternative is to wait!

Hyperlinks Or Text Do Not Appear On Web Pages

Hyperlinks Or Text Do Not Appear On Web Pages

If IE4 loads a page but doesn't display hyperlinks or text, one of these problems may be to blame:

- *Underline links is turned off*—Check the Advanced pane of the Internet Options dialog box to see if Underline Links has been set to Never. If this is the situation, turn on the Underline Links option.

- *Background and text colors are set to the same color*—If you have configured IE4 to override the text or background color for a Web page, it's possible that both the background and text colors are currently set to the same color. You may need to change your configuration and allow the Web page to display its own colors before you can see the links.

- *There is an HTML page error*—The author may have improperly coded the Web page. Try loading another page to see whether the problem disappears.

Pages Take Minutes To Load (Or IE4 Stops Completely)

Pages Take Minutes To Load (Or IE4 Stops) Completely

If IE4 takes an inordinate amount of time loading a page (or stops completely and appears to lock up), check the following potential problems:

- *The server is heavily loaded*—If you're connected to a particularly popular Web server, it may be sluggish and take longer to load pages. Consider calling during the off hours of midnight to 8 am.

- *The dial-up connection is slow*—Your modem may have negotiated a slower connection, like 24Kbps or 26.4Kbps, for this Web session. Check the speed of your connection by resting your mouse pointer on top of the dial-up icon in the Taskbar. If your modem is slower than your typical speed, disconnect and redial.

- *Your ISP's equipment has failed*—If the sluggish behavior continues, call your ISP's technical support and check to see whether or not its server computer is experiencing a problem.

A Hyperlink Returns An Error

If you click on a link and receive only an error message, you may be experiencing one of these problems:

- *The hyperlink target has moved*—The target file or Web page may have been moved to another server. If this is the case, you cannot follow the link.

- *The server has been disconnected*—The Web server hosting the link target may be offline for backup or maintenance, or it may be locked up—try connecting again at a later time.

- *There is an HTML page error*—The page's author may have typed the hyperlink incorrectly. If this is the case, you cannot follow the link.

Using Windows 98 Disk Compression

In Brief

Want to easily tell how long a person has been using computers? Ask how much space his or her newly installed business application, utility program, or game takes up on the hard drive: If the person has been using computers for at least two or three years, you'll get a disgusted shake of the head and a complaint about how programs used to take up 10MB of space. "Now anything I install on my PC takes up at least 100MB!"

It's true—even the smallest programs written for Windows 98 often feature some sort of animation, stereo sound, or music. The latest and greatest games typically feature digital video and digitized speech that can occupy literally hundreds of megabytes of hard drive territory. If you're lucky and you've bought a PC within the last few months, it probably has anywhere from 4GB to 12GB of hard drive storage. However, if you're working with an older hard drive of less than 1GB, you'll probably need to keep an eye on your drive's total capacity to make sure you can install that next program.

If your hard drive is running out of space, Windows 98 allows you to clean up temporary files. You can also uninstall programs to make room for new applications or spend several hundred dollars to replace your existing hard drive (or add it as a secondary drive). However, the best solution for a hard drive that suffers from chronically low amounts of free space is *disk compression*. Windows 98 provides you with a program called DriveSpace 3 that can compress the contents of a hard drive, providing up to twice the original space of the uncompressed drive.

Within Windows 98, a compressed drive is treated exactly like an uncompressed drive, so you don't need to make any changes to your applications or data. If you're using a PC with a Pentium-class processor, you should notice little or no delay in running compressed programs or accessing data on compressed drives.

TIP: *Disk compression has actually been around since the days of DOS 6 and 6.22. Older disk compression utilities, however, were slower, took more resources, and weren't very well-integrated with DOS or Windows 3.x. It was easier to lose data and harder to access compressed drives (especially removable media)—and you had to use special utilities to scan your disk or defragment your compressed drives. DriveSpace 3 has eliminated all that. All of the disk utilities and applications provided with Windows 98 automatically recognize and use compressed drives.*

This chapter is devoted to DriveSpace 3 disk compression—
how to safely compress a drive, how to adjust compression
settings, how to mount and unmount a compressed drive, and
how to diagnose problems that may arise when you are using a
compressed drive.

Immediate Solutions

Compressing A Drive The Right Way

DriveSpace 3 can create compressed drives with up to a 2GB capacity from an uncompressed drive. There are two methods of compressing a disk:

- *Compress the entire drive, including existing data.* If you choose to compress your entire original drive, you'll have a drive with approximately double the capacity and that still holds your existing data. If you decide to compress the entire drive, the compression process outlined in the next section will take much longer than if you simply compress your free space (because DriveSpace 3 must also compress your programs and data). Keep in mind that some Windows 98 applications cannot run from a compressed drive.

- *Compress the free space on your drive to create a new empty drive.* Using this method, the data on the original drive remains uncompressed (as I said previously, some Windows 98 applications cannot run from a compressed drive), but the free space on the original drive becomes a brand new compressed drive with approximately double the space.

TIP: Before compressing anything, MAKE SURE that the data on the drive you're compressing has been completely backed up! A good backup is essential. Although the compression process is automatic and reasonably foolproof—it can even be interrupted by a power failure without losing any data—only a full backup can ensure that your data is safe in case of catastrophic error.

DriveSpace 3 has limitations, however. You can't compress hard drives that have been converted to FAT32, nor can you create a new compressed drive with the free space on a removable media drive. However, DriveSpace 3 is reasonably backward-compatible, so if you have compressed floppies, Zip disks, or Jaz disks using DoubleSpace or an earlier version of DriveSpace, Windows 98 should be able to read them (or you can upgrade them, as I'll discuss later in this chapter).

Compressing An Entire Drive With Data

To compress an entire drive on your Windows 98 system with DriveSpace 3, follow these steps:

1. Click on Start|Programs|Accessories|System Tools and then click on DriveSpace. The DriveSpace 3 opening screen appears, as shown in Figure 11.1. The screen displays all of the current compressed and uncompressed drives on your system.

2. Click on the drive you want to compress and then select Drive|Compress from the menu.

3. DriveSpace 3 displays the very informative Compress A Drive dialog box. It tells you how much free space the selected drive currently has, as well as how much it will have once the process has been completed. Figure 11.2 illustrates an example using the floppy drive A: as the drive to be compressed. (Remember that you can compress floppies and removable media like Zip drives as well.)

4. Click on Options to display the Compression Options dialog box, which presents you with the following three options:

    *   *Drive Letter Of Host Drive*—DriveSpace 3 creates a new drive letter for your uncompressed *host drive*, which contains the compressed data and any uncompressed files that are required to access the data. If you're connected to a network and have a series of network drive letters, make sure to select a drive letter from the drop-down list that is not currently in use.

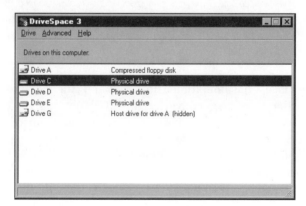

Figure 11.1   DriveSpace 3 displays all of the compressed and uncompressed drives on your system.

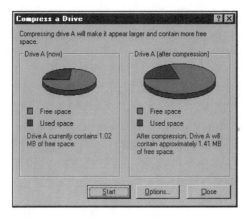

Figure 11.2   *DriveSpace 3 uses pie charts to help you understand how much space you'll save.*

- *Free Space On Host Drive*—You can specify the amount of uncompressed free space that will be available on the host drive after DriveSpace 3 has finished. If you're not compressing your boot drive and your Windows swap file is not located on the compressed drive, you can type "0.0" into this field and dedicate the entire host drive to compressed data.

- *Use DoubleSpace-Compatible Format*—As I mentioned previously, integrated disk compression was also available in DOS 6, 6.22, and Windows 95. If you're going to access any compressed data under any of these operating systems—which used an older version of disk compression called DoubleSpace—then enable this checkbox. If you will read and write compressed data only under Windows 98, leave this box unchecked.

5. Are all options set? If so, click on OK to return to the Compress A Drive dialog box and then click on Start.

6. Windows 98 prompts you for confirmation before beginning the compression process. To begin compressing data, click on Compress Now; to back up the files on the drive before compression (which I highly recommend), click on the Back Up Files button to launch Microsoft Backup or another backup program.

Depending on the number of open files and your Windows 98 properties, DriveSpace 3 may have to reboot your PC to begin the compression process. Once the process begins, the program should

not be interrupted. Depending on the amount of data being compressed and the speed of your computer, the compression process can take anywhere from a few minutes to one or two hours.
(It makes sense to start the DriveSpace 3 compression process to
run unattended during the weekend or on an evening that you'll
be away from your PC.)

After the compression process has completed successfully, DriveSpace 3 reboots your PC back into normal Windows 98
and reports the new amount of free space available on the compressed drive.

Compressing Free Space On An Existing Drive

You can also compress the free space on an existing drive with
DriveSpace 3, creating a new, empty drive. To do so, follow these
steps:

1. Click on Start|Programs|Accessories|System Tools and
   then click on DriveSpace. The DriveSpace 3 opening
   screen appears.

2. Click on the drive that contains the free space you want to
   compress and then select Advanced|Create Empty from
   the menu.

3. By default, Windows 98 uses all of the free space on the
   specified drive to create your new compressed drive. If you
   would like to leave some of the space free and uncompressed on the existing drive, enter a smaller amount in the
   Using field.

4. Click on Start to begin the compression process.

After the compressed drive has been created, DriveSpace 3 reboots
your PC back into normal Windows 98 and reports the new amount
of free space available on your new compressed drive.

Optimizing Compression Settings

The previous sections described how to create compressed drives
with the default DriveSpace 3 settings; however, DriveSpace 3
also offers a variety of compression settings that you can adjust
after you've created a compressed drive. Generally, you can configure your compressed drive to provide either the fastest possible data transfer or even more free space (or you can choose a

setting that operates somewhere in between). In this section, I'll discuss how you can optimize the speed or storage space of your compressed drives.

Understanding Compression Formats

DriveSpace 3 offers four levels of compression:

- *UltraPack compression*—UltraPack format is the compression champion, providing the most free space. However, storing a file in UltraPack format requires you to run Compression Agent as a manual or scheduled task, so UltraPack doesn't appear as a choice for your default DriveSpace 3 compression format.

TIP: *UltraPack compression requires more time to uncompress files than HiPack does, so it's a good idea to use it only for those "archive" files you won't access very often.*

- *HiPack compression*—HiPack compression provides you with an average of about 15 percent more free space than Standard compression, but it requires a faster CPU and more system resources. Microsoft recommends that you use HiPack compression only on a Pentium-based computer.

- *Standard compression*—This is the same level of compression attained with older disk compression software like DoubleSpace and earlier versions of DriveSpace. It's a good compromise between the most possible free space and the fastest possible performance.

- *No compression*—You can actually turn compression off on a compressed drive. Although the drive itself is still compressed, this setting provides the best performance.

Selecting A Default Compression Format

You can select the default level of compression to use from the Advanced menu. To do so, follow these steps:

1. Click on Start|Programs|Accessories|System Tools|DriveSpace.

2. Click on Advanced|Settings from the menu to display the Disk Compression Settings dialog box, shown in Figure 11.3.

3. Click on the compression option that best fits your preferences for better performance or more free space on the compressed drive. You have the following four choices:

Figure 11.3   Configuring global settings for DriveSpace 3.

- *HiPack Compression*—If you have a fast Pentium or Pentium II PC and you'd like to obtain as much free space as possible from your compressed drives, select this method as your default. Windows 98 and DriveSpace 3 work together to compress your files automatically "behind the scenes." Also, the data is uncompressed automatically when a program calls for it.

- *Standard Compression*—Pick this compression method to achieve the most free space with the best possible performance. Once again, files are compressed and uncompressed automatically as they're written to disk and accessed by other programs.

- *No Compression, Unless Drive Is At Least n% Full*—This is a good setting for those PC owners who want the best possible performance but would like DriveSpace 3 to begin compressing files when their hard drive is almost full. If you pick this option, DriveSpace 3 leaves all files uncompressed until your drive reaches the threshold you specify in the % Full field; when this threshold is reached, DriveSpace 3 begins to apply Standard compression.

- *No Compression (Fastest)*—For those PC owners with plenty of free space, this option leaves all files uncompressed for the best possible performance with the fastest file transfer time.

4. Click on OK to save your default compression method and return to the DriveSpace 3 main screen.

Configuring Compression Agent

Compression Agent is a stand-alone program that allows you to apply all forms of compression (including the UltraPack compression format) to specific files on your drive. You can also use Compression Agent to convert files from UltraPack back to HiPack compression.

The Agent can be run manually, or you can schedule it with Task Scheduler to run unattended; the Windows 98 Tune-Up Wizard can also schedule Compression Agent to run at regular intervals. (You'll find more information on Task Scheduler in Chapter 9, and Chapter 14 covers the Tune-Up Wizard in depth.)

TIP: *If you like, Compression Agent can also compress those files that you saved with a DriveSpace 3 default of uncompressed. You can, therefore, write new files as uncompressed for best hard drive performance, and then Compression Agent can compress those files for you while you're not using your PC.*

To configure Compression Agent, you must have at least one compressed drive currently active on your system. Follow these steps to configure the Agent:

1. Click on Start|Programs|Accessories|System Tools|
   Compression Agent. The Agent displays the information
   screen, shown in Figure 11.4. It provides approximate
   figures for the amount of free space provided by UltraPack,
   HiPack, and no compression.

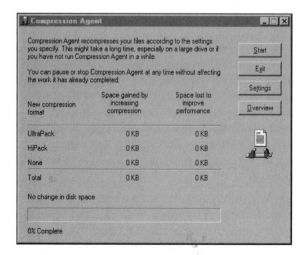

Figure 11.4   The Compression Agent information screen.

2. Click on Settings to display the Compression Agent Settings dialog box.

3. Select the files you would like to compress with UltraPack. You have three options:

   - *Do Not Use UltraPack*—If space is not a concern on your system and you'd prefer better performance, select this option; Compression Agent does not compress any files using the UltraPack method.

   - *UltraPack All Files*—This is the option to select if you need every possible byte squeezed out of your com- pressed drive. Compression Agent applies UltraPack compression to every file. Avoid this option if you're running Windows 98 on a PC with an 80486 CPU—your computer doesn't have the speed to decompress these files without a noticeable delay.

   - *UltraPack Only Those Files Not Used In n Days*—Use this option to apply UltraPack compression to rarely used files; for example, data files for last year's income taxes or clipart that you don't use very often. If you select this option, you can enter the number of days as the threshold. Any executable files that you haven't run or data files that an application hasn't accessed in at least that many days will be compressed.

4. Next, specify whether remaining files that are not com- pressed with UltraPack should be compressed with HiPack. If you select Yes, you'll achieve better compression; if you select No, you'll enjoy the fastest possible performance. As a rule, if you need additional space, pick Yes. If you have plenty of free space, select No.

5. Do you need to exclude any files from compression or use a different type of compression? If so, click on the Exceptions button and then click on Add. Compression Agent allows you to browse and select files, folders, and files with a certain extension that should be compressed using a different method. Click on OK when you've added all files, folders, and extensions that should be excluded.

TIP: *Generally, there's no need to exclude application executable files from HiPack compression if your PC is a Pentium running at 166MHz or faster. However, it's usually a bad idea to use UltraPack compression on application executable files; it simply takes your PC too long to prepare and launch a program compressed with UltraPack.*

---

6. If you want, you can also set a minimum threshold for applying UltraPack compression. Click on the Advanced button and then specify a minimum amount (in megabytes) in the Do Not Reduce Any File's Compression Level If There Is Less Than x Mb Of Free Disk Space field. If this threshold is reached, Compression Agent does not automatically reduce UltraPack compression to HiPack format. To completely disable the reduction feature within Compression Agent, enable the Leave All UltraPacked Files In UltraPack Format field. Doing so ensures that all Ultra-Packed files remain in UltraPack format. Click on OK to accept your settings.

7. Enable the Save These Settings As The New Default Settings checkbox. Compression Agent uses the settings you've specified each time it runs.

8. Click on OK to exit the Compression Agent Settings dialog box and return to the Compression Agent display screen.

You can now run Compression Agent by clicking on the Start button, or you can use Task Scheduler or the Windows 98 Tune-Up Wizard to schedule Compression Agent to run at regular intervals.

Uncompressing A Drive

If you add a new, larger hard drive to your system, you may find yourself with plenty of space and no need for disk compression. As long as a compressed drive has enough free space to hold all of the data, you can uncompress it for maximum performance. To do so, follow these steps:

1. Click on Start|Programs|Accessories|System Tools and click on DriveSpace. The DriveSpace 3 opening screen appears.

2. Click on the compressed drive you want to uncompress and then select Drive|Uncompress from the menu.

3. Windows 98 prompts you for confirmation before beginning the decompression process. To back up the files on the drive before uncompressing them (a very good idea), click on the Back Up Files button to launch Microsoft Backup or another backup program.

4. Click on Start to begin the decompression process.

After the drive has been decompressed, DriveSpace 3 reboots your PC back into normal Windows 98.

Adjusting The Size Of A Compressed Drive

In most circumstances, your host drive actually has no uncompressed free space available at all; it is completely dedicated to the compressed volume file that holds the data for the compressed drive. However, from time to time, you may need to adjust the ratio of free space from a compressed drive to its host drive. For example, you may need additional uncompressed space on the host drive for holding real-mode drivers used during system startup; if this uncompressed space is not available, a specific application may not run on a compressed drive.

DriveSpace 3 allows you to control how much free space is allocated to both drives through an easy-to-use slider control. Follow these steps to adjust the free space available on a compressed drive:

1. Click on Start|Programs|Accessories|System Tools and then click on DriveSpace. The DriveSpace 3 opening screen appears.

2. Click on the compressed drive you want to resize and then select Drive|Adjust Free Space. DriveSpace 3 displays the Adjust Free Space dialog box, shown in Figure 11.5.

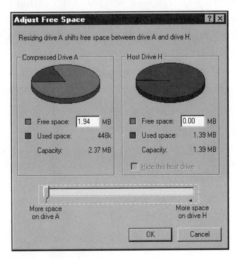

Figure 11.5   Adjusting the free space available on a compressed drive.

3. Click on and drag the slider control at the bottom of the dialog box in the direction of the drive that should receive more space. DriveSpace 3 automatically updates the pie chart to reflect your change; the values for Free Space, Used Space, and Capacity also change for both drives.

4. When you're satisfied with the distribution of free space between the two drives, click on OK.

Depending on the amount of free space you're adding, DriveSpace 3 may have to defragment your compressed drive—it starts the Disk Defragmenter program automatically.

Adjusting The Compression Ratio

You may know that some types of data and executable files can be compressed to a higher degree than others. For example, database files are usually highly compressible, whereas many image file formats have built-in compression and do not shrink very much when compressed. Because of these variances in the compression ratio, DriveSpace 3 can only estimate the actual amount of free space remaining on a compressed drive—the program has no idea what type of files you'll add to the drive and how well they'll compress.

If your compressed drive holds a large number of files that don't match the default compression ratio of 2 to 1, Windows 98 could conceivably run out of free space (even though it has reported that there is enough room to save a file). In such a case, you could run into problems in your applications or even disk errors like lost clusters or cross-linked files. Luckily, ScanDisk can recognize and repair errors on compressed drives, so you can recover from such disk problems.

To prevent such difficulties from happening, DriveSpace 3 allows you to adjust the estimated compression ratio for a specific compressed drive. You can set a more realistic ratio, and the amount of free space reported will be more accurate. To adjust the compression ratio, follow these steps:

1. Click on Start|Programs|Accessories|System Tools and then click on DriveSpace. The DriveSpace 3 opening screen appears.

2. Click on the compressed drive you want to adjust and then select Advanced|Change Ratio from the menu. DriveSpace 3 displays the Compression Ratio dialog box. The top ratio is the actual compression ratio calculated by DriveSpace 3; if your compressed drive currently contains a representative mix of file types that you'll use in the future, use this value as your estimate of the compression ratio.

3. Click on and drag the slider control at the bottom of the dialog box in the correct direction (the left side is a ratio of 1 to 1, whereas the right side of the slider control is 64 to 1). Alternately, you can simply click on the Estimated field and type in the number directly.

4. When you're finished and the estimated ratio is correct, click on OK.

Mounting And Unmounting Compressed Drives

Unlike an uncompressed drive, a compressed volume file (or CVF) must be mounted (or activated) for Windows 98 to recognize it (*mounting* is an old mainframe computer term that refers to loading a tape or disk unit into a drive when requested by a program). Until you mount a compressed drive, your PC cannot read data from or write data to that drive.

Windows 98 automatically mounts all fixed compressed disk drives, but not removable media drives. You can configure Windows 98 to automatically mount all removable media compressed drives, or you can mount removable compressed drives manually.

Mounting Compressed Drives Automatically

To configure Windows 98 for automatic mounting, follow these steps:

1. Click on Start|Programs|Accessories|System Tools and then click on DriveSpace.

2. Select Advanced|Settings from the menu to display the Disk Compression Settings dialog box (refer to Figure 11.4).

3. Enable the Automatically Mount New Compressed Drives checkbox.

4. Click on OK to return to the DriveSpace 3 menu.

Mounting Compressed Drives Manually

To mount a compressed fixed disk drive or removable media drive manually, follow these steps:

1. Click on Start|Programs|Accessories|System Tools and then click on DriveSpace.

2. Click on the drive you would like to mount and then select Advanced|Mount from the menu. DriveSpace 3 displays a confirmation message when the process has completed.

3. Click on OK to return to the DriveSpace 3 menu.

Unmounting Compressed Drives Manually

To unmount a compressed fixed disk drive or removable media drive manually, follow these steps:

1. Click on Start|Programs|Accessories|System Tools and then click on DriveSpace.

2. Click on the drive you would like to unmount and then select Advanced|Unmount from the menu. DriveSpace 3 displays a confirmation message when the process has completed.

3. Click on OK to return to the DriveSpace 3 menu.

Formatting A Drive

If necessary, you can format a compressed drive; doing so erases all files and data, just like traditional formatting clears an uncom-0pressed drive. To format a compressed drive and remove all of its contents in a single step, follow these steps:

1. Click on Start|Programs|Accessories|System Tools and then click on DriveSpace. The DriveSpace 3 opening screen appears.

TIP: Remember that you need to mount compressed drives, including compressed removable media drives, before you can read or format them.

2. Click on the compressed drive you want to adjust and then select Drive|Format from the menu.

3. DriveSpace prompts you for confirmation before formatting. Click on Yes to begin the process or No to cancel the operation without formatting the drive.

Upgrading A Compressed Drive

As I mentioned previously in this chapter, DriveSpace 3 can read compressed disks created by older versions of DriveSpace, as well as by the DoubleSpace compression system used by DOS 6 and 6.22. The DriveSpace 3 Standard compression format is the same as the format these older compression utilities used.

However, the HiPack and UltraPack formats are not compatible with these older utilities. Therefore, you must upgrade compressed removable media drives created with DoubleSpace and older versions of DriveSpace before you can apply HiPack or UltraPack compression to them. For this reason, DriveSpace 3 provides an Upgrade function. To upgrade a compressed drive created with an older compression utility, follow these steps:

1. If necessary, load the compressed drive. The drive must be mounted before you can upgrade it.

2. Click on Start|Programs|Accessories|System Tools and then click on DriveSpace. The DriveSpace 3 opening screen appears.

3. Click on the compressed drive you want to adjust and then select Drive|Upgrade from the menu. DriveSpace 3 displays a completion message when the upgrade process is finished.

Troubleshooting

Troubleshooting Compression Problems

Although disk compression under Windows 98 is as nearly fool-proof as possible, plenty of problems can still occur. The trouble-shooting tips in this section may help you solve some of the errors that might arise with compressed disks.

WARNING! Do not attempt to modify or edit a DriveSpace 3 compressed volume file. Any change you make to a CVF is likely to result in lost data (or even the loss of the entire compressed drive)—for this reason, Windows 98 treats compressed volume files with the file attributes Read-Only, Hidden, and System. You can, however, use ScanDisk to check compressed drives for errors as well as safely repair them.

Windows Cannot Create The MSDOSSYS.TMP File

If you're compressing your C: drive and DriveSpace 3 returns an error that it cannot create the MSDOSSYS.TMP file, one of these problems may be the culprit:

- *More than 512 files are in the root directory.* DriveSpace 3 can't create the temporary files necessary to complete the compression process; you've reached the maximum number of files allowed in your root directory. Delete several files that you don't need from your C: root directory and try the compression step again.

- *The drive is out of space.* DriveSpace 3 doesn't have enough free disk space to create the necessary temporary files. Delete any programs and data files that you don't need and try again.

ScanDisk Returns Drive Error Messages

If you receive an error message telling you to run ScanDisk when you are compressing a drive, creating a new drive, uncompressing a drive, or upgrading a drive, consider the following possible problems:

- *There is a disk error.* The drive may have lost clusters or cross-linked files; allow ScanDisk to repair these errors before you continue.

Windows Cannot Create The MSDOSSYS.TMP File

ScanDisk Returns Drive Error Messages

- *The path name is too long.* The drive may contain a folder that has a path with more than 66 characters; DriveSpace 3 can't handle such a folder when you're compressing a drive, creating a new drive, uncompressing a drive, or upgrading a drive. You must locate any folders on the drive with path names longer than 66 characters and relocate them to another drive using Explorer (or move them to another location on the same drive, as long as the pathname is shorter than 66 characters). After the DriveSpace 3 function is completed, you can return the folders to their original location.

Windows 98
Cannot
Read A
Compressed
Drive

Windows 98 Cannot Read A Compressed Drive

If Windows 98 doesn't display a drive letter for a compressed, fixed, or removable drive, check for these possible problems:

- *The drive is not mounted.* Windows 98 can't access a compressed drive until it has been mounted (including floppies and removable media drives). To mount a drive, follow the instructions in the "Mounting And Unmounting Compressed Drives" section earlier in this chapter.

- *Changes were made to the CVF.* If you've edited or modified the compressed volume file on the host drive, it may be impossible to read data from the compressed drive.

- *Surface errors are on the host drive.* Restart your PC and use your emergency disk. After your computer has finished booting, run a thorough scan on all drives and repair any errors with the following command line:

```
scandisk /all
```

- *The DBLSPACE.BIN file is missing.* Restart your PC, press F8 to display the Startup menu, and then select Safe Mode Command Prompt Only. Create a new file by typing in these two commands and then rebooting your PC:

```
attrib -s -h -r drvspace.bin
copy drvspace.bin dblspace.bin
```

DriveSpace 3
Does Not
Compress
A Drive

DriveSpace 3 Does Not Compress A Drive

If DriveSpace 3 refuses to compress a drive, one of these problems is the likely cause:

- *The drive has been converted to FAT32.* DriveSpace 3 can recognize a drive using FAT32, but it can't convert the drive. Unfortunately, FAT32 can't be converted back to FAT16, so there's really nothing that you can do.

- *The drive has already been compressed.* If the drive has been compressed with DoubleSpace or an earlier version of DriveSpace, you can't compress it—however, you can upgrade the drive to DriveSpace 3.

- *The drive uses removable media.* DriveSpace 3 does not allow you to create a new compressed drive with the free space on a removable media drive; you can, however, compress the entire removable media drive.

Compressed Drive Is Out Of Space

If a compressed drive has run out of free space (whether it still reports free space remaining or not), check these possible problems:

- *The compression ratio is incorrect.* Follow the instructions in the "Adjusting The Compression Ratio" section earlier in this chapter to adjust the compression ratio for the compressed drive; if the ratio is too high, Windows 98 estimates too much free space on the drive.

- *Compression Agent is not using UltraPack.* If Compression Agent automatically converts UltraPack files into HiPack format, the amount of free space will shrink (and can actually run out when you attempt to save a file). Follow the instructions in the "Configuring Compression Agent" section earlier in this chapter to configure Compression Agent for UltraPack compression.

Compressed Drive Is Out Of Space

Chapter 12

Optimizing Windows 98 Virtual Memory

In Brief

In the previous chapter, I discussed how to compress your hard drive real estate to make more room for today's monster Windows applications—however, that's only half of the solution. Today's applications also crave memory... and although RAM prices have plummeted over the last few years, most of us still can't boast that we have 64 or 128MB to use with programs like Adobe Photoshop or AutoCAD.

If an application needs more system RAM than your PC can provide, Windows 98 comes to the rescue with *virtual memory*. Rather than storing data in RAM, the data is temporarily stored on your hard drive until the program needs it. If you recall the days of DOS programs (and how you constantly had to juggle high memory, extended memory, and expanded memory), you know that a virtually unlimited pool of system memory is a *very* good thing.

By default, Windows 98 handles virtual memory automatically, but allowing Windows 98 to take care of things by itself isn't always the best choice. Depending on your Windows applications, the amount of physical RAM you've installed in your PC, and the speed of your hard drive, you may be able to manually configure your virtual memory for even better performance.

In this chapter, you will optimize the virtual memory system within Windows 98 and learn how to solve problems stemming from insufficient memory or mismanaged virtual memory.

Immediate Solutions

Understanding Virtual Memory

Windows 98 can allocate virtual memory automatically—in fact, quite a bit of activity is going on behind the scenes as you use Windows 98, and much of it is due to your computer's constantly changing requirements for memory. As applications and operating system tasks require more memory, Windows 98 dynamically expands the size of the virtual memory buffer—or *swapfile*—on your hard drive. As you close these applications and finish these tasks, your PC needs less virtual memory, and the swapfile shrinks to provide you with more free hard drive space.

TIP: *The Windows 98 swapfile is named WIN386.SWP, and you'll find it in the root directory of the drive where you installed Windows 98. If you do allow Windows 98 to manage virtual memory for you, make sure that the drive where this file is stored has plenty of free space so that the file can expand as necessary.*

To check your swapfile settings, follow these steps:

1. Right-click on My Computer and then choose Properties from the menu. The System Properties dialog box appears.

2. Click on the Performance tab and then click on the Virtual Memory button to display the Virtual Memory dialog box, shown in Figure 12.1.

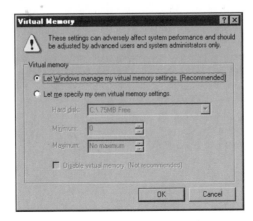

Figure 12.1 *Displaying virtual memory settings under Windows 98.*

There are three modes for virtual memory use:

- *Let Windows Manage My Virtual Memory Settings (Recommended)*—This is the correct selection for most computers running Windows 98. The operating system will dynamically expand and contract the swapfile whenever necessary, providing you with practically unlimited virtual memory.

- *Let Me Specify My Own Virtual Memory Settings*—In the Hard Disk field, you can select the drive where your system swapfile will be stored. In the Minimum and Maximum checkboxes, you can select the minimum and maximum swapfile sizes.

- *Disable Virtual Memory (Not Recommended)*—Because Windows 98 requires 16MB of memory all by itself—before you start to load those memory-hungry applications—disabling virtual memory is almost certain to slow your PC down and render it incapable of running most programs. I use this setting only when debugging memory handling within a Windows application.

3. Click on OK to close the Virtual Memory dialog box and then click on OK to close the System Properties dialog box.

I recommend you allow Windows 98 to handle virtual memory if your PC meets the following minimum criteria:

- At least 200MB of free hard drive space

- At least 32MB of system RAM

- A hard drive with an access time of less than 12 milliseconds connected to a PCI or SCSI hard drive controller

Specifying Custom Virtual Memory Settings

"OK, Mark, you've told me that Windows 98 should be allowed to manage its own virtual memory—why should I consider taking manual control by specifying my own virtual memory settings?" Once again, there are exceptions to the rule. In any of the following situations, you'll probably be better off specifying your own settings:

- *You have less than 32MB of RAM.* If your PC has less than 32MB of system RAM, Windows 98 will be constantly resizing your swapfile. Although nothing is inherently wrong with constant swapfile activity, it eats system resources and can put additional wear and tear on your hard drive. Moreover, your PC will be spending a lot of time managing your swapfile, which causes the overall performance of Windows 98 to suffer.

- *Your hardware is slow.* If your PC has a slower file *subsystem* (a fancy way of referring to both your hard drive and your hard drive controller), any long period of virtual memory activity will slow down your PC. By a "slower" file subsystem, I refer to a hard drive with an access time of 13 milliseconds or higher, or a PC with an ISA hard drive controller instead of a PCI controller.

- *Your hard drive space is tight.* If your PC's hard drives are very close to full, Windows 98 will not be able to expand the swapfile very much—but it will continue to try, which impacts the performance of your computer.

In the following section, I will demonstrate how you can adjust your virtual memory settings to make the best of all three of these situations. Each situation offers a different insight into how virtual memory works, and how you can sometimes do a better job managing it than Windows 98 can.

Optimizing Virtual Memory: Less Than 32MB Of RAM

If your PC has less than 32MB of system RAM, I recommend first that you upgrade your machine to at least 32MB. Windows 98 runs much more efficiently and your system will respond faster if you give the operating system some additional elbowroom. Memory is much less expensive than it used to be, and anyone with a basic knowledge of computer assembly can easily install RAM.

Until then, however, follow these steps to adjust your virtual memory settings and reduce the wear and tear on your hard drive:

1. Right-click on My Computer and then choose Properties from the menu. The System Properties dialog box appears.

2. Click on the Performance tab and then click on the Virtual Memory button to display the Virtual Memory dialog box (refer to Figure 12.1).

3. Click on the Let Me Specify My Own Virtual Memory Settings option.

4. Select a hard drive on your system with at least 100MB of free space (if you have more than one drive with that much free space, choose the drive with the fastest access time).

5. Click on the Minimum scrolling list and then select 64MB.

6. Click on the Maximum scrolling list and then select No Maximum.

7. Click on OK to close the Virtual Memory dialog box and then click on OK to close the System Properties dialog box.

In this situation, your goal is to minimize the amount of dynamic swapfile resizing that Windows 98 requires, which will optimize your PC's performance. To do so, you specified a minimum size for the swapfile. Windows 98 will never shrink the swapfile below this value, so your swapfile is always ready to "take up the slack" until you can upgrade your PC with more RAM.

Note, however, that you did *not* select a maximum value, so the operating system can expand the swapfile to accommodate programs that require even more memory.

TIP: *Although the minimum of 64MB will work in most situations, you may need to adjust your minimum virtual memory size before it works perfectly. I recommend starting with 64MB. If Windows 98 is still slowing down or running out of memory, experiment and increase the minimum figure until the problems disappear.*

Optimizing Virtual Memory: Slow Hardware

If you're running Windows 98 on an older PC, you may not have a speedy hard drive or high-performance PCI hard drive controller. Consequently, any data that's written to or read from your hard drive can become a potential bottleneck (especially in multitasking situations where your PC is running more than one application at once).

However, you can reduce the impact of slower file transfer speeds on your Windows 98 swapfile by optimizing your virtual memory settings. To do so, follow these steps:

1. Right-click on My Computer and then choose Properties from the menu. The System Properties dialog box appears.

2. Click on the Performance tab and then click on the Virtual Memory button to display the Virtual Memory dialog box.

3. Click on the Let Me Specify My Own Virtual Memory Settings option.

4. Select a hard drive on your system with at least 100MB of free space (if you have more than one drive with that much free space, choose the drive with the fastest access time).

5. Click on the Minimum scrolling list and select 80MB.

6. Click on the Maximum scrolling list and then 80 MB.

7. Click on OK to close the Virtual Memory dialog box and then click on OK to close the System Properties dialog box.

Again, our goal is to minimize the amount of dynamic swapfile resizing that Windows 98 requires, which will reduce the time spent reading and writing through your slower file subsystem. Because both the Minimum and Maximum swapfile sizes are the same, we are (in effect) "disabling" the dynamic resize feature in favor of a larger, static swapfile. Windows 98 will maintain the swapfile at 80MB, which means less disk activity.

TIP: *A swapfile of 80MB should be enough in most situations (especially if you have 32MB or more of system RAM), but you may need to adjust your "static" virtual memory size before it works perfectly. I recommend starting with 80MB; if Windows 98 runs out of virtual memory, experiment and increase the Minimum and Maximum settings until the problems disappear. (Remember that the Minimum and Maximum figures should be the same for this technique to work).*

Optimizing Virtual Memory: Free-Space Restrictions

This third example addresses those running Windows 98 with very little additional hard drive space to spare: For example, if you're running Windows 98 on a laptop. If your PC has less than 50MB of free space remaining after you've installed Windows 98 (or you've been running Windows 98 with such space restrictions for some time), you know that you need to conserve every byte of hard drive territory.

You might consider compressing your hard drive with DriveSpace 3 before you decide to buy a brand new drive (refer to Chapter 11 for full details on disk compression). However, in the meantime, you can follow these steps to reduce the size of your virtual memory swapfile to make sure that it doesn't grow too large:

1. Right-click on My Computer and then choose Properties from the menu. The System Properties dialog box appears.

2. Click on the Performance tab and then click on the Virtual Memory button to display the Virtual Memory dialog box.

3. Click on the Let Me Specify My Own Virtual Memory Settings option.

4. Select the hard drive on your system with the most free space.

5. Click on the Minimum scrolling list and then select 0MB.

6. Click on the Maximum scrolling list and then select a maximum number of megabytes between 32 and 64, depending upon the amount of free space remaining.

7. Click on OK to close the Virtual Memory dialog box and then click on OK to close the System Properties dialog box.

In this case, you're taking control of the virtual memory settings to prevent Windows 98 from allocating too much of your hard drive space to the dynamic swapfile. With these settings, the swapfile is limited to a certain maximum, but it can shrink whenever possible (which will save you additional space).

Of course, this technique will make it harder for you to run larger Windows 98 applications that require huge amounts of system RAM. If, however, you spend the large majority of your time surfing the Internet or answering your email, you can safely reclaim much of the space that would otherwise be dedicated to your swapfile.

TIP: *Although the maximum amount of required system RAM will vary according to the programs you run, you can still experiment and increase the Maximum figure until the problems disappear—you'll simply lose more free space on your hard drive.*

Disabling Virtual Memory

Although Windows 98 will allow you to disable virtual memory entirely, I don't recommend doing so if you intend to run any programs at all. If you need to disable virtual memory for some reason, follow these steps:

1. Right-click on My Computer and then choose Properties from the menu. The System Properties dialog box appears.

2. Click on the Performance tab and then click on the Virtual Memory button to display the Virtual Memory dialog box (refer to Figure 12.1).

3. Click on the Disable Virtual Memory (Not Recommended) checkbox to enable it.

4. Click on OK to close the Virtual Memory dialog box and then click on OK to close the System Properties dialog box.

Adjusting DOS Program Memory Usage

As I mentioned earlier in this chapter, the Windows 98 operating system and its 32-bit applications have all but eliminated the dreaded "Out of Memory" errors that once plagued DOS programs. With virtual memory, your Windows applications can use megabytes of memory that DOS programmers would have thought impossible.

Most of us run at least one or two legacy DOS programs, which means that those memory problems can still crop up. In this section, I will discuss how you can prevent DOS programs from running out of memory within Windows 98.

TIP: *You may be wondering how much memory a specific DOS program requires—if you still have the program's manual, it should list the amount of memory needed. If you don't have the manual, you may need to experiment before you know exactly how much free memory is required in the DOS window for a certain program to operate.*

Adjusting Conventional Memory For DOS Programs

All DOS programs require a certain amount of *conventional* memory, the familiar 640K portion of system RAM that used to be a standard in the IBM world. To adjust the amount of conventional memory that Windows 98 allocates to a DOS program, follow these steps:

1. Click on My Computer and then browse through your system until you have located the desired DOS program.

2. Right-click on the program icon to display the program's Properties dialog box, similar to the example shown in Figure 12.2.

3. Click on the Memory tab to display the Memory pane, similar to the example shown in Figure 12.3.

4. In the Conventional Memory section, click on the Total drop-down list and then select the maximum amount of conventional memory (in kilobytes) the program requires. If you're unsure what this figure is, choose 640K, or select Auto and Windows 98 will attempt to determine the program's memory needs automatically.

5. The DOS program COMMAND.COM, which is invoked to run DOS programs and batch files within Windows, requires a number of bytes of data to be reserved for its own use; this memory allocation represents the DOS *initial environment*. Click on the Initial Environment drop-down list and then select a value; alternately, select Auto and Windows 98 will allocate the amount of memory specified in the **SHELL=** statement within your CONFIG.SYS file.

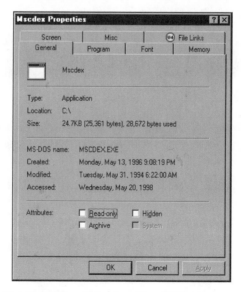

Figure 12.2   The Properties dialog box for a DOS program.

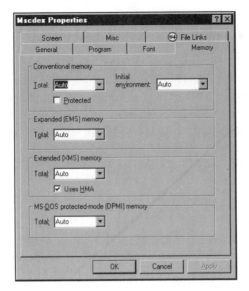

Figure 12.3   Adjusting memory options for a DOS program.

6. In the ancient days of DOS PCs, many DOS programs used
    various programming "tricks" to sidestep or modify system
    memory. These techniques were fine under DOS, but as you
    may imagine, they can cause lockups or other strange behavior
    within Windows 98, and you could potentially lose data within
    other programs. To protect your Windows 98 system memory
    from any DOS-program modification, enable the Protected
    checkbox. (Doing so will cause the program's performance to
    slow slightly, so I recommend you use this setting only in
    situations where a DOS program is causing memory-corrup-
    tion problems throughout the rest of Windows 98.)

7. Click on OK to save your changes and close the program's
    Properties dialog box.

Adjusting Expanded (EMS) And Extended (XMS) Memory For DOS Programs

Expanded and *extended* memory were two "extensions" for conventional memory within DOS; as programs began to demand
much more than 640K, they could call upon expanded and extended memory to store additional data. To adjust the amount of
expanded and extended memory that Windows 98 will allocate to
a DOS program, follow these steps:

1. Click on My Computer and then browse through your
    system until you've located the desired DOS program.

2. Right-click on the program icon to display the program's Properties dialog box.

3. Click on the Memory tab to display the Memory pane.

4. In the Expanded (EMS) Memory section of the Memory pane, click on the Total drop-down list and then select the maximum amount of expanded memory (in kilobytes) the program requires. If you're unsure about how much expanded memory the program requires, choose 2048K or select Auto and Windows 98 will attempt to determine the program's memory needs automatically.

5. In the Extended (XMS) Memory section of the Memory pane, click on the Total drop-down list and then select the maximum amount of extended memory (in kilobytes) the program requires. If you're unsure about how much expanded memory the program requires, choose 4096K or select Auto and Windows 98 will attempt to determine how much extended memory the program needs for you.

6. If the program uses the DOS High Memory Area (usually abbreviated as HMA) to store data, enable the Uses HMA checkbox. (Note that a program can only use the HMA if nothing else is taking up that memory location, and many DOS device drivers and Windows 98 system utilities can claim it during the startup sequence.)

7. Click on OK to save your changes and close the program's Properties dialog box.

Adjusting Protected-Mode (DPMI) Memory For DOS Programs

DOS programs that used DPMI (*DOS Protected-Mode Interface, or just protected-mode*) memory had access to all the RAM in your PC. Older DOS-based, high-resolution games, which may demand that you allocate several megabytes of DPMI memory, are a good example. Follow these steps to adjust DPMI memory:

1. Click on My Computer and then browse through your system until you've located the desired DOS program.

2. Right-click on the program icon to display the program's Properties dialog box.

3. Click on the Memory tab to display the Memory pane.

4. In the MS-DOS Protected-Mode (DPMI) Memory section of the Memory pane, click on the Total drop-down list and then select the maximum amount of DPMI memory (in kilobytes) the program requires. If you're unsure about how much protected-mode memory the program requires, choose 8192K or select Auto and Windows 98 will attempt to determine the program's memory needs automatically.

5. Click on OK to save your changes and close the program's Properties dialog box.

Troubleshooting

Troubleshooting Memory And Swapfile Problems

Memory problems can occur from the moment you turn on your PC, so the tips in this troubleshooting section will refer to errors displayed while you are booting your PC as well as to Windows 98 virtual memory errors.

PC Displays Parity Errors Or Memory Errors While Booting Up

If your PC displays an error message while booting up (usually during the memory test or immediately afterwards), consider these possible problems:

- *Memory is mismatched.* Most PC motherboards require RAM chips of the same speed and type (parity, EDO, or SDRAM). Make sure that your memory chips are compatible before you install them.

- *Memory was installed incorrectly.* Each RAM chip must be firmly seated to make good contact with the motherboard; check each chip to make sure that it is correctly seated and facing the proper direction.

- *Memory is malfunctioning.* Although it's rare for a memory chip to fail, it can happen. If you suspect that one of your RAM boards is bad, take it to a local computer repair shop and let the technicians determine whether you have a bad chip.

- *Your CMOS battery is dead.* Older computers stored the amount of installed memory as a part of your CMOS data. If your CMOS battery fails or your computer loses its CMOS data, you may have to re-enter your RAM specifications.

Windows 98 Reports Low Disk Space On Swapfile Drive

If Windows 98 alerts you to a lack of hard drive space on the drive that contains your virtual memory swapfile, follow the instructions in the "Optimizing Virtual Memory: Free-Space Restrictions" section earlier in this chapter.

PC Displays Parity Errors Or Memory Errors While Booting Up

Windows 98 Reports Low Disk Space On Swapfile Drive

315

Windows 98 Constantly Accesses Your Hard Drive

If you have less than 32MB of RAM and Windows 98 is constantly reading and writing data to your virtual memory swapfile, follow the instructions in the "Optimizing Virtual Memory: Less Than 32MB Of RAM" section earlier in this chapter.

DOS Programs Report Insufficient Conventional Memory

Are your DOS programs requesting more conventional memory when you run them within Windows 98? One of these problems is the likely cause:

- *Windows 98's Conventional Memory setting is set too low.* Follow the instructions in the "Adjusting Conventional Memory For DOS Programs" section earlier in this chapter and specify 640K.

- *Windows 98's Auto Conventional Memory setting is allocating too little memory.* Follow the instructions in the "Adjusting Conventional Memory For DOS Programs" section earlier in this chapter and specify 640K instead of Auto.

- *16-bit driver statements are in CONFIG.SYS.* If your CONFIG.SYS file still loads 16-bit DOS drivers, they're likely taking up conventional memory that could be allocated to your program instead. Refer to Chapter 1 for complete instructions on how to "clean up" your CONFIG.SYS file.

- *16-bit TSRs are loaded in AUTOEXEC.BAT.* Any 16-bit TSR (or *memory-resident*) program loaded into background operation by your AUTOEXEC.BAT program will occupy conventional memory. It may also conflict with Windows 98 or your Windows applications, so I recommend that you remove it. (As an example, many DOS-based, virus-scanning programs were loaded as TSRs that remained in memory for as long as the PC was running.) Refer to Chapter 1 for complete instructions on how to "clean up" your AUTOEXEC.BAT file.

DOS
Programs
Report
Protected-
Mode
Memory
Problems

DOS Programs Report Protected-Mode Memory Problems

If your DOS games return errors indicating problems with protected-mode memory, check these possible problems:

- *Windows 98's DPMI Memory setting is set too low.* Follow the instructions in the "Adjusting Protected-Mode (DPMI) Memory For DOS Programs" section earlier in this chapter and specify 8192K. Try running the DOS program again. If the problem reoccurs, repeat the process and specify a larger amount of DPMI memory until the problem disappears.

- *Windows 98's Auto DPMI Memory setting is allocating too little memory.* Follow the instructions in the "Adjusting Protected-Mode (DPMI) Memory For DOS Programs" section earlier in this chapter and specify 10240K instead of Auto. Try running the DOS program again—if the problem reoccurs, repeat the process and specify a larger amount of DPMI memory until the problem disappears.

Hardware Configuration In Windows 98

In Brief

One of the design advantages of the first IBM PC was its open architecture—unheard of at the time—that allowed you to expand the capabilities of your computer by adding standard expansion cards. Unlike Apple, Atari, and Commodore, whose personal computers were modular, IBM opened the door for new devices and new technology as the PC matured.

Unfortunately, the classic IBM PC has now matured into a computing monster that its original designers could never have imagined in their wildest dreams. Some of the standards that have survived along with it are hopelessly outdated, leading to countless headaches and hardware configuration problems. For example:

• Only four COM ports for serial communications and you can't use COM1 and COM3 at the same time?

• A maximum of only four IDE devices?

• Hard drives limited to 512MB partitions?

Remember those adapter cards? Now they're "arguing" with each other over DMA and IRQ settings. Instead of one or two adapter cards, which the original IBM PC could easily handle, you may very well have five or six in your PC right now!

Before you sell your PC and buy an abacus, don't panic—luckily, newer standards like USB and plug and play are making it easier to connect and configure your hardware. Your old friend Windows 98 helps configure your hardware automatically, whenever possible.

In this chapter, I avoid all the technojargon and confusing acronyms and show you how to use the power of Windows 98 to automate your hardware configuration chores. I'll also discuss how you can add and remove hardware from your PC and—of course—how you can troubleshoot hardware problems and solve them in as little time as possible.

Immediate Solutions

Adding A Device

Windows 98 allows automatic hardware configuration for most peripherals and components that you can add to your PC. Some new peripherals, such as printers or modems, can be detected automatically during the startup sequence. Other devices, such as most adapter cards, require you to run the Add New Hardware Wizard before Windows 98 recognizes them.

We've covered in detail how to install printers (Chapter 7) and modems (Chapter 8), so let's follow the process you will use when adding a device such as a SCSI card, hard drive, or serial card. To do so, follow these steps:

1. Click on Start|Settings.

2. Click on Control Panel to open the Control Panel window and then double-click on the Add New Hardware icon to run the New Hardware Wizard, as shown in Figure 13.1. Close all other Windows applications you might have opened and then click on Next to continue.

3. On the next screen, the Wizard reminds you that your screen may go blank while Windows 98 searches for plug-and-play adapter cards and peripherals. Click on Next to continue.

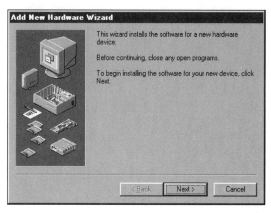

Figure 13.1   The Add New Hardware Wizard's opening screen.

4. After a few seconds, the Wizard reports any new plug-and-play devices that it found that can be installed, as shown in Figure 13.2. At this point, you have two choices of action, depending on what devices were detected:

   • *The device is in the list.* Select the Yes, The Device Is In The List option. Click on the item name and then click on Next to continue. On the last Wizard screen, click on Finish to begin the installation process. (Windows 98 may prompt you to insert your original Windows 98 CD-ROM or the driver disk that came with the device.) You have now added your plug-and-play hardware; you can skip the rest of this section.

   • *The device isn't in the list.* If the device you're installing isn't in the list, Windows 98 can still find it—however, the device doesn't support plug and play, so you'll have to do a little more work. Click on the No, The Device Isn't In The List option and then click on Next to continue.

TIP: *Note that some of these devices may have already been installed, but they may be experiencing problems. You know a problem exists if the icon next to the device name has a yellow exclamation point or a red checkmark on it. The Wizard displays these malfunctioning parts because you can often re-install the specific device within the Wizard to solve the problem.*

---

5. The Wizard now prompts you to choose between an automatic search for your new hardware and a manual search through a list. In most cases, I recommend that you select Yes and allow Windows 98 to search for new hardware.

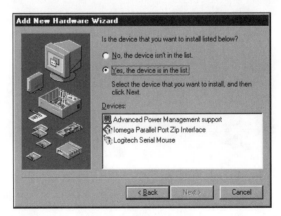

Figure 13.2   Displaying new plug-and-play devices within Windows 98.

However, if you've already tried an automatic search and it didn't locate the new device, you should try again and select your new hardware from a list as described in Step 6.

6. *If you selected the automatic search method*—The Wizard warns you that the search process may take several minutes on older PCs; however, a progress bar is displayed to let you know how the search is progressing. If your PC freezes or locks up for several minutes during the process, you can reboot the system by pressing the Alt, Control, and Delete keys at the same time. Then try selecting your hardware from a list. Click on Next to continue.

   If you select your hardware from a list—The Wizard displays a scrolling list of hardware categories. Click on the correct category to select it (for example, Mouse or CD-ROM Drive) and then click on Next to continue.

7. *If you selected the automatic search method*—After Windows 98 has completed the search, you can display a list of the devices it found. If your new device was found and it appears in the Detected list, click on Finish to complete the process. If your new device was *not* found, click on Cancel, and start this process over at Step 1; when you reach Step 5, click on the No, I Want To Select The Hardware From A List option and continue.

   If you select your hardware from a list—The Wizard builds a device database and displays the make and model screen shown in Figure 13.3. If the device is a brand new model, the manufacturer should include a driver compatible with

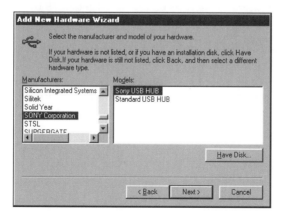

Figure 13.3   Selecting a new hardware device manually from a list.

Windows 98. If you have a Windows 3.1 or Windows 95 driver on disk, you can also try the older driver. Click on Have Disk to browse your system and load the driver. If you have no driver software at all, pick the correct manufacturer and select the closest model to yours. For example, if you're installing a model 670 and it doesn't have a driver entry, try the model 650 or 680. Click on Next to confirm your selection and finish the process.

Windows 98 may require you to reboot your PC before the new hardware can be activated.

Changing Device Properties

As with files, folders, and programs, Windows 98 assigns a number of properties to each hardware device within your PC. Some of these properties enable or disable certain features available on the device—for example, the Autoinsert notification setting for CD-ROM drives. Others control the hardware resources allocated to that device. You may find yourself using these options often at the request of a technical support person or your network system administrator.

In this section, I demonstrate how to display and change the feature settings for a typical device under Windows 98—in this case, a CD recorder. To do so, follow these steps:

1. Right-click on My Computer and select Properties to display the System Properties dialog box, then click on the Device Manager tab to display the Device Manager pane, as shown in Figure 13.4.

2. Click on the plus sign next to the entry for the correct device category to expand the branch and display the corresponding devices. (For our example, you would click on the CDROM entry.)

3. Click on the device you want to change to highlight it. If your device appears in the Device Manager list with a yellow exclamation point or a red checkmark, you may have a conflict with another device. The other device may also have a yellow exclamation point next to it.

4. Click on Properties to display the Properties dialog box, as shown in Figure 13.5, and then click on the General tab. The

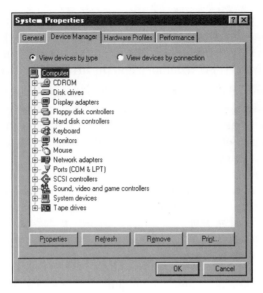

Figure 13.4   Displaying the categories for hardware devices.

General pane usually lists the manufacturer, the hardware version, and device status, so you can quickly tell whether this particular device is working properly.

5. From time to time, you may need to update a device driver with a new version to add new functionality or to correct driver problems. To do so, click on the Driver tab and then

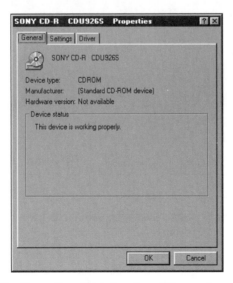

Figure 13.5   The Properties dialog box for a CD recorder.

click on Update Driver to check for newer drivers for the device; Windows 98 launches the Update Device Drivers Wizard. The Driver pane also displays the driver manufacturer, the version number, and the driver's file date.

6. As you might have guessed, most of the settings you can change appear on the Settings pane. Every type of hardware device has a different list of settings, so there is no one generic Settings pane. Figure 13.6 shows a typical Settings pane for a SCSI CD recorder.

WARNING! *If a device is currently working fine, there's no reason to modify any settings unless you have a specific need to change something. I strongly recommend that you resist the temptation to experiment with hardware settings because any change you make here will probably alter the behavior of that device under Windows 98 (usually for the worse).*

7. When you have made the required changes to the device settings, click on OK to exit the device's Properties dialog box and then click on OK to exit the System Properties dialog box. If you made any changes, you must reboot Windows 98.

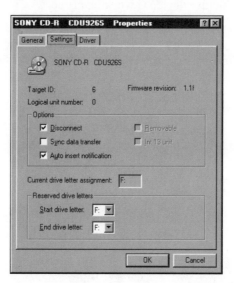

Figure 13.6   This Settings pane allows you to configure the features of a SCSI CD recorder.

Configuring Hardware Resources

Uh-oh... here come the buzzwords. If you've ever installed PC hardware, you've heard of the acronyms DMA (*Direct Memory Address*) and IRQ (*Interrupt ReQuest*), and you might have had to change these settings in the past on at least one device you've installed. However, what do these settings really *do*?

Here's the layman's explanation (the one that doesn't require a degree in electrical engineering): Adapter cards and devices that you connect to your PC need some method of communicating with your PC—the device needs to receive instructions and commands from Windows 98, and Windows 98 expects data in return. That's the function that hardware addresses such as DMA and IRQ perform; they act as mailboxes for the transfer of data between your PC and its devices.

The need for individual hardware addresses also explains why each device you install in your PC needs its own unique DMA and IRQ settings: If two devices try to share the same settings, Windows 98 has no idea to whom it's talking, and the two devices "argue" over the commands they receive. (That's why your PC often locks up because of hardware conflicts—both devices simply stop working until the problem is fixed.)

In Windows 98, the limited number of DMA and IRQ addresses are called *hardware resources,* and your favorite operating system tries its best to automatically allocate resources among your various devices. In this section, I will show you how to set a device for automatic resource allocation, as well as how you can configure a device manually with specific settings.

TIP: *Does your new hardware device have its own Windows 98 installation program? If so, use it when installing the device—the installation program will probably help you avoid hardware conflicts, especially if the device supports plug and play.*

Using Automatic Resource Settings

As you'd expect, it's far easier to allow Windows 98 to automatically configure the hardware resources for a device than to do the job manually. Windows 98 can automatically configure any plug-and-play device, and it also can make a darn accurate guess for a device that doesn't support plug and play. To automatically configure a hardware resource, take the following steps:

1. Right-click on My Computer to display the System Properties dialog box and then click on the Device Manager tab to
   display the Device Manager pane.

2. Click on the plus sign next to the entry for the correct
   device category to expand the branch and display the
   corresponding devices.

3. Click on the device you want to change to highlight it. (If
   your device appears in the Device Manager list with a
   yellow exclamation point or a red checkmark, you may have
   a conflict with another device. The other device may also
   have a yellow exclamation point next to it.)

4. Click on Properties to display the Properties dialog box and
   then click on the Resources tab. In Figure 13.7, you see the
   Resources pane for a Sound Blaster 16-bit sound card with
   plug-and-play support (sound cards are a traditional source
   of trouble if they're not properly configured). Notice the
   Conflicting Device List at the bottom of the dialog box: If
   Windows 98 has detected a resource conflict between the
   device you're modifying and another piece of hardware,
   details about the problem should appear in this list.

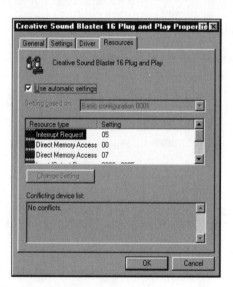

**Figure 13.7   The Resources pane allows you to modify
hardware resources.**

TIP: *Some devices don't have resource settings—for example, CD-ROM drives and hard drives, which are actually accessed through your IDE or SCSI controller's resources. If you open the Properties dialog box for a specific device and it doesn't have a Resources tab, check the resources for the device's adapter card instead.*

---

5. Enable the Use Automatic Settings checkbox at the top of the Resources pane.

6. Click on OK to exit the device's Properties dialog box and then click on OK to exit the System Properties dialog box. Depending upon the device you modified, Windows 98 may require you to reboot.

Setting Resource Settings Manually

So, a device that doesn't support plug and play is causing you trouble? Configuring resource settings manually usually involves experimenting with different combinations of settings. (In the days of DOS, the configuration process required reboot after reboot to determine whether or not you had made the right choice.) Windows 98 removes much of the frustration and almost all of the rebooting from this process, so it typically takes no more than a couple of minutes to resolve a conflict. To manually configure resource settings, follow these steps:

1. Right-click on My Computer to display the System Properties dialog box and then click on the Device Manager tab to display the Device Manager pane.

2. Click on the plus sign next to the entry for the correct device category to expand the branch and display the corresponding devices.

3. Click on the device you want to change to highlight it. (If your device is causing a resource conflict, it will likely appear in the Device Manager list with a yellow exclamation point or a red checkmark, and the other device will probably also be flagged with one of these symbols.)

4. Click on Properties to display the Properties dialog box and then click on the Resources tab. Notice the Conflicting Device List at the bottom of the dialog box—if Windows 98 has detected a resource conflict between the device you're modifying and another piece of hardware, details about the problem should appear in this list.

> **TIP:** *Some devices don't have resource settings—for example, CD-ROM drives and hard drives, which are actually accessed through your IDE or SCSI controller's resources. If you open the Properties dialog box for a specific device and it doesn't have a Resources tab, check the resources for the device's adapter card instead.*

5. Disable the Use Automatic Settings checkbox at the top of the Resources pane.

6. Windows 98 provides a number of *resource configurations* for the device. Each configuration provides a complete group of alternate resource settings, making it easy to experiment. To select an alternate configuration, click on the Setting scrolling list, select the desired group, and then skip to Step 8. Otherwise, go to Step 7.

> **TIP:** *The default configuration group—Basic configuration 0001—often works for both of the devices that are causing the conflict; check the other device and see if it needs to be reset to Basic configuration 0001.*

7. To change a specific resource, click on the resource entry in the Resource Type scrolling list to highlight it and then click on the Change Setting button. Windows 98 displays the Edit dialog box, as shown in Figure 13.8. Click on the arrows next to the Value field to change the setting. If Windows 98 can identify a resource conflict, it displays details in the Conflict information window. If the setting you have selected conflicts with another device in your system, choose another value until you've found one with no conflicts, and then click on OK to accept it.

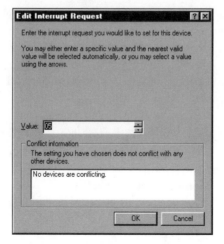

Figure 13.8   Specifying an individual resource value.

8. If Windows 98 reports no conflicts on the Resources pane, try your new settings. Click on OK to exit the device's Properties dialog box, click on OK to exit the System Properties dialog box, and then allow Windows 98 to reboot.

9. Check the operation of your device. If it appears to be working correctly, right-click on My Computer to display the System Properties dialog box and then click on the Device Manager tab. If the entry for the hardware device doesn't have a yellow exclamation point or a red checkmark, you're done! Click on OK to exit the System Properties dialog box.

On the other hand, if the device isn't working or the Device Manager entry for the device still reports a conflict, it's time to repeat the process (beginning at Step 1 in this section) with another configuration group; alternately, you could modify an individual value. Remember that most hardware devices on your PC can operate just fine with any one of a number of different resource settings, so experimentation is the key.

Removing A Device

If you remove a hardware device from your system, Windows 98 doesn't automatically remove the entry for that device within the Device Manager list. This can pose a problem, especially if you're upgrading and the replacement device needs to use the same hardware resources as the hardware you removed. To avoid device conflicts and ensure that your PC has access to all of its available hardware resources, you should remove a device from your Device Manager if you have permanently removed it from your PC. To remove a device, follow these steps:

1. Right-click on My Computer to display the System Properties dialog box and then click on the Device Manager tab to display the Device Manager pane.

2. Click on the plus sign next to the entry for the device category that holds the device you want to remove.

3. Click on the device you want to remove to highlight it and then click on the Remove button.

4. Click on OK to exit the System Properties dialog box. Depending on the device you removed, Windows 98 may require you to reboot.

Troubleshooting

Troubleshooting Hardware Problems

The words "it's a hardware problem" can strike fear into the heart of even the bravest and most knowledgeable PC owners, and for good reason: Troubleshooting hardware problems can be time-consuming and exasperating!

In this section, I will try to identify some of the common hardware problems you might encounter on a PC running Windows 98 and offer possible solutions.

TIP: These problems are generalized and do not address a specific device like a modem or a printer—if you're looking for troubleshooting tips for a specific piece of hardware, refer to the chapter covering that device.

Windows 98 Locks Up During The Startup Sequence

If Windows 98 freezes during the startup sequence, check for the following possible hardware trouble areas:

- *There is a hardware conflict.* Boot Windows 98 in Safe mode and check the Device Manager pane. If one or more devices indicate a conflict, follow the instructions in this chapter to resolve it.

- *Windows 98 is using an incorrect device driver.* A hardware device can lock up your system if Windows 98 attempts to load the wrong driver. Boot Windows 98 in Safe mode and check the Device Manager pane to determine which device is causing the problem. Remove the device, then boot normally and reinstall the device with the latest driver from the manufacturer.

- *A program in your StartUp folder is locking up.* Check any programs that you may be running from your Windows 98 StartUp folder. If one of these programs is causing problems and locking up, remove it from the folder. (For complete details on StartUp programs and how to remove them, see Chapter 9.)

Windows 98 Locks Up During The Startup Sequence

Related solution:	Found in:
Deleting A Startup Program	Chapter 9

Windows 98 Locks Up After The Startup Sequence

If Windows 98 freezes regularly after a certain time has passed—perhaps an hour or two—one of the following hardware problems may be the source of the trouble:

- *Your CPU fan is broken.* The buildup of heat over a few minutes can cause lockups on today's super-fast Pentium and Pentium II-class CPUs. Remove the cover from your PC and make sure that the CPU fan is turning; if not, replace it with a new fan.

- *Virtual memory has been disabled.* Have you assigned your own virtual memory settings (or even disabled virtual memory entirely)? Running out of space on your swapfile drive can cause Windows 98 to freeze until you delete files to create space. Check the drive that contains your swapfile and make sure that it has sufficient free space to hold the maximum size you configured. (Chapter 12 includes all the details on virtual memory and the Windows 98 swapfile.)

- *Your computer's components are overheating.* Like your CPU, other components within your PC can fail after a few minutes of operation if they overheat. Remove your PC's case and check to make sure that the power supply's fan is turning; if not, replace it with a new power supply. Additionally, you should make sure that your PC is located in an area with adequate airflow.

TIP: *I strongly recommend that you open your PC's case at least once a year and remove the accumulated dust that can coat your motherboard and adapter cards. This coat of dust can act as an insulating blanket; the heat generated by the electrical components in your PC can shorten the life of your PC or cause lockups. The best tool for the job is a disposable can of compressed air, which can blow the dust off without damaging anything. Most stores carrying computer products also stock compressed air.*

- *There is a hardware conflict.* Some hardware conflicts between two pieces of hardware occur only when you try to actually use either device (for example, a mouse and modem), so they won't lock up your system during the startup sequence. Boot Windows 98 in Safe mode and check the Device Manager pane. If one or more devices indicate a conflict, follow the instructions in this chapter to resolve it.

- *Your motherboard's BIOS is incompatible with a new device.* Not every hardware device you install is completely compatible with many of the advanced features available on the latest PC motherboards (especially older hardware). If you just upgraded a piece of hardware and your computer begins locking up regularly, consult your motherboard's manual on how to disable advanced features such as video memory management, UltraDMA, and high-speed CPU cache. Experiment by disabling these features to see if your new device works properly. In the worst case, you may have to remove the upgrade device until you can contact the manufacturer's technical support department.

Related solutions:	Found in:
Understanding Virtual Memory	Chapter 12
Specifying Custom Virtual Memory Settings	Chapter 12
Disabling Virtual Memory	Chapter 12
Adjusting DOS Program Memory Usage	Chapter 12
Troubleshooting Memory And Swapfile Problems	Chapter 12

Windows 98 Does Not Recognize A Plug-And-Play Device

If Windows 98 fails to recognize that you've installed a plug-and-play device, consider the following possible problems:

- *You installed the plug-and-play device improperly.* If the manufacturer supplied any diagnostic software, run it to see if you've correctly installed the device. If you're adding an internal adapter card, it should be firmly seated in the slot.

- *You don't have plug-and-play support.* Older motherboards may not fully support the plug-and-play standard—check your motherboard's manual. You may be able to add full plug-and-play support to your motherboard by upgrading the BIOS.

- *A hardware conflict exists.* Even plug-and-play devices can cause hardware conflicts, especially when they try to share resources with devices that don't support the plug-and-play standard. Boot Windows 98 in Safe mode and check the Device Manager pane. If one or more devices indicate a conflict, follow the instructions in this chapter to resolve it.

- *You are having connection or power problems.* For plug and play to work on an external device, it must be properly connected and turned on before you boot Windows 98. If you turn on the device after Windows 98 is already running, it may not recognize that the device is present. Make sure that the external device is turned on and connected, then restart Windows 98.

Windows 98 Does Not Recognize A Plug-And-Play Device

Windows 98
Does Not
Recognize A
Device
Without
Plug And Play

Windows 98 Does Not Recognize A Device Without Plug And Play

If you can't access a hardware device under Windows 98 and the device doesn't support plug and play, one of these problems may be to blame:

- *There is a hardware conflict.* Boot Windows 98 in Safe mode and check the Device Manager pane. If one or more devices indicate a conflict, follow the instructions in this chapter to resolve it.

- *You installed the device improperly.* Run any diagnostic software provided by the manufacturer to check your installation, and check any jumpers you had to set on the card to make sure that you moved them to the correct positions. If you're adding an internal adapter card, it should be firmly seated in the slot.

- *The device has been disabled within your current Hardware Profile.* Open the Device Manager pane and display the General properties for the device. Make sure that the Exists In All Hardware Profiles checkbox is enabled and that the Disable In This Hardware Profile checkbox is disabled.

- *You are having connection or power problems.* External devices must be properly connected and turned on before you boot Windows 98. If you turn the device on after Windows 98 is already running, it may not recognize that the device is present. Make sure that the external device is turned on and connected, then restart Windows 98.

An IDE Device Does Not Work

If an IDE device such as a CD-ROM, hard drive, or tape backup drive is experiencing problems, consider one of these possible problems:

- *The master/slave jumper is incorrectly set.* This is by far the most common problem you encounter when installing an IDE device. If you have two IDE devices on the same cable, one must be assigned as "master in a two-drive system", whereas the other must be assigned as a "slave". If you have only one IDE device on the cable, it should be set to Master In A Single Drive System (or some similar setting—exact wording differs from manufacturer to manufacturer). Consult your IDE device's manual for more information on how to set the jumpers on your device for master/slave operation.

- *The secondary IDE has been disabled.* By default, most motherboards and IDE controller cards disable the secondary IDE connector. If you're adding an IDE device to the secondary IDE connector on your system, make sure that you change the jumper or set the BIOS switch to enable it.

- *You are operating two devices simultaneously.* Unfortunately, the IDE specification doesn't allow more than one device to be active at once on an IDE connector. Therefore, if you connect both an IDE hard drive and an IDE CD-ROM on the same cable, only one can be reading data during the same time. This normally isn't a problem because your PC reads data very quickly, but it can slow your system. If your hard drive controller or motherboard offers a secondary IDE connector, use the primary IDE connector for your hard drive and the secondary IDE connector for your CD-ROM drive or tape backup.

- *The BIOS is improperly set.* If an IDE hard drive is configured for the wrong IDE mode (which affects the speed of your drive), it can write data incorrectly. If your hard drive is regularly reporting corrupted files with no apparent cause, an improperly set BIOS is the likely candidate. Check your hard drive's manual for the proper mode, and refer to your motherboard's manual for instructions on how to set that mode within your PC's BIOS.

- *The device is disabled within your current Hardware Profile.* Open the Device Manager pane and display the General properties for the device. Make sure that the Exists In All Hardware Profiles checkbox is enabled, and that the Disable In This Hardware Profile checkbox is disabled.

- *You are having connection or power problems.* Check your IDE cables to make sure that the marked wire on the cable mates with Pin 1 on the device connector. Also, make sure that your IDE device is hooked up to the computer's power supply.

A SCSI Device Does Not Work

A SCSI Device Does Not Work

Do you have a misbehaving SCSI device? Here's a list of potential problems and their solutions:

- *The SCSI device is improperly terminated.* Every SCSI device on your system must be set correctly for termination; in effect, termination indicates to your SCSI adapter card that no more devices are available on that end of the SCSI cable. If you have only one device and a SCSI adapter card, they should both be terminated. If you have any external SCSI devices, the last device on the external cable should be terminated. Most SCSI devices use either a switch or a simple resistor pack for termination. Check your device's manual and your SCSI adapter card's manual for more information.

- *You don't have a unique SCSI ID.* Along with proper termination, it's essential that each of your SCSI devices be assigned a unique SCSI ID number (your SCSI adapter card also needs a unique ID). Check each device and reassign a new unique number to any devices sharing the same SCSI ID.

- *The device is disabled within your current Hardware Profile.* Open the Device Manager pane and display the General properties for the device. Make sure that the Exists In All Hardware Profiles checkbox is enabled, and that the Disable In This Hardware Profile checkbox is disabled.

- *You are having connection or power problems.* Check your internal SCSI cables to make sure that the marked wire on the cable mates with Pin 1 on the device connector. Also, make sure that your SCSI device is hooked up to the computer's power supply (or for external devices, that the power supply is connected to both the device and the wall socket).

Chapter 14

Using The Windows 98 Tune-Up Wizard

In Brief

The Windows 98 Tune-Up Wizard is a dream come true for most PC owners, many of whom have never performed any routine maintenance on their systems. To keep your Windows 98 system running smoothly, you need to run programs like Disk Defragmenter and ScanDisk regularly. You could put both of these programs in your StartUp folder, but you don't need to run these tasks every time you boot your computer. Besides, running these programs from the StartUp folder wouldn't automate them, and it would take far too long for your PC to complete the startup sequence.

On the other hand, the Wizard makes it easy to set up a regular automated schedule so that Windows 98 performs these tasks when you're not using your PC. A typical maintenance schedule includes programs that are necessary to do the following:

- Keep your PC running at top speed
- Maximize the amount of free space on your drives
- Check your hard drives for file errors
- Compress files with UltraPack compression

In this chapter, I will help you configure your own maintenance schedule with the Windows 98 Tune-Up Wizard, using both the Express and the Custom setup modes. You will also learn how to add additional tasks to your maintenance schedule using the Task Scheduler.

Immediate Solutions

Creating A Maintenance Schedule

The Windows 98 Tune-Up Wizard offers two modes of operation:

- *Express*—In Express mode (the default), the Wizard selects the most common maintenance tasks for you automatically, and you can select from one of three preset time slots to run your maintenance.

- *Custom*—In Custom mode, you choose which maintenance tasks you want the Wizard to configure and schedule them to run at exactly the time(s) you specify.

In this section, I cover both modes of operation, step by step.

Using The Wizard: Express Mode

Looking for the easiest and fastest method of building a maintenance schedule? If so, run the Windows 98 Tune-Up Wizard in Express mode. To do so, follow these steps:

1. Click on Start|Programs|Accessories|System Tools|Windows Tune-Up. Windows 98 displays the Maintenance Wizard opening screen, as shown in Figure 14.1.

2. Click on Express and then click on Next to continue. The Wizard displays the schedule screen shown in Figure 14.2.

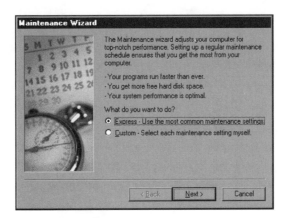

Figure 14.1   Selecting Express or Custom mode in the Maintenance Wizard.

345

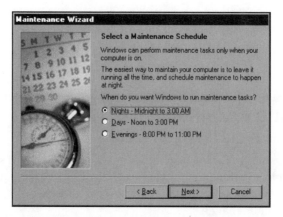

Figure 14.2   You can schedule maintenance for nights, days, or evenings.

3. You can schedule maintenance tasks for one of three times of the day (or if you're editing a schedule that already exists, four periods). Choose one of the following periods and then click on Next to continue:

- *Nights*—Select this option to run maintenance tasks between midnight and 3:00 A.M.

- *Days*—Pick this option if you want to run your maintenance tasks between noon and 3:00 P.M.

- *Evenings*—Choose this option to run your maintenance tasks between 8:00 P.M. and 11:00 P.M.

- *Custom*—If you're editing an existing maintenance schedule and you want to keep your current time, choose this option.

TIP: *If you want to set a different time slot for your maintenance tasks, just pick the closest period here; you can edit these default settings and change the time slot later, after you've finished using the Wizard.*

---

4. The Wizard displays a confirmation screen, shown in Figure 14.3, that lists the tasks to be scheduled and reminds you to leave your PC running during the maintenance time slot. The Express tasks are as follows:

- *Speed up your most frequently used programs*—Windows 98 launches the Disk Defragmenter program to speed up your hard drive.

- *Check hard disk for errors*—The Wizard schedules ScanDisk to check your hard drive for file errors.

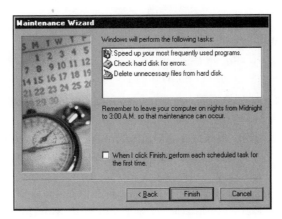

Figure 14.3   *The Wizard displays the maintenance tasks to be performed in Express mode.*

- *Delete unnecessary files from hard disk*—Windows 98 runs the Disk Cleanup program to erase temporary files from your drive and create additional free space.

5. If you want to see the maintenance tasks in action, the Wizard can perform them immediately after you have created your schedule. To do so, click on the When I Click Finish, Perform Each Scheduled Task For The First Time checkbox to enable this option.

6. Click on Finish to complete the process. The Wizard creates the maintenance schedule and launches the Task Scheduler program (if necessary). If you enabled the checkbox in Step 5, each maintenance task that you selected will then run automatically.

Using The Wizard: Custom Mode

If you want more control over what applications run during your maintenance schedule, run the Windows 98 Tune-Up Wizard in Custom mode by following these steps:

1. Click on Start|Programs|Accessories|System Tools|Windows Tune-Up to display the Maintenance Wizard opening screen.

2. Click on Custom and then click on Next to continue. The Wizard displays the schedule screen.

3. You can configure maintenance tasks for one of three periods (if you're editing an existing schedule, you also can pick a fourth period). Choose one of the following periods and then click on Next to continue:

- *Nights*—Select this option to run your tasks between midnight and 3:00 A.M.

- *Days*—Select this option to run your maintenance tasks between noon and 3:00 P.M.

- *Evenings*—Choose this option to run your maintenance tasks between 8:00 P.M. and 11:00 P.M.

- *Custom*—If you're editing an existing maintenance schedule and you want to keep your current time period, choose this option.

4. Next, the Wizard allows you to enable and disable programs that launch automatically when you run Windows 98, as shown in Figure 14.4. If your PC is running a program at startup that you don't need, disable the checkbox next to the program name. Disabling a program does not remove it from your startup sequence, so you can re-enable a program later by running the Windows 98 Tune-Up Wizard a second time. Click on Next to continue.

5. The Wizard displays the screen shown in Figure 14.5. Here, you can schedule the first of your maintenance tasks: Disk Defragmenter. If you select the No, Do Not Defragment My Disk option, this task is skipped. To add defragmenting to your maintenance schedule, click on the Yes, Defragment My Disk Regularly option.

   The Wizard selects a default time for defragmenting based upon the time setting you selected earlier. If this is the time you want, you're done on this Wizard screen. If you need to reschedule the defragmenting task, click on Reschedule and

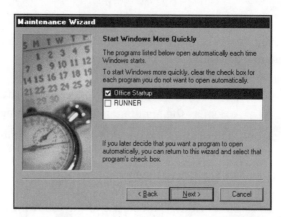

Figure 14.4   The Wizard makes it easy to enable and disable programs that run automatically during the startup sequence.

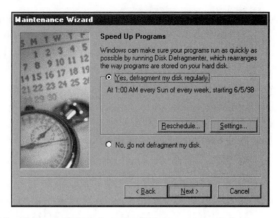

Figure 14.5   Adding disk defragmenting to your maintenance schedule.

then select a schedule based on time (Daily, Weekly, or
Monthly), One Time Only, Whenever Windows 98 Boots Up,
or Whenever You Log On To This Computer. For more
information about these settings, refer to the section titled
"Changing Task Settings" in Chapter 9.

You can also change the settings for the Disk Defragmenter
program from within the Wizard. Click on Settings to
display the Scheduled Settings For Disk Defragmenter
dialog box. Select one or all of your hard drives from the
drop-down list and then enable the Rearrange Program Files
So My Programs Start Faster checkbox. Click on OK to
return to the Wizard and save your changes.

After you've made any necessary changes to the task
schedule and the settings for Disk Defragmenter, click on
Next to continue.

6. Follow the instructions in Step 5 for the next Wizard screen,
    which controls the ScanDisk task; it's very similar to the
    previous screen. If you need details on the various settings
    for ScanDisk, see the section titled "Troubleshooting With
    ScanDisk" in Chapter 3. Click on Next to continue.

7. The last task to configure is the Disk Cleanup program;
    once again, follow the instructions in Step 5. On the Delete
    Unnecessary Files screen, the Types Of Files To Remove list
    displays the types of files that will be erased to restore free
    space. If you need to specify different file types, click on
    Settings and then select them from the list. When you have
    configured everything to your satisfaction, click on Next.

8. If you'd like to perform the first maintenance immediately, the Wizard can perform it automatically after you have created your schedule. To do so, click on the When I Finish, Perform Each Scheduled Task For The First Time checkbox.

9. Click on Finish to complete the process; the Wizard creates the maintenance schedule and launches the Task Scheduler program (if necessary). If you enabled the checkbox in Step 8, each of the maintenance tasks runs automatically.

Editing Your Maintenance Schedule

If you've already created a maintenance schedule and you need to update it—for example, if you need to use your PC during the time period you had selected earlier—it's easy to modify your schedule. You can re-run the Windows 98 Tune-Up Wizard to change time periods and settings, but you can only schedule three tasks in your maintenance schedule. With the Task Scheduler, however, you can add tasks that aren't included among the Wizard's standard maintenance tasks.

Editing Your Maintenance Schedule With The Wizard

To modify your existing maintenance schedule using the Windows 98 Tune-Up Wizard, follow these steps:

1. Click on Start|Programs|Accessories|System Tools|Windows Tune-Up. Windows 98 displays the dialog box shown in Figure 14.6.

2. Click on the Change My Maintenance Settings Or Schedule option and then click on OK to continue.

3. The Windows 98 Tune-Up Wizard opening screen appears. Follow the instructions for either Express or Custom mode in the "Creating A Maintenance Schedule" section earlier in

Figure 14.6   By clicking on the Change My Maintenance Settings Or Schedule option, you can easily edit an existing maintenance schedule.

this chapter. The Wizard allows you to keep your existing schedule and settings or modify them as necessary.

Editing Your Maintenance Schedule With The Task Scheduler

To modify your existing maintenance schedule using the Task Scheduler, follow the instructions in the section titled "Scheduling A Task" in Chapter 9.

Why add new tasks to the maintenance schedule the Windows 98 Tune-Up Wizard created? You may need to run a number of programs on a daily basis that the Wizard doesn't include. These tasks can include the following:

- Compressing files with UltraPack compression, using the DriveSpace 3 Compression Agent. (Chapter 11 discusses disk compression in detail, including more about the Compression Agent.)

- Checking for viruses with a commercial anti-virus program.

TIP: *Are you running Windows 98 without a good anti-virus program? Fire up your Web browser and connect to Network Associates at www.nai.com. You can download an evaluation version of my favorite anti-virus package, McAfee's VirusScan, and try before you buy!*

- Backing up system files or an entire hard drive to tape, Zip drive, or another removable medium.

- Automated uploading or downloading of data and files across the Internet to a host computer.

Launching Your Maintenance Schedule Manually

Launching Your Maintenance Schedule Manually

If you need to perform your maintenance tasks manually, follow these steps:

1. Click on Start|Programs|Accessories|System Tools|Windows Tune-Up. Windows 98 displays the dialog box that prompts you for your choice of action.

2. Click on the Perform Maintenance Now option and then click on OK to continue.

The Task Scheduler immediately launches your maintenance tasks.

351

Troubleshooting

Troubleshooting Maintenance Schedule Problems

In this section, I'll cover common problems that can occur with scheduled maintenance events and possible solutions.

Maintenance Task Does Not Launch

If you've scheduled a task and it did not run when it should have, check these possible problems:

- *The Task Scheduler is turned off or paused.* Turning off or pausing the Task Scheduler prevents any scheduled tasks from running. Follow the instructions in Chapter 9 to activate the Task Scheduler program.

- *The system clock is incorrectly set.* Check your system clock to make sure that your PC is set to the right time. To display the system date and time, click on Start|Settings|Control Panel to display the Control Panel and then click on Date/Time to display the Date/Time Properties dialog box. Alternately, you can right-click on the time display on the right side of the Windows 98 Taskbar to set the time and date.

- *The system was suspended or turned off.* Many computers cannot launch scheduled programs if your system is suspended (or, of course, if your system is turned off). Make sure that your PC is running and that Suspend mode is disabled so that the Task Scheduler can run your maintenance tasks.

- *The JOB file was deleted.* Check your \WINDOWS\TASKS folder for a JOB file—without one, no scheduled tasks run. If you have accidentally deleted this file, run the Windows 98 Tune-Up Wizard again to generate another JOB file.

Maintenance Task Does Not Run Successfully

If a scheduled maintenance task runs but does not finish successfully, check these possible problems:

- *The program requires manual intervention.* If the program requires you to select menu choices or press buttons, you probably shouldn't use it as a maintenance program—check

Maintenance Task Does Not Launch

Maintenance Task Does Not Run Successfully

to see if you can configure the program to run without requiring manual intervention.

- *The program requires removable media.* If your maintenance schedule includes data on any removable media drive, make sure that media is properly loaded into the drive before the maintenance tasks run.

Index

B

C

mode, 261
security zones
adding Web sites, 259-260
configuring, 258
definition, 257
removing Web sites, 260
security levels, customizing, 258-259
security levels, definition, 258
zone types, 257-258
sounds, disabling, 256
temporary Internet files
definition, 252
storing, 253-254
tracking pages you've visited, 254
troubleshooting
connection disconnects, 272
DNS failure, 273
failure to connect, 271
graphics don't load, 273-274
hyperlink errors, 275
hyperlinks missing from Web
pages, 274
ISP equipment failure, 273
modem does not respond, 271
multimedia files don't play, 273-274
password incorrect, 272
TCP/IP settings incorrect, 273
text missing from Web pages, 274
URL is incorrect, 273
user information incorrect, 272
Web pages load slowly or stop, 274
wrong network protocol, 272
videos, disabling, 256
Web site for, 267
Internet logon, with dial-up
scripts, 218-219
Internet Zone, 257
Interrupt ReQuest (IRQ). *See* Hardware
resources, configuring.
IRQ (Interrupt ReQuest). *See* Hardware
resources, configuring.
ISP logon. *See* Internet logon, with
dial-up scripts.

J

Jasc Software, 12
Java options, 261-262

K

Keyboards
alternate languages
adding, 151-152
removing, 152
switching between, 152-153
character-repeat settings, 149-150
ergonomic, 147
overview, 147-148
troubleshooting, 158-159

L

LoadTop startup option, 7
Local Intranet Zone, 257
Location entries
creating, 203-205
removing, 203
selecting, 202-203
Locked baud rate, 195
Logged option, Startup menu, 11
Logging, 11, 28-29
Logging modem activity, 200
Logo startup option, 7
Logon profiles missing, 56
Logos. *See* Startup/shutdown logos.
LOGO.SYS file, displaying at startup, 7
Lost clusters, 89-90
Low-level drivers, loading to top of
conventional memory, 7

M

Magnetic interference, 111
Maintenance schedules
creating, 345-350
editing, 350-351
launching, 351
troubleshooting, 353-354
McAfee VirusScan, Web site for, 351
Memory. *See* Virtual memory.
Menus (desktop)
customizing
Favorites menu, 43-45
Programs menu, 43-45
Start menu, 43
slow display, troubleshooting, 104

R

Read-only files, troubleshooting, 59
Recording devices, selecting, 124-126
Recording properties, customizing, 129
Recording sounds, 137-138
Recycle Bin
configuring across all hard
drives, 77-78
configuring for a specific hard drive, 78
disabling, 79
global settings, configuring, 77-78
Refresh rate
definition, 100
selecting, 102
troubleshooting, 111
Registry, scanning for errors, 30
REM (remark) statement, 16

S

Safe mode
booting, with network support, 8, 10, 11
displaying a warning message, 6
graphics limitations, 112
troubleshooting startup problems, 28
Safe Mode Command Prompt Only
option, Startup menu, 11
Safe Mode option, Startup menu, 11
Safe Mode with Network option,
Startup menu, 11
ScanDisk
advanced options, 87-89
application lockups, 89
automating. *See* Tune-Up Wizard.
backups, 85-86
cross-links, 89-90
incorrect shutdown, 89-90
legacy DOS programs, 90
lost clusters, 89-90
naming problems, 90
old disk utilities, 90
power failures, 90
running automatically, 87
running manually, 86-87
surface damage, 90
ScanDisk, running after improper
shutdown, 5
SCANREG program, 30

Scheduled Task Wizard, 233-236
Scheduling tasks. *See also* Tune-Up
Wizard.
agent programs
definition, 231
installing and configuring, 241
backup agents
definition, 231
installing and configuring, 241
changing a task, 237
creating tasks, 233-236
deleting tasks, 236-237
launching tasks during idle time, 236
notification of missing tasks, 239
power management for laptops, 236
Scheduled Task Wizard, 233-236
scheduled tasks, definition, 230
startup folder programs
adding, 239-240
definition, 230-231
deleting, 240-241
task scheduler
pausing, 238
starting/stopping, 237-238
troubleshooting, 243-245
Screen resolution
color depth mismatch, 111
definition, 99
selecting, 100-101
too high, 112-113
troubleshooting, 112-113
Scripts, dial-up, 218-219
SCSI devices, double buffering, 7
SCSI hardware, configuring
device chains, checking, 75-76
SCSI disconnect, enabling, 76
SCSI settings, optimizing, 76-77
SCSI Sync Data Transfer, setting, 76-77
troubleshooting
cabling incorrect, 85
device ID not unique, 85
driver not installed, 85
hardware conflicts, 84-85
SCSI adapter not recognized, 83-84
SCSI chain improperly
terminated, 85
SCSI device does not work, 339-340
SCSI device not recognized, 84-85
Seagate, Web site for, 231
Search engines, shortcut to, 39

My Computer, 58-59
read-only files, 59
stretched images, 55
Windows background, 55
Windows Explorer, 58-59
wrong program launches, 58
Troubleshooting audio problems
audio from only one speaker, 142
bad cable connections, 142
hardware conflicts, 141-142
MCI driver errors, 143
no audio at all, 141-142
no CD audio, 142-143
no power to speakers, 142
volume control too low, 142
Troubleshooting automation
task did not launch, 243-244
task did not quit, 244-245
task did not run successfully, 244
Troubleshooting compression problems
compression ratio incorrect, 297
CVF file was changed, 296
DBLSPACE.BIN file missing, 296
disk surface errors, 296
drive not mounted, 296
drive space shortage, 297
DriveSpace 3 does not compress a
drive, 296-297
path name too long, 296
ScanDisk returns drive errors, 295-296
unable to create MSDOSSYS.TMP
file, 295
unable to read compressed drive, 296
Troubleshooting disk access
application lockup, 89
backups, 85-86
cross-links, 89-90
incorrect shutdown, 89-90
legacy DOS programs, 90
lost clusters, 89-90
naming problems, 90
old disk utilities, 90
power failures, 90
ScanDisk
advanced options, 87-89
running automatically, 87
running manually, 86-87
surface damage, 90
Troubleshooting graphics
blank screen, 112-113

color depth/screen resolution
mismatch, 111
colors blink, 113
colors look grainy, 113
colors shift, 113
DirectX drivers not properly
installed, 113
dithering, 113
dot pitch, 111, 112
flickering display, 111
fonts are truncated, 113
fuzzy display, 111
improper refresh rate, 111
insufficient video RAM, 112
magnetic interference, 111
Safe Mode limitations, 112
screen resolution too high, 112-113
startup sequence stalls, 112-113
video driver incompatibilities, 113
Troubleshooting hardware problems.
See also Troubleshooting SCSI
hardware problems.
device not recognized, 337-338
dust, 336
IDE device does not work, 338-339
lockup after startup, 336-337
lockup during startup, 335
overheating, 336
Troubleshooting Internet Explorer 4.0
connection disconnects, 272
DNS failure, 273
failure to connect, 271
graphics don't load, 273-274
hyperlink errors, 275
hyperlinks missing from Web pages, 274
ISP equipment failure, 273
modem does not respond, 271
multimedia files don't play, 273-274
password incorrect, 272
TCP/IP settings incorrect, 273
text missing from Web pages, 274
URL is incorrect, 273
user information incorrect, 272
Web pages load slowly or stop, 274
wrong network protocol, 272
Troubleshooting keyboard, 158-159
Troubleshooting modems
call waiting, 223-224
COM port conflicts, 222
dial-up connections cannot access
modem, 224-225

367

V

Video cards
  acceleration, configuring, 103-104
  RAM, displaying, 102
  RAM requirements, 101-102
  troubleshooting
    animation slows or locks up, 104
    desktop improperly redrawn, 104
    mouse pointer disappears, 104
    slow menu display, 104
Video clips. *See* Digital video.
Video drivers. *See also* Monitor drivers.
  incompatibilities, 113
  selecting, 98-99
  updating, 95-97
Video (monitor)
  24-bit color
    advantages of, 100
    definition, 99
  color depth
    definition, 99
    screen resolution mismatch, 111
    selecting, 101-102
  color management, 109-110
  flickering display, 111
  fuzzy display, 111
  monitor profiles, 109-110
  pixels, definition, 99
  recommended for DVD viewing, 81
  refresh rate
    definition, 100
    selecting, 102
    troubleshooting, 111
  restart after changes, disabling, 105
  screen resolution
    color depth mismatch, 111
    definition, 99
    selecting, 100-101
    too high, 112-113
  system colors, changing, 106-108
  system fonts, changing, 102-103, 106-108
  true color
    definition, 99
Videos, disabling, 256
Virtual memory
  conventional memory,
    adjusting, 309-311
  custom settings, reasons for, 304-305

  definition, 301
  disabling, 309
  for DOS programs, 309-313
  expanded memory (EMS), adjusting,
    311-312
  extended memory (XMS), adjusting,
    311-312
  free-space restrictions, 307-308
  for PCs with less than 32MB RAM,
    305-306
  protected-mode memory (DPMI),
    adjusting, 312-313
  for slow hardware, 306-307
  swapfiles
    checking settings of, 303-304
    definition, 303
    dynamic resizing, 307
    recommended size, 307
    troubleshooting, 315-317
  troubleshooting
    excessive hard drive access, 316
    insufficient conventional
      memory, 316
    low disk space on swapfile, 315-316
    memory errors while booting, 315
    parity errors while booting, 315
    protected-mode memory (DPMI)
      problems, 316-317
  WIN386.SWP file, 303
Volume Control, displaying on the
  taskbar, 126
Volume Control dialog box,
  customizing, 122-123
Volume controls, setting, 119-121

W

Wallpaper
  active, removing, 35
  HTML, adding, 39
Web addresses
  list of favorite sites, 39
  listing favorites, 39
  listing recently visited, 40
Web browsers. *See* Explorer bars,
  adding.
Web items on desktop
  adding, 38-39
  disabling, 37

X

GET ON THE ROAD
TO CERTIFICATION SUCCESS

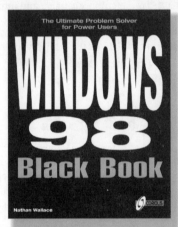